# Understanding Mobility as a Service (MaaS)

D1829175

# Understanding Mobility as a Service (MaaS)

## Past, Present and Future

David A. Hensher

Chinh Q. Ho

Corinne Mulley

John D. Nelson

Göran Smith

Yale Z. Wong

ELSEVIER

Elsevier
Radarweg 29, PO Box 211, 1000 AE Amsterdam, Netherlands
The Boulevard, Langford Lane, Kidlington, Oxford OX5 1GB, United Kingdom
50 Hampshire Street, 5th Floor, Cambridge, MA 02139, United States

© 2020 Elsevier Inc. All rights reserved.

No part of this publication may be reproduced or transmitted in any form or by any means, electronic or mechanical, including photocopying, recording, or any information storage and retrieval system, without permission in writing from the publisher. Details on how to seek permission, further information about the Publisher's permissions policies and our arrangements with organizations such as the Copyright Clearance Center and the Copyright Licensing Agency, can be found at our website: www.elsevier.com/permissions.

This book and the individual contributions contained in it are protected under copyright by the Publisher (other than as may be noted herein).

**Notices**
Knowledge and best practice in this field are constantly changing. As new research and experience broaden our understanding, changes in research methods, professional practices, or medical treatment may become necessary.

Practitioners and researchers must always rely on their own experience and knowledge in evaluating and using any information, methods, compounds, or experiments described herein. In using such information or methods they should be mindful of their own safety and the safety of others, including parties for whom they have a professional responsibility.

To the fullest extent of the law, neither the Publisher nor the authors, contributors, or editors, assume any liability for any injury and/or damage to persons or property as a matter of products liability, negligence or otherwise, or from any use or operation of any methods, products, instructions, or ideas contained in the material herein.

**Library of Congress Cataloging-in-Publication Data**
A catalog record for this book is available from the Library of Congress

**British Library Cataloguing-in-Publication Data**
A catalogue record for this book is available from the British Library

ISBN: 978-0-12-820044-5

For information on all Elsevier publications
visit our website at https://www.elsevier.com/books-and-journals

*Publisher:* Joe Hayton
*Acquisitions Editor:* Brian Romer
*Editorial Project Manager:* Sara Valentino
*Production Project Manager:* Omer Mukthar
*Cover Designer:* Miles Hitchen

Typeset by SPi Global, India

Working together to grow libraries in developing countries
www.elsevier.com • www.bookaid.org

# Contents

# About the authors

**David A. Hensher** is Professor of Management and Founding Director of the Institute of Transport and Logistics Studies (ITLS) at The University of Sydney. David is a Fellow of the Australian Academy of Social Sciences, Recipient of the 2009 International Association of Travel Behaviour Research (IATBR) Lifetime Achievement Award in recognition for his long-standing and exceptional contribution to IATBR as well as to the wider travel behaviour community; Recipient of the 2006 Engineers Australia Transport Medal for lifelong contribution to transportation, recipient of the Smart 2013 Premier Award for Excellence in Supply Chain Management, the 2014 Institute of Transportation Engineers (Australia and New Zealand) Transport Profession Award, and the 2016 Award for Outstanding Research as part of the inaugural University of Sydney Vice-Chancellor's Awards for Excellence. David is also the recipient of the 2019 John Shaw Medal which honours an industry champion who has made a lasting contribution to Australia's roads. In 2018 David was selected as one of 25 academics at the University of Sydney who have made a significant impact through engaging with industry and government. He has published over 650 papers in leading international transport and economics journals as well as 16 books. He has over 54,000 citations of his contributions in Google scholar and a Scopus H-index of 65.

**Chinh Q. Ho** is Senior Lecturer in Applied Spatial Data Analytics in the Institute of Transport and Logistics Studies (ITLS) at The University of Sydney. He has a research track record with 30+ journal articles, five book chapters and 12 fully refereed conference papers (three winning the best paper award) in the areas of logistics and transport, statistical modelling and big data. Acting as a member of scientific and technical committee, Chinh has provided strategic and operational advice on urban and regional planning, including economic analysis of transport infrastructure projects in Vietnam, urban mobility for developing world, and public transport and demand modelling issues in Australia. His research interests cover four main areas: (1) integrated land use and transport planning (ILUT), (2) spatial analysis of big data, (3) emerging transport technologies such as mobility as a service (MaaS) and driverless vehicles, (4) modelling group decisions.

**Corinne Mulley** was the inaugural Chair of Public Transport at the Institute of Transport and Logistics Studies at The University of Sydney, now Professor Emerita. Corinne is a transport economist, active in transport research at the interface of transport policy and economics, concentrating on specific issues relating to public transport. She has provided both practical and strategic advice to local and national governments on transport evaluation, including economic impact analysis, benchmarking, rural transport issues, public transport management, and on Mobility as a Service (MaaS). Professor Mulley's research is motivated by a need to provide evidence for policy initiatives and, whilst in Sydney, created links with the federal government, for example serving as an expert on the Public Transport Committee, the National Infrastructure Audit for Infrastructure Australia and the Long Term Master Plan for the NSW state government. Corinne continues to be engaged in research looking widely at BRT issues, value capture, regional transport flexible transport services with Transport for NSW, studies understanding travel behaviour and studies involving Mobility as a Service (MaaS) in different contexts.

**John D. Nelson** is Chair in Public Transport at the Institute of Transport and Logistics Studies (ITLS), The University of Sydney (from February 2019) and has previously held senior academic positions at the University of Aberdeen and Newcastle University. John is particularly interested in the application and evaluation of new technologies to improve transport systems (with a particular focus on public transport and shared transport solutions) as well as the policy frameworks and regulatory regimes necessary to achieve sustainable mobility. His research is funded by the UK Research Councils, Innovate UK, the European Commission and industry. He is a past Chairman of the Universities' Transport Study Group (UTSG), which promotes transport teaching and research across the United Kingdom and Ireland, served as Scientific Director for the ITS European Congress in Glasgow (2016) and is a founder member of MaaS Scotland. He is Series Editor for Routledge's Transport and Mobility and Transport and Society book series.

**Göran Smith** is a regional developer at Region Västra Götaland (Sweden) and industrial Ph.D. candidate at Chalmers University of Technology. Additionally, he holds a position as a Research Associate at the Institute of Transport and Logistics Studies at The University of Sydney. In his doctoral project, which is tied to K2—the Swedish Knowledge Centre for Public Transport, he studies the development and diffusion of Mobility as a Service (MaaS) in the Nordic countries. The main objectives are to create better understanding of disruptive and collaborative innovation processes, and of how the public sector can govern such processes so that they bring value to involved actors as well as to society. Beyond theoretical contributions, Göran's research will create a basis for long-term strategic decisions regarding Region Västra Götaland's future roles in MaaS.

**Yale Z. Wong** is Doctoral Candidate and Research Associate at the Institute of Transport and Logistics Studies (ITLS) at The University of Sydney Business School. Yale's research focus encompasses three core facets in future mobility, transport contracts and bus operations. A major area of work for Yale is to market test the mobility as a service (MaaS) proposition with the aim to understand what the community demands and businesses are willing to provide. Yale won the David Willis Prize (2018), ITLS Research Prize (2018), and was selected by Intelligent Transport Systems (ITS) Australia as Youth Ambassador to the World Congress (2019), and as recipient of the Young Professional Award (2019). In addition, Yale undertakes a range of advisory and consultancy work with clients ranging from bus operators to industry bodies, vehicle suppliers and local government. Having previously worked in bus operations with experience in network planning and service development, Yale continues to be called upon regularly by the bus industry in his now strategic capacity looking to the future of the bus industry in an era of disruption and change.

# Foreword

This book has been written specifically to provide an easy to access contribution to the growing interest in Mobility as a Service (MaaS). Although there are many outlets for research contributions, the publications are often not accessible to those who do not have a subscription to academic journals or libraries that subscribe. We saw an opportunity to bring together, in a readable form, the developments in MaaS to date that can be easily accessed by industry, government and consultants.

We thank Andre Pinto of ITLS for his role in formatting our book and coordinating with Elsevier and Daniel Reck (Institute for Transport Planning and Systems (IVT), ETH Zürich, Switzerland) for reading the penultimate draft and providing very useful comments.

We dedicate this book as a contribution to the Volvo Research and Educational Foundations (VREF) Bus Rapid Transit (BRT+) Centre of Excellence (http://www.brt.cl/) and the iMOVE Cooperative Research Centre (CRC) (https://imoveaustralia.com/).

# Testimonials

*This book is an important contribution to the growing interest in MaaS and provides a thoroughly researched reference source. The book is an enjoyable read and should be on the bookshelves of all professionals interested in getting an up to date briefing of the MaaS journey to date. The authors have really gone through the materials existing to date and point out level of understanding we have at the moment. In particular the chapter 2.5 in which modal efficiency and the rationale for integration is discussed is an important contribution to knowledge. I commend the authors for this stimulating book.*

Sampo Hietanen, Founder CEO—MaaS Global

*This book is an important contribution to the growing interest in Mobility-as-a-Service (MaaS). It should be an important reference for academics as well as practitioners in clarifying the concept as well as providing an up to date summary of research on MaaS. Even though all chapters are important contributions, I found the chapter on institutional barriers and governance particularly interesting to read in that it not only describes the challenges associated with but proposes strategies by which the development and diffusion of MaaS could be addressed. I commend the authors for an interesting and stimulating book.*

I.C. MariAnne Karlsson, Professor and Head of Division of Design & Human Factors, Department of Industrial and Materials Science—Chalmers University of Technology

*This book is a critical examination of MaaS globally and shows a coherent depth of research that we have not seen to date. It will become the definitive source for MaaS and its honesty and analysis means that it will be a benchmark for the state of MaaS. The chapter on pilot programs for MaaS provides a holistic review of global initiatives that draws on some of the successes and limited wins for MaaS and shows why MaaS has started to work and in some instances why it hasn't succeeded as well as planned, but this feeds directly into the next chapter that then asks the critical question for businesses and cities alike 'What is the potential for MaaS'. I recommend that this book becomes essential reading and reference for all mobility professionals.*

Andy Taylor, Strategy Director—Cubic Transportation Systems, Inc.

Chapter 1

# Overview

## Chapter outline



---

*The world of transportation is going through disruption that is technology-enabled but fundamentally demand-driven. Based on all the signals I see and hear, MaaS has moved onto the when stage.*

Sampo Hietanen, Founder of MaaS Global, 'Sampo's Blog: Scaling MaaS requires tweaking reality', 6 September 2019

## 1.1 Introduction

We live in an exciting world where technology driving change in the passenger transport sector has led to almost daily commentary in the transport literature, including grey material and the popular press. The words "There has never been a more exciting time in the world of transportation" are uttered, or prevailing views held to such sentiment, in any gathering of transport professionals—be they industry, government or academic. A central theme is the way that digitally supported technological change has opened up opportunities to consider new ways of delivering services under the mantra of what has become known as Mobility as a Service (MaaS). The term MaaS was first popularised during the European Congress on Intelligent Transport Systems in Helsinki in 2014 and described as "… a system, in which a comprehensive range of mobility services are provided to customers by mobility operators" (Heikkilä, 2014, p. 8), and as "… a mobility distribution model in which a customer's major transportation needs are met over one interface and are offered by a service provider" (Hietanen, 2014, p. 1).

Digital technologies like smartphones, the internet of things and big data analytics, coupled with demographic change, is ushering in a new future in transportation, with disruptive ramifications for many stakeholders, especially operators and regulators, plus new service expectations by citizens. This transformation has enabled as a pre-condition, the evolution of MaaS into a concept that promotes the integration of transport services to provide one-stop access through a common interface (Mukhtar-Landgren et al., 2016) (Fig. 1.1).

Understanding Mobility as a Service (MaaS). https://doi.org/10.1016/B978-0-12-820044-5.00001-4
© 2020 Elsevier Inc. All rights reserved.

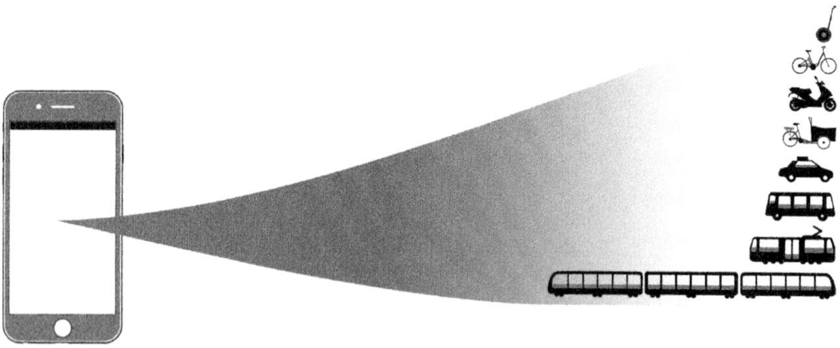

**FIG. 1.1** Principle visualisation of MaaS. *(Source: Smith, G., Hensher, D.A., 2019. Towards a framework for Mobility-as-a-Service policies. Paper Presented at the Thredbo 16—The International Conference Series on Competition and Ownership in Land Passenger Transport, Singapore.)*

In terms of transport policy, MaaS is often at the centre of the popular view on future collaborative and connected mobility in the presence of driver-operated and driverless vehicles, notably car and bus; and is seen as a way in the short run to reduce emissions and in the long run to reduce car ownership, and other negative externalities, by enabling citizens to satisfy their mobility needs without having to own assets such as an automobile. Storme et al. (2020) however, in a pilot study undertaken in Ghent, Belgium report how a group of car owning participants were offered mobility budgets to replace their private car use. Regrettably, although respondents were happy to explore MaaS type options, reductions in private car use were not forthcoming, suggesting the interplay between MaaS and private car use may be more complex than currently appreciated.

For a concept that has only been in existence for 5 years, MaaS has received considerable attention from decision-makers (for example, the Finnish government which has implemented new transport regulations which arguably is largely designed to facilitate MaaS developments, cf. Mukhtar-Landgren and Smith, 2019; Smith et al., 2018b), practitioners (examples are MaaS start-ups including MaaS Global in Finland, EC2B in Sweden and Moovel in Germany—see Chapter 3) as well as researchers (e.g. Hensher, 2017; Jittrapirom et al., 2017; Sochor et al., 2016; Wong et al., 2020; Mulley, 2017; Kamargianni et al., 2016a,b, 2018a,b; Kamargianni and Matyas, 2017). Still, the knowledge of MaaS is nascent, and we are yet to find evidence of how the alleged mobility and societal benefits of MaaS can truly be captured (Smith and Hensher, 2019), leading to the common reference of MaaS as 'rhetoric and hype'.

The rise of transportation network companies (TNCs) providing ridesharing, carsharing and bikesharing, and more latterly scooter sharing, and the new propositions being announced seemingly every other day in both developed and developing economies embodies the pace and scale of this change. MaaS is seen as the umbrella that can integrate all of the emerging services and public transport, taking the debate on modal substitutes and complements to a higher level. As part of these developments, MaaS has become the catch-all of innovation, and has grown to encompass the broad suite of changes associated with future mobility, delivered through multi-modal technological platforms. Very often, proponents regard TNC-driven innovation [e.g. Uber, Ola (with Indian origins), Grab (South East Asia's equivalent of Uber)] and mobile applications which provide only a more advanced informational and ticketing interface as MaaS—this is something questioned in this book (see Chapter 3).

There have been massive venture capital raisings (Uber being a much publicised example), with a plethora of start-ups, hostile takeovers and substantial investments by many technology, automotive and financial enterprises. Governments are also jumping on the bandwagon, as trials of on demand public transport and autonomous (electric) vehicles in particular become ever more ubiquitous (see Chapters 3 and 4), many as unimodal trials. Government and politicians associate themselves with trials, many of which have been limited in scope and test only constituent components of the full MaaS proposition. Think tanks, consultancies and industry suppliers are releasing white papers regularly; and governments and lobbyists are publishing policy documents to showcase their vision and influence debate (Smith and Hensher, 2019). The contemporary reality may be best described as an "adrenal rush" (Hensher, 2017, p. 86) governed by hyperbole and conjecture. The future is increasingly painted as a technologically deterministic utopia designed to revolutionise and herald a new era of smart transport for all.

The 'commercialisation' of MaaS, which is seen by many as a new entrepreneurial opportunity despite a sustainable business model yet to be found, raises many questions on societal governance (see Chapter 8). If, as is possible, many competing MaaS companies emerge, how will this resonate with a future where a 'unified transport app for the world' is promised to support portability wherever the customer travels? Vested interests and battles over who owns the user relationship (control of the customer) are already starting to surface, with specific views for example of Uber about maintaining their branding. What is urgently required is a standards-based, coalition approach—a MaaS ecosystem—in much the same way as technical standards were developed, for example, for smart cards.

Fig. 1.2 shows, MaaS has been characterised by different levels of integration, discussed further in Chapter 3, ranging from unimodal services through to greater collaboration through multimodal linking which we call *High level MaaS* in the presence of subscription bundles and *Low level MaaS* under a fully integrate PAYG offering. Examples of MaaS offers in real markets (including pilots and trials) are presented and discussed in other chapters, especially Chapters 3 and 4.

MaaS can also be seen as a tool spearheading modal integration. The integration of specific modes is motivated by the need to improve network efficiency, as illustrated by Chapter 2's modal efficiency framework (also see

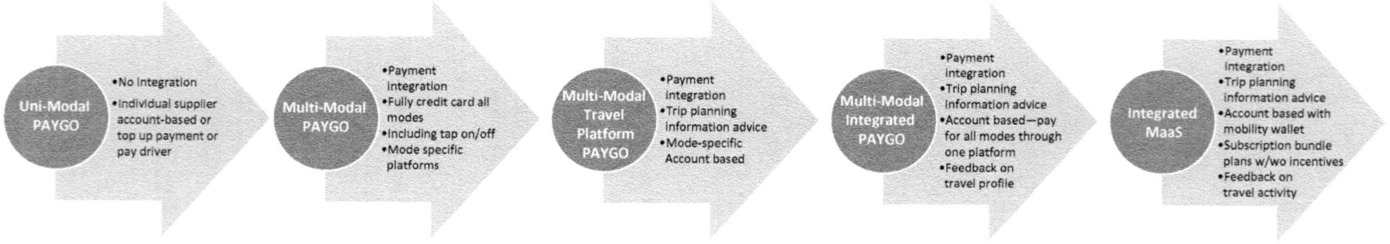


**FIG. 1.2** The evolution to integrated high level MaaS.

Wong et al., 2020). Emerging transport services (like the unfettered deployment of autonomous cars) might result in greater single-occupancy vehicles (and, indeed, deadheading zero-occupancy vehicles) and hence congestion. MaaS brings together all temporally efficient modes (i.e. non-ownership modes) across a range of spatial efficiencies and deploys them in a way which befits the geographic environment including consideration of location-specific financial incentives. The recent developments in digital platforms facilitate this integration and future regulatory intervention must ensure that the modes deployed provide a transition consistent with broader land use and societal regimes (Fig. 1.3).

The message in this book is best described by a common theme when talking with those interested in intelligent mobility solutions: namely that there is little detail on how best to implement MaaS to achieve both business and societal objectives, despite the rhetoric and hype as to the potential of MaaS. This book makes clear (Chapters 2 and 3) that MaaS is not a black and white concept but one that exists on a spectrum. Singular mobility services and mobility technologies definitely *do not* constitute MaaS but beyond this there are degrees of 'MaaS-ness'. Positively put, this book aims to take stock of where we are at present and what are some of the big challenges in the future in making MaaS an appealing reality.

It is likely that readers will, after reading this book, implicitly if not explicitly form a view of scepticism or support. We predict that many readers will move along the spectrum from left (scepticism) to right (support) and vice versa, and even back and forth in deciding on their degree of scepticism or support. Indeed, in writing this book the authors have found that they too have also revised their prior position(s), but where they have ended to date is best left a mystery to avoid at least biasing the responses of readers.

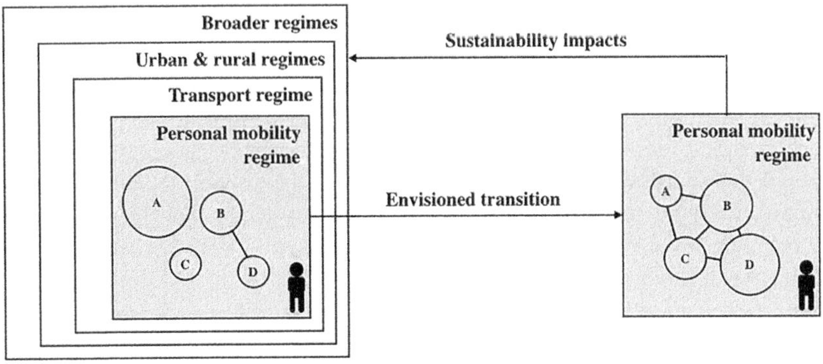


**FIG. 1.3** MaaS conceptualised from a transition perspective. *(Source: Smith, G., Hensher, D.A., 2019. Towards a framework for Mobility-as-a-Service policies. Paper Presented at the Thredbo 16—The International Conference Series on Competition and Ownership in Land Passenger Transport, Singapore.)*

## 1.2 Themes to contemplate

Before providing an overview of the following chapters we present, through a series of contexts and questions (C&Qs), some high agenda themes that are discussed in more detail throughout the chapters of the book. These fit within a MaaS topology that recognises the critical levels of integration: information, booking and payment, mobility packages, and policy (Sochor et al., 2018 and Fig. 1.1).

The first theme relates to the key participants in a MaaS ecosystem include the customer, the MaaS provider or integrator, the data provider and the transport operator, and Government. Chapter 3 reviews the global debate around these stakeholders including the emerging roles and where champions delivering leadership might come from.

A second theme relates to the way in which recent years have witnessed much MaaS-related experimentation and many trials have come and gone, whilst many more MaaS trials are under development or ongoing. A Lack of evaluation means lessons learnt from these trials are missing. Addressing this gap, Chapter 4 seeks to capture experience with MaaS trials to date based on a review of the setups, processes and outcomes of five seminal (and well documented) MaaS trials and, in proposing parameters for MaaS experimentation and research, explores the lessons that can be learnt from past and on-going MaaS trials and how should this information be used to design future MaaS trials to facilitate structured evaluation to best inform transport policymaking?

Chapters 3 and 4 address the theme of how the digital technology platforms are sufficiently ready to progress pilots, trails and ongoing MaaS schemes, including understanding the revealed preferences of customers about the wanted elements of a MaaS bundle. Chapter 5 develops a wider understanding of what customers want through the examination of the literature and presentation of stated preference experiments which are not so limited by geography, modal offering and/or the degree of integration of live pilot or operational schemes.

MaaS of course is much more than an App and a subscription plan. If public transport is to be at the heart of MaaS then we need to create circumstances where it is natural for public transport operators to seamlessly integrate with first and last mile solutions, enabling the customer to have the opportunity to plan, pay and execute trips according to their personal preferences. Chapter 5 provides a synthesis of what has been learnt to date about consumer preferences, providing some discussion of what success might look like for MaaS from a consumer perspective and what incentives might be needed to attract interest in a MaaS subscription package.

In terms of success on the supply side, firms must collaborate (either as operators of physical services, technology suppliers or financial investors) and there always exists commercial issues like cost/revenue sharing between responsible stakeholders, choice of branding and control/ownership of the customer. At a broader scale are the issues of uniformity and interoperability between regions and operators. What is needed is a national vision for MaaS as in Finland (cf. Smith et al. 2018b, 2019a) and operationalised through regulation to ensure competition and a 'level' playing field. These are recurring themes in Chapters 2 and 6.

The MaaS concept has proven difficult to realise beyond short-term and small-scale trials. The theme of governance and institutional barriers in the development and diffusion of MaaS is taken up in Chapter 7. Chapter 7 also discusses how to ensure 'joined up' government can act in defining a legislative framework for delivery.

A separate theme concerns whether MaaS can survive in rural and regional environments or modes, there is lower more generally low density origin–destination contexts, where, although physical space is more readily available and so may accommodate a greater mix of point-to-point offerings using less spatially intensive densities. This is taken up in Chapter 3 which identifies that pilots and operational schemes have been preponderantly in the urban areas, identifying a debate as to whether MaaS can survive in the less dense areas.

There is often a lot of stigma around mainstream public transport. This theme is explored in Chapters 2 and 8 as our definitions and experiences of public transport will be fundamentally different with MaaS. In particular, the emphasis with MaaS will be to move away from transportation consumed via asset ownership (i.e. purchase of a private car) to one based on buying a transportation service (via a subscription or pay-as-you-go (PAYGO) model. MaaS constitutes all non-ownership modes including traditional (mass transit) public transport but the difference here is that it also encompasses these emerging shared mobility services (ridesharing, carsharing, bikesharing).

The redefining of public transport will lead to changes in the way public transport services are procured by government is a theme addressed by Chapter 6. One of the greatest pendulum swings relates to the role of the public and private sectors and how this relationship is defined through contracts. A move to a MaaS setting brings changes to the status quo and challenges for a future institutional regime, with much reform occurring in the public transport contracting space.

Moving on to a wider context for MaaS, the book considers how autonomous and electric technologies might impact our cities if these modes become mature during the next 20 years. Congestion, as an important societal 'evil' might not improve as discussed in Chapter 8. The sharing culture, with its many manifestations, which is central to MaaS remains an issue as discussed in Chapter 2, might be the greatest constraint towards greater network efficiency.

A final theme concerns the aspiration for MaaS to have a stronger take in major cities with promises of reducing single occupancy car journeys. The pricing model and the regulatory overlay implemented to 'nudge' people towards particular modes, as suggested in Chapter 8 will be critical in determining the outcome. Many MaaS service providers might have a bias towards point-to-point transportation modes (taxis and ridesharing) since they are usually more profitable, and might encourage their users to shift from shared modes and mass transit as explored by Chapter 6.

## 1.3 Structure of the following chapters

Chapter 2 'What is MaaS and how it fits into the transport landscape' brings together a number of initial think pieces completed by the ITLS research team (Hensher, 2017, 2018a,b; Mulley, 2017; Wong et al., 2020) which set up the framework, vision and context for our subsequent programme of empirical and quantitative research market testing and envisioning a future under MaaS. Defining the starting point of our journey in this book, the chapter develops the need and rationale for MaaS, in the context of a changing mobility landscape. The chapter begins with some commentary on the hype and rhetoric which has accompanied the MaaS proposition in recent years. Greater clarity is brought to the MaaS concept, dispelling some of the myths which have circulated around the transport fraternity. Next, disruptors like new mobility services, technologies and businesses are presented, along with their associated impacts on the transport landscape. In particular, this relates to modal mix scenarios which might have unintended consequences on road capacity, congestion and the urban form. The concept of *modal efficiency* is developed through a conceptual framework situating both existing and emerging modes of transport around spatial and temporal dimensions. MaaS is presented as a vision to integrate temporally efficient modes across a range of spatial efficiencies, deployed according to geographic context and in doing so enhancing the operation of the transport network. Some final commentary on sharing is presented along with reflections on how a MaaS future might be realised.

Chapter 3 'Global debate and experience with MaaS' sets the current debate and experience in the context of the early roots of MaaS. It begins by looking at the background, noting in particular the enabling role of technological change and the developments in the service-sharing economy which have encouraged wide scale on-demand mobility services and the emergence of MaaS. The various definitions of MaaS that have been proposed in both the academic and professional literature are reviewed: the co-definition of MaaS remains elusive in terms of finding a definition which is universally accepted. The representation of MaaS via 'levels of integration' is considered and global development charted by analysing a selection of existing and former MaaS schemes in terms of their status and levels of integration. More detailed attention is given to three locations closely associated with the early development and growth of schemes (i.e. Finland, Sweden, and UK). Finally, reflections on the global debate relating to the development of MaaS are offered, drawing on the experience to date and analysis of the schemes discussed.

The main purpose of Chapter 4 'MaaS trials—what have we learnt?' is to establish the practical experience of MaaS thus far. It seeks to capture experience with MaaS trials to date. Five specific cases are selected for in-depth assessment; two from Sweden (UbiGo and EC2B in Gothenberg); one from Finland (Whim in Helsinki); one from Germany (MobiFlat in Augsburg); and one from Australia (Tripi in Sydney). In contrast to the bulk of MaaS and MaaS-like trials, the selected trials have been thoroughly documented, evaluated and disseminated to a wider audience. Following a review of the setups, processes and outcomes of the four selected trials, the chapter discusses key lessons learnt from these, and from the global pool of MaaS trials, noting that most trials have thus far been small-scale in terms of geographical coverage, longevity and numbers and variety of users, and that their context has varied significantly. Lastly, based on the discussion of lessons learnt, avenues for future MaaS experimentation and research are proposed, with a call for more MaaS trials as well as full-scale implementations.

As MaaS continues to evolve, a key driver for its success will be the market demand and user's willingness to pay for mobility services. Chapter 5 'What do we know about market interest and potential uptake?' examines the demand for MaaS products where travellers can either pre-pay for their mobility services bundled into a MaaS plan or Pay-as-they-go through a smartphone app that offers one-stop access to multiple modes of transport as well as providing journey planning, ticketing, and billing in real-time. Using state-of-the-art stated preference surveys conducted in Sydney, Australia and Tyneside, UK via face-to-face interviews, we aim to shed light on several key unknowns including potential uptake of MaaS and its likely impact on travel behaviour. This includes how MaaS adopters would access public transport services in the future and how drivers may question the necessity of their own cars in the presence of MaaS and vice versa. Stated preference methods offer a powerful behavioural tool to understand potential preferences for MaaS products and are especially informative in guiding, to some extent, the design of bundles.

From the user perspective, this chapter draws implications for policy makers and MaaS innovators around the business model to follow, the level of discount required to obtain commercially viable products, the necessity of cross-subsidy in providing MaaS, and the likely market segments of MaaS offerings. Based on the user's willingness to pay estimates, we also discuss issues around packaging such as how best to bundle, cost and market mobility plans to end users to obtain sustainable goals and a high take-up rate before exploring the ways in which MaaS might be introduced to the market in Chapter 6.

Chapter 6 'How might MaaS be best introduced to the market?' complements Chapter 3 by turning the focus from the demander to the supplier interface. Supply-side issues around the service delivery of mobility as a service (MaaS) is an important but often neglected aspect in the transport futures discussions, as compared with the demand-side issues covered in Chapter 5. This chapter begins by reviewing how governments procure transportation, particularly relating to how the allocation of responsibilities between the public and private sectors have changed in recent years. Commentary is made on the role of partnerships, especially between public transport operators and transportation network companies in the provision of more integrated and multimodal service offerings. The idea of a broker/aggregator bringing together specialised mobility and other value-add businesses is then established in the context of delivering MaaS. Brokers (or aggregators) need to think about funding sources and use various arguments to justify the long term business model potential, including the value to citizens of integration, the value of sustainable offers to society (especially the view of government and how it relates to their strategic goals), and the prospect of government using MaaS to reprice the use of roads in particular (hidden road user charging).

The chapter considers different approaches to business models as part of this service delivery ecosystem, sharing some barriers to implementation as well as empirical evidence for how the business community might wish to deliver MaaS.

Despite an overwhelming interest in Mobility-as-a-Service (MaaS) within the transport sector in recent years, very few such services are hitherto operational. In order to improve the understanding of why the MaaS concept has proven difficult to realise, Chapter 7 sets out to map key institutional barriers. Chapter 7 'Institutional barriers and governance' draws on documented MaaS activities in general, but on the convoluted development processes in Sweden in particular (e.g. Sochor et al., 2016; Smith et al. 2017, 2018a, 2019b,c). It finds that the development and diffusion of MaaS faces manifold barriers at several different institutional levels. This indicates that the process of realising MaaS will require vast and swift actions from a multitude of public and private actors. Given that the overarching aim is that the diffusion of MaaS should contribute to policy objectives, this imposes an immense governance challenge on the public sector. The chapter concludes by proposing five tactics that public sector authorities could implement to address the identified institutional barriers, and thus facilitate the development and diffusion of MaaS.

Chapter 8 'MaaS and issues impacting on broader transport and societal goals' steps away from the details of MaaS customer and supplier models to the societal setting in which evolving MaaS offerings should be assessed. The chapter synthesises the role that government might or should play in the evolving MaaS market to ensure that societal outcomes are supported. These include the great potential to deliver new transport services, improve road safety, alleviate congestion and increase productivity. It focusses on a number of costs and benefits that define the contribution to efficiency and equity of transport services within a network, specifically accessibility, traffic flow and subsidy implications. MaaS, as one popular interpretation of future collaborative and connected mobility services, must be considered under both the presence and absence of autonomous vehicles (AVs) as well as the extent to which we can change society to adopt a sharing culture. This chapter considers the future of MaaS with and without autonomous vehicles (car, bus and shuttles) since the inclusion of AVs has specific implications on the impact that a MaaS subscription plan has on the modal mix and its pricing in the transport network system.

Chapter 9 on 'Future challenges' recaps the contribution of this book by revisiting the questions of the global debate identified in Chapter 3 to examine how many of these questions now have answers, to identify those areas where there are 'still more questions than answers', and to compile a list of unanswered questions which need to be the preoccupation of future researchers. The conclusions of this book highlight that a MaaS future embraces a very appealing mobility strategy; however we are in the very early days in our understanding of how best to facilitate a MaaS future. Needing more research is an inevitable conclusion.

Chapter 2

# What is MaaS and how it fits into the transport landscape

Chapter outline



## 2.1 Introduction

The digital era has been hailed as the 'fourth' industrial revolution. Advances in digital technologies and their increasingly widespread availability are enabling us to realise new ways of delivering and accessing transport services. A desire to leverage these opportunities to realise "smart" cities (Lyons, 2016) has become the new order of the day. The rise of transportation network companies (TNCs) which have developed digital platforms to match demanders and suppliers, and to provide ridehailing, carsharing, bikesharing and microtransit embodies the pace and scale of this change. As discussed in Chapter 1, the world bears witness to massive venture capital raisings, with a plethora of new startups established, hostile takeovers and huge investments by some of the world's largest technology, automotive and financial enterprises. The desire to be innovative has become almost an end in itself—a part of the government agenda and narrative for politicians incumbent and aspiring. The future being painted is a technologically deterministic utopia which is said to revolutionise and herald a new era of transportation for all.

Understanding Mobility as a Service (MaaS). https://doi.org/10.1016/B978-0-12-820044-5.00002-6
© 2020 Elsevier Inc. All rights reserved.

MaaS has often emerged as an all-encompassing concept of these developments, and often confounded with singular modes or a technological platform. Chapter 1 addressed the hype which is often associated with the most dogmatic MaaS proponents. What is generally missing, however, is a convincing premise and rationale motivating the MaaS concept. It is often assumed (especially amongst players in private industry) that MaaS and advances in intelligent mobility are a precondition for a more desirable future corresponding with improved sustainability and accessibility for all humanity. However, there are fundamental unknowns which could affect whether MaaS makes this positive contribution. How might an integrated MaaS offering which bundles TNC-provided shared mobility services impact on the use of public transport, for instance? Could there be a danger that more people are enticed onto single-occupancy vehicles, especially with the advent of autonomous technologies? How might this affect land use and residential location in the longer term? Many of these effects are expected to be highly context-dependent. MaaS has at times offered itself as the solution, when in fact what is required is a clear definition of the problem statement in question.

The purpose of this chapter is therefore to establish a vision and rationale for MaaS in the context of an emerging future—including identifying any pitfalls unfettered deployment of technologies might bring and link this with the societal objectives espoused by government. Section 2.2 brings clarity to the MaaS proposition, challenging some of the hype and rhetoric which has dominated the topic in recent years. Section 2.3 introduces an emerging transport paradigm, driven by new mobility services, technologies and businesses. Section 2.4 places these disruptors in the context of how they might impact the mix of modes used for travel, with significant and adverse implications on road capacity, increasing congestion and in the longer term impacting urban form. The concept of *modal efficiency* is illustrated in Section 2.5 through a conceptual framework situating both existing and emerging modes of transport around spatial and temporal dimensions. Section 2.6 suggests how a MaaS future premised on shared mobility and modal integration constitutes a major opportunity to improve the transport realm. Some final commentary on demographic change and the sharing culture is provided in Section 2.7, before the chapter is brought to a conclusion in Section 2.8.

## 2.2 Conceptualising MaaS: Bringing clarity to the proposition

Five years ago, the term "mobility as a service" was very much unheard of beyond a few select entrepreneurs in Finland. In the years since, it has entered the transport and technology lexicon and become widely promoted, as the concept has caught the interest of transport operators, regulators, academics and other industry stakeholders alike, across both developed and developing economies. Whilst the MaaS proposition has never enjoyed a single fixed definition, the proliferation of the term across the transport fraternity has led it to become a 'buzzword' of sorts, similar to other overused descriptors like "smart" and "sustainable". Whilst Chapter 3 examines the commonalities of the definitions of MaaS (drawing on a broad range of literature sources and Chapter 1), this section aims to clarify what MaaS *is not* whilst also presenting some historical incarnations of the idea under former guises.

MaaS is often confounded with concepts like mobility on-demand (MOD), flexible transport services (FTS) and flexible mobility on-demand (FMOD). MOD, FTS and FMOD are just some examples of the plethora of services which have garnered significant attention, but (importantly) are not MaaS, describing only individual mobility services (see Section 2.3). The US is particularly susceptible to this confusion (particularly synonymising MaaS with ridehailing), given it being the birthplace of TNC giants Uber and Lyft (with their dominating market power), and the relatively recency of the term "MaaS" imported from Europe. Sometimes, transportation as a service (TaaS) is used in place of MaaS in the US. In Australia, the growing interest in government-sponsored on demand services has seen many private operators offer up a microtransit service under the name of MaaS, due to a lack of understanding of the concept and desire to join the latest 'craze' or 'bandwagon'. Ridehailing and microtransit all constitute mobility *services* which could form a component of a multimodal mobility *as a service* proposition. Describing MaaS as merely a technology (usually a better journey planner) is also problematic, since technology is only one key *enabler* of MaaS. Describing what is not MaaS as MaaS risks degrading the entire concept.

Today's widespread adoption of the "mobility as a service" terminology may be attributed to a group of Finnish entrepreneurs, most notable of which being Sampo Hietanen, widely proclaimed as the "father of mobility as a service". Mr. Hietanen is a civil engineer with a background in telecommunications and intelligent transport systems, and a former CEO of ITS Finland who went on to found several startups in these fields. He first proposed the MaaS concept back in 2006, inspired by the business model in the telecommunications sector. Under his advocacy (and that of his contemporaries), the MaaS terminology received a boost in recognition during the European Congress on ITS in Helsinki, 2014. Mr. Hietanen also advised a Masters student whose dissertation Heikkilä (2014) represents the first appearance of the MaaS term in the scientific literature (as referred to in Chapter 1), before its gradual adoption by the rest of the academy. Mr. Hietanen also went on to help reform the *Finnish Transport Code* (introduced as part of enabling legislation to support the development of digitally-led business models) as well as gain global recognition through his startup MaaS Finland (now MaaS Global).

Whilst many herald the concept as novel and innovative, important contributions from notably Mulley (2017) and Lyons et al. (2019) also note that MaaS is an evolution of the decades-old idea of mobility management. Mobility management has at its core the idea of matching the preferences of end users with service suppliers, via a clearinghouse mechanism for information and financial transactions (similar to a broker/aggregator as will be introduced in Chapter 6). The virtual agency approach of mobility management has formed a key part of the flexible transport literature and provision of demand-responsive service (Mulley and Nelson, 2009). The key difference in the mobility management era is that it pre-dated the modern proliferation of smartphones and instantaneous communication which makes many of the integration visions possible. Mulley (2017) therefore describes MaaS as simply "technology-enabled Mobility Management". Whilst there have been technological breakthroughs, the organisational and business model breakthroughs that will enable the widespread realisation of MaaS are in many respects still absent. Similarly, Lyons et al. (2019) offer that MaaS is evolutionary, rather than revolutionary, drawing back to functions described by (as an example) advanced traveller information systems (ATIS) in the pre-smartphone era. The aims of MaaS are also likened to what has been held as government policy for decades—e.g. "integration within and between different types of transport" as published in the UK government's 1998 White Paper *A New Deal for Transport* (Department of the Environment and Regions, 1998). Professor Lyons therefore posits MaaS as in many ways "old wine in new bottles". Finally, Pangbourne et al. (2020) also questions the role of rhetoric in the debate on how MaaS might become mainstream (see also Chapter 9).

A major theoretical contribution around the design and implementation of MaaS may be related to the *three Bs* "budgets, bundles and brokers" initially proposed in Hensher (2017, p. 91). Bundles relate to mobility packages which customers purchase, granting them a defined volume of access to different modes of transportation, often quantified in kilometre or hour terms. Brokers, also known as aggregators or intermediaries, integrate independent suppliers of transportation, and emerge as a new stakeholder in a business model as part of an ecosystem for delivering MaaS. Evidently, bundles capture a demand phenomenon and brokers a service delivery or supply-side issue. Budgets is cross-cutting and relates to how demand and supply ought to be considered by way of the preferences (including financial preference or willingness-to-pay) of relevant stakeholders. Chapters 5 and 6 collectively consider these *three Bs* with respect to demand and supply side issues.

Utriainen and Pöllänen (2018) offers an excellent review of the (then) existing MaaS literature, pointing to three primary foci of research to date: (i) establishing taxonomy and the role of different modes within the MaaS service offering; (ii) findings from MaaS pilots and trials; and (iii) the expected effects of MaaS on travel behaviour and government policy. A lot of this literature content follows in the subsequent chapters, beginning with the global debate and experience with MaaS (Chapter 3), demand-side issues (Chapter 5), then supply-side issues (Chapter 6). Before doing so, however, it is essential to define a single idea which encompasses an overarching vision for MaaS. Usually, this relates to the nature of ownership and use of the private car. As an example,

Mulley (2017) describes MaaS as the shift from owned physical assets such as a car to the service nature of mobility, consistent with the 'servitisation' of the economy. Audouin and Finger (2018) describes MaaS as a "'post car' system", where MaaS means *beyond* the private car. In both instances, the MaaS platform is an optimisation engine which enables this vision by combining modes and ensuring excellent customer experience. The purpose of this chapter is to present this overarching vision, but first it is necessary to contextualise this in the setting of the nexus of disruptors bringing rapid change to the mobility landscape.

## 2.3 Genesis for MaaS: Emerging transport disruptors

This nexus of disruptors may be broadly categorised under new mobility services, technologies and businesses. These developments offer enormous benefits like greater choice in mobility offerings for the community, but also runs the risk of unintended consequences linked to adverse effects on road capacity, congestion and urban form which can compromise the ideals of sustainable cities. A particular area of interest is how these services and technologies integrate or compete with high capacity public transport, as well as their effects on travel demand, private vehicle ownership and usage.

A plethora of new mobility services (Shaheen and Chan, 2016) have come online as a result of digital platforms (enabled by the widespread proliferation of smartphones) which TNCs have developed to match supply and demand and use sophisticated pricing signals to nudge travel behaviour and to accommodate any imbalances in supply in real-time. There exists a wide spectrum of such services and SAE International (2018) offers a taxonomy of shared mobility modes and key enabling technologies. Perhaps the most prevalent is ridehailing which has infamously disrupted taxi incumbents. Early evidence has been mixed but more often points to ridehailing competing with, rather than complementing public transport (Alemi et al., 2018; Rayle et al., 2016), though this depends on specific geographic environments and demographics. Indeed, ridehailing TNCs have identified public transport as a growth market through which they seek to penetrate, as evidenced by Uber's filing to the US Securities and Exchange Commission (SEC) as part of their initial public offering in 2019. There also exists evidence pointing to increased congestion as ridehailing vehicles circulate in search of trips (Alexander and González, 2015; Schaller, 2017).

One of the major critiques of ridehailing is that they fail to increase vehicle occupancies. A wave of ridesharing (or carpooling) schemes have hence developed, enhanced by ever more sophisticated ride matching capabilities (Amey et al., 2011; Teubner and Flath, 2015). In these cases, the driver shares the same (or similar) destination as the passenger(s), and in doing so reduces the number of cars on the road. A scaled-up version of such proposition has been described as microtransit (originally known as demand-responsive transport in their non-digital form). These are either provided commercially (e.g. UberPool, GrabShare, LyftLine), or as government-contracted on demand bus services. How these types of flexible services might provide an alternative to poorly occupied, expensive fixed route bus services is of real interest. Many incumbent bus operators are collaborating with TNCs and platform providers in an effort to 'uberise' their services (Boone et al., 2018; Wong, 2018). The business implications of this trend is explored in Chapter 6.

A number of new mobility services are also premised on the sharing of assets. Carsharing, for instance, offered under various ownership (peer-to-peer/fleet managed) and operating models (return-to-base/one-way/roaming) have come online (Shaheen et al., 2018), with carshare members even shown to increase their use of public transport and active modes (Martin and Shaheen, 2011). Another emerging service segment has been termed as 'micromobility'—short distance transport like bicycle and scooter sharing (sometimes called personal mobility devices). There exists enormous potential for this market to replace traditional motorised modes since a large proportion (e.g. 60% of trips in the US) are of a short distance of 5 miles or less (CB Insights, 2016). However, current evidence shows many e-scooter trips averaging just 1–1.5 miles (Noland, 2019), thereby displacing previous walking trips and questioning the likelihood that they can replace motorised modes. Further, regulatory issues linked to vandalism, theft and bans have accompanied their entry to market.

Whilst many of these shared mobility services are not new, having been trialled/tested in limited capacities over past decades, real time ride-matching algorithms and other new mobility technologies have made them more successful in attracting massive venture capital investments as evidenced by the growth of global behemoths Uber as well as SoftBank as the primary investor behind many ventures around the world. Indeed, the near universal penetration of smartphones has been hailed by many as the single greatest innovation for transportation in the last decade. Many proponents (though somewhat speculative and led by technology giants like Tesla and Uber) have argued that technologies like artificial intelligence, connected and autonomous vehicles will enhance the efficient use of vehicle and infrastructure assets and reduce congestion (linked to their ability to platoon—see also Chapter 8). The decoupling of labour costs from service quantity will bring a step-change in the cost-effective provision of public transport (although what form this will take remains to be seen). There also runs the risk that the influx of more personalised transport services can bring negative consequences in the absence of appropriate pricing and regulation. For instance, empty vehicles deadheading, induced demand and greater point-to-point service provision could increase traffic congestion and urban sprawl—issues explored in Section 2.4. Research is hence being advanced using the stated choice methodology (Daziano et al., 2017; Kyriakidis et al., 2015; Payre et al., 2014) to understand acceptability and the public's willingness-to-pay for driverless cars. This will help inform their operation/ownership model which are key unknowns in the move towards a driverless future.

The final disruptor is the emergence of new mobility businesses which are leveraging these technologies to deliver the innovative services introduced. Already, a plethora of companies whose core business has not traditionally been associated with the delivery of transportation services are foraying into the sector. Many existing companies need to adapt to change and disruption—including rethinking who their customers might be in the future. The need to develop new business models may lead to the creation of entire new industries (Teece, 2010). As an example, the rise of ridehailing has brought about a host of related businesses in data management and technology suppliers building (for instance) digital platforms connecting demanders and suppliers. In a report by McKinsey and Bloomberg (2016), the authors describe the potential knock-on effects across sectors for some of these trends, as well as how the boundaries between and within sectors might erode and sectors converge. One of the most potent examples of innovation and boundary blurring comes from the automotive manufacturing industry as the sector recognises the need to diversify their revenue stream. The shift from vehicle ownership to access may mean that selling cars might not be their core business in the future. Another example are incumbent bus operators who are struggling to see their value proposition beyond being an organiser of labour (which will be challenging in a driverless world) and hence aim to transform into 'total' transport providers (Stanley et al., 2019). The role of a mobility broker/aggregator within a MaaS context is described in Chapter 6.

In general, the nexus of emerging mobility services, technologies and businesses brings about a host of risks and opportunities. Table 2.1 summarises

**TABLE 2.1** Summary of the disruptive drivers and their implications for the transport ecosystem, as discussed in Section 2.3.

| | (1) New mobility technologies | (2) New mobility businesses | (3) New mobility services |
|---|---|---|---|
| Drivers | Artificial intelligence | New market entrants | Application-enabled ridesharing/carsharing |
| | Autonomous vehicles | Venture-capital backed propositions | Micromobility options |
| | Electric vehicles | Move from asset ownership to access as a service | Microtransit options |
| Impacts | Unfettered deployment of autonomous cars | Incumbent businesses no longer relevant | Enhanced freedom and opportunities |
| | Reduced cost resulting in induced demand for travel | Businesses need to disrupt themselves or risk being disrupted | Negative impacts on public transport patronage |
| | Changing definitions of liability and ethics | Blurring of sector boundaries | Higher service level expectations (for reduced cost) |

some of the drivers of this future as well as their impacts as described in this section. In terms of the direction of causality, new mobility technologies (1) are being used by new mobility businesses (2) to offer new mobility services (3). The next section will consider some possible scenarios for how these disruptors might impact on the transport network.

## 2.4 What could this mean for the transport landscape?

The key question remains what these emerging services, technologies and businesses will mean for our cities and our communities. A major unknown is how new services might be synergetic or competitive to existing fixed route public transport (Veeneman, 2019). Unintended consequences are linked to the possible influx of point-to-point transportation, especially as autonomous technologies come online, and based on the present model of universal vehicle ownership. The possible demise of fixed route public transport, replaced by personalised point-to-point transport services will bring challenges with respect to ensuring adequate road capacity, as well as to curtail congestion and to enable the development of sustainable urban forms.

In order to consider the efficacy of the changing mobility landscape, it is important to step back and understand why humanity has evolved to live in cities. Cities exist as a solution to the transportation problem, by bringing people and activities together in close proximity, so as to garner economies of agglomeration and scope. Traffic congestion and externalities are a function of cities agglomerating at a rate where the transport system has not kept up, and is very much a failure linked to success. Roads and road-based land uses like parking account for 30% or more of the urban land use—this is an oft-cited figure which varies considerably with up to two thirds of land use being devoted to transportation in cities like Los Angeles. Cities exist as systems where there are competing demands on land use and so road space is limited, calling on the need for the most efficient use of this scarce commodity. This section details two scenarios of transport modal development which has been promulgated by technology giants and describes why they might be problematic for the urban realm.

### 2.4.1 Modal displacement: Effect of TNCs and personalised modes

Modal displacement embodies a scenario where fixed route public transport becomes less prominent in the urban realm. The underlying rationale for fixed route public transport (more technically, mass transit), is to transport people from different origins to different destinations on a single vehicle (Walker, 2012), which although adds an access/egress component, ensures that the use of the vehicle (and road space) is spatially efficient by carrying volume. As described, many TNCs have a stated objective to replace public transport through price and quality competition. Buses operating in mixed traffic are particularly vulnerable to this, whilst railways with dedicated right-of-way might be harder to displace.

One of the greatest concerns is the downward spiral (process of cumulative causation) as quality public transport becomes gradually degraded. To start with, TNCs do not compete on a level playing field since they subcontract drivers and do not treat them as employees (thereby avoiding minimum wages and on-costs like benefits and taxes). This helps them obtain a price advantage to disrupt the taxi industry and threaten public transport viability by first picking the cream and undercutting heavily profitable bus routes. Governments can no longer internally cross-subsidise (in a regulated market) between profitable routes and those it supports as a community service obligation. Increasingly, governments will have less money to run services and the reduction in quantity and quality further brings about a reduction in patronage. This entices more people to use TNCs. This modal displacement cycle is illustrated in Fig. 2.1.

Whilst TNCs may bring a lot of impacts on the existing public transport sector, there is also a move amongst bus operators and government authorities to 'uberise' their fixed route services into on demand (microtransit) incarnations (Mulley and Kronsell, 2018). The motivation here might be to reduce service costs, especially during evening and weekend periods where

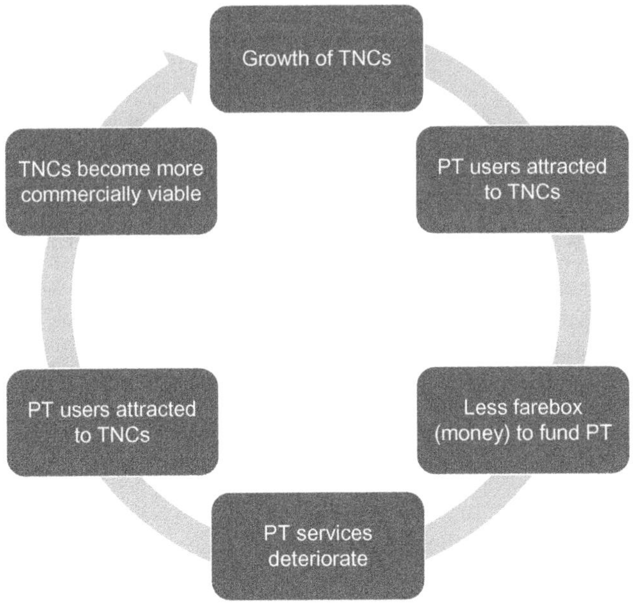


**FIG. 2.1** Process of cumulative causation where public transport (PT) is eventually displaced by TNC-provided services.

passenger loads are low. This has been the impetus for the flexible transport movement going as far back as the 1960s (initially as dial-a-ride), which has been met with considerable challenges in how they have not been able to endure (Mulley and Nelson, 2009; Walker, 2012). Indeed, Currie and Fournier (2019) found in a global review of demand-responsive services that half of all such services have failed. Cost savings are often negative due to the additional vehicle kilometres (hence labour) and fleet required, whilst any savings from digital dispatching capabilities have been marginal. Many demand-responsive propositions have also been implemented on top of existing fixed route services without adequate reform of the entire network structure (Mulley and Daniels, 2012). This reality might change in an autonomous future and studies like Becker et al. (2020) are quantifying exactly what savings autonomous buses could entail.

Whilst demand-responsive transport has merits in particular geographic (and temporal) circumstances, it is important that they do not replace fixed routes, stops and schedules as a means of providing high capacity transport in cities. Not only do more personalised services result in more road space being needed to provide the same transport capacity, the smaller vehicles will also result in greater vehicle kilometres travelled, with implications on emissions and congestion. Smaller vehicles contravene economies of scale which are the central supporting blocks of cities, and encourage lower population density and (by extension) urban sprawl. Greater point-to-point transport will also replace the present access/egress component in terms of the walk to public transport stops and stations with motorised transport; and this has impacts on health and social inclusion. The challenge, therefore, is to ensure that public transport modes are not displaced, but rather TNC modes are provided to support fixed route public transport as the core. MaaS offers itself as an opportunity to achieve this ideal. Section 2.6 explains the objective further.

### 2.4.2 Modal convergence: Effect of autonomous technologies

The modal convergence scenario describes a future where the mix of modes presently available in the network all converge into a universal automated taxi service (sometimes described as robo-taxis or taxibots). Such a future has been viewed as a panacea (driven by technologists and futurists) to deliver universal point-to-point services at a low cost. Enoch (2015) is one prominent proponent who envisages this modal convergence future. Illustrated in Fig. 2.2, the scenario proposes that the three different modal families which exist today will all converge into a universal automated taxi system. Cars, representing low occupancy and privately-owned vehicles, become displaced due to the increasing cost of ownership and greater awareness amongst the community of the externalities of private transport. Buses, capturing high occupancy and fleet-managed systems, disappear due to end users' desire for point-to-point or more personalised services. Finally, taxis, which are low occupancy and fleet-managed, are displaced

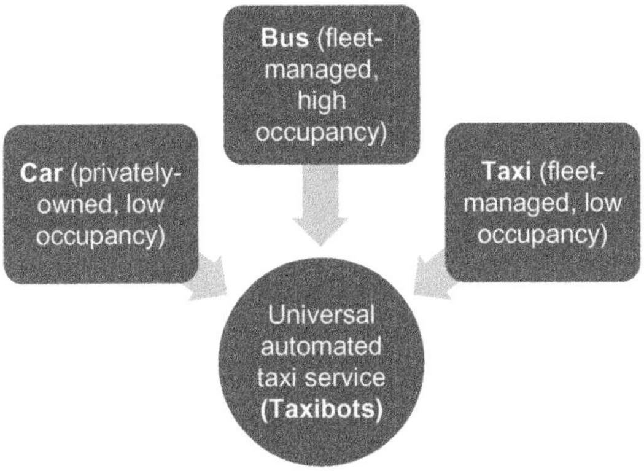


**FIG. 2.2** Convergence of different categories of urban passenger transport modes. *(Adapted from Enoch, M.P., 2015. How a rapid modal convergence into a universal automated taxi service could be the future for local passenger transport. Tech. Anal. Strat. Manag. 27(8), 910–924.)*

due to customers' desire for lower cost travel. The replacement is by a new category of low occupancy and fleet-managed vehicles (taxibots).

Although Enoch (2015) recognises that modal convergence will bring increased vehicle kilometres, the severe binding constraint of road space being a scarce commodity in dense urban environments is not recognised. Point-to-point transportation is not scalable—they are by definition low volume and associated with sole or low occupancy vehicles. All of these take up more road space per passenger transported. Another limitation in the Enoch (2015) hypothesis is the assumption that people will choose to access autonomous vehicles via a fleet-managed (taxi) model—a far more efficient model than when they are privately owned. However, this is based on people transcending car culture, car ownership and car pride and willing to make cars no longer a status symbol (though many argue this is already happening amongst the young—see Section 2.7). Another model as put forward by Elon Musk (2016) is where autonomous vehicles are privately held but hired out when not in use for driverless ridehailing. Whilst this might be preferred to full private ownership, spatial and temporal peaking issues come to mind as with the case of one-way/roaming carsharing and dockless bikesharing.

The promise of autonomous vehicles including the Enoch (2015) modal convergence future is premised on the fallacy that this will bring "uncongested mobility for all" (Zachariah et al., 2014). A number of simulation studies have attempted to model the impacts of an automated taxi regime on road congestion (see Chapter 8 for more details). Martinez and Crist (2015), in a study on Lisbon, Portugal, found that whilst only a quarter of the existing car fleet will be required, these will be utilised far more extensively throughout the day. The study showed minor increases in average travel times, based on local streets absorbing much of the traffic increase (as opposed to arterials and distributors). Not only does this disregard the road hierarchy, it will turn over local communities where pedestrians ought to have priority to motorised modes and bring with it associated noise, air and urban amenity externalities. In another simulation study on the road network of Austin, Texas, Fagnant et al. (2015) showed each shared autonomous vehicle being able to replace 9.3 conventional vehicles, with each vehicle averaging 26 trips per day over 8 hours, as compared to 3 trips over 1 hour under the present privately-owned regime. Total vehicle miles travelled will increase by 8%, accounting for unoccupied/empty-vehicle travel. Another study by Maciejewski and Bischoff (2016) on a network model of Berlin, Germany, concluded no flow capacity improvements and recommended against the wholesale introduction of autonomous taxis due to the large scale congestion impacts it will bring.

What is often neglected in these conversations is the communal issues of amenity (its intrinsic value), as well as recognition of feedback loops and induced demand. Induced demand might arise from three scenarios. Firstly, existing drivers might choose to travel further and more often due to time freed up en route—this is linked to location choice over the medium term and the idea of Marchetti's Constant (Marchetti, 1994). Secondly, non-drivers can now join the network, thereby increasing the number of cars on the roads (Harper et al., 2016). Finally, there will be an influx of zero-occupancy vehicles dead running to avoid parking or to reposition for their next trip. Clearly, these are a complex set of scenarios where even the best network models, which show (in whatever limited way) that modal convergence and modal displacement can function in cities, need to be supported by naturalistic experiments of human behaviour to understand these feedback effects. For instance, Harb et al. (2018) conducted a revealed preference study of the demand impacts of autonomous vehicles on people (by in effect giving them a free chauffeur) and found participants travelling some 76% more kilometres than they previously did. In the longer term, the urban form may morph to reflect the increased accessibility, with feedback effects on congestion (Hensher, 2018b and Chapter 8).

Despite this, there is a place for autonomous taxis but the question is in what settings? Clearly, cities require a multimodal offering linked to land use—and MaaS is a facilitator of enhanced multimodality. The next section will motivate the need for a multimodal future by examining the various efficiencies of different modes of transport.

## 2.5 Modal efficiency and the rationale for integration

All modes of transportation may be defined as a function of space and time and may be situated amongst spatial and temporal efficiency dimensions, as measures of their ability to reap economies of scale in the utilisation of the transportation asset. Spatial efficiency is defined as the number of people carried per unit area and may be measured as the number of passengers carried per vehicle/train consist (or per unit road space equivalent). Note the caveat that a vehicle's capacity and its loading can be immensely different, particularly during different

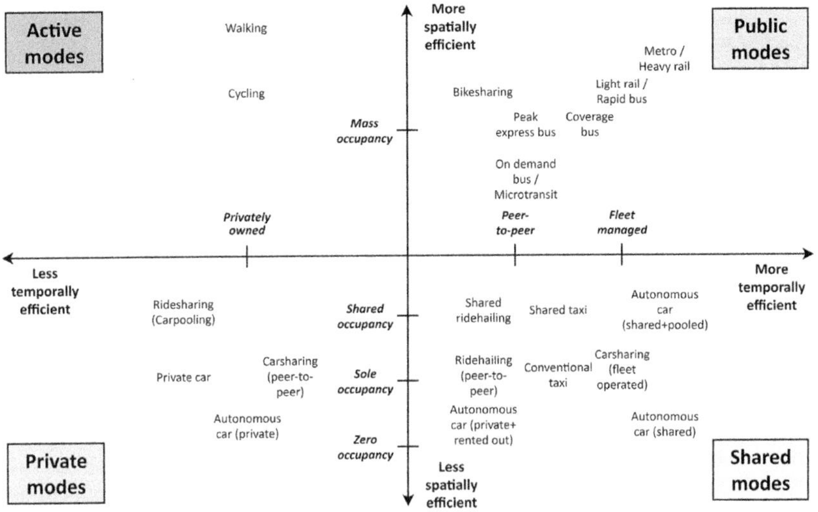


**FIG. 2.3** The modal efficiency framework situates public, private, active, and shared modes with respect to their spatial and temporal efficiencies. Both modal displacement and modal convergence scenarios developed see the centre of mass reside in the bottom right, shared modes quadrant (Wong et al., 2020).

times of the day. Temporal efficiency considers whether the vehicle is mobile or idle, and is measured by the proportion of time a vehicle spends on the road (in revenue service for public transport). Fig. 2.3 illustrates these dimensions and situates public, private, active and shared modes in each quadrant within the space–time plane. Axes scales are estimated and intended to be illustrative only.

The modal efficiency framework is divided into four quadrants, each of which captures a spatial and temporal efficiency combination. In the top right are both spatially and temporally efficient public modes. These encompass bus and rail mass transit, which carry large amounts of people in a single vehicle (or train consist), as well as ply the network around the clock. More specifically, the temporal efficiency of public transport may be measured by metrics like the operational peak-to-base ratio (explored in Section 2.6 on Temporal Opportunities). Naturally, metro/heavy rail carry the most people (even super dense crush loads in India and Japan), followed by different classes of bus services (along with light rail). Microtransit and demand-responsive buses feature as less spatially/temporally efficient public transport, as they use smaller vehicles and many operate at peak periods and in the peak direction only.

On the other side of the ledger are private modes, which are neither spatially nor temporally efficient. Private modes revolve around the private car which average just 1.2 people per vehicle (an oft-cited figure for developed economy journey-to-work travel) and sit idle (unproductive) the other 95% of the time. Ridesharing (or carpooling) also exists in this quadrant, being slightly more spatially efficient (shared occupancy), but still not temporally efficient (since they remain privately owned).

The shared modes quadrant has received the most attention of late (see Section 2.3), and capture a range of temporally efficient but spatially inefficient modes. Previously only available as conventional and (in some markets) shared taxis (a *shared public* mode), a range of TNC-provided new mobility services have now joined the quadrant. Ridehailing, which operate similarly to taxis, have the same spatial efficiency but are less temporally efficient since they are often run by drivers as a side job. This compares with taxis which might even operate multiple shifts in fleet-owned environments. Carsharing, as compared with private vehicles, are more temporally efficient (but not as much as taxis), and even more so in fleet-managed than peer-to-peer form. One reason for this is that in the latter case there are more transaction costs associated with screening and less convenient positioning/availability, resulting in a lower utilisation of vehicles. A lot of interest (and presented in Section 2.4) revolves around the impact of autonomous cars, whose efficiency may be considered as a function of their ownership and operating models. In general, they can be considered less spatially efficient due to the amount of time repositioning (deadheading) with zero occupancy, though this improves if they are not privately-held but rather operated as part of a fleet (in this latter case temporal efficiency also improves). When autonomous cars are used as microtransit (pooled trips), then their spatial efficiency improves further—as is the case with all shared modes.

For completeness, active modes like walking and cycling are added to the framework. Both are very spatially efficient, but they are placed in the less temporally efficient side although this is not entirely relevant since the requirement for vehicle assets is minor (or non-existent). Whilst they play an immensely important role in CBD-type environments, active modes are more limited for longer distance travel.

Whilst the framework is designed to be purely illustrative, it nevertheless provides a powerful visual representation in terms of the spatial–temporal modal mix and link to a desired policy setting. In general, the recommendation is to increase spatial and temporary efficiencies wherever possible. As such, private mode travel should be shifted to the shared modes quadrant, and shared modes moved to public modes, wherever the geographic environment allows this. The next sections will consider this link with geography, and how MaaS might be a key enabler in the move up this spectrum. The very real worry is that the opposite might be happening, especially with public modes being displaced by shared modes (or autonomous taxis in the future), as has been suggested in Section 2.4.

### 2.5.1 How might MaaS vary between different geographic contexts?

One of the key questions concerns how MaaS might look in different geographic settings and cultures in which it is introduced. Taking two extremes, one can consider on one hand private car *first* cities (1A), such as in North America and

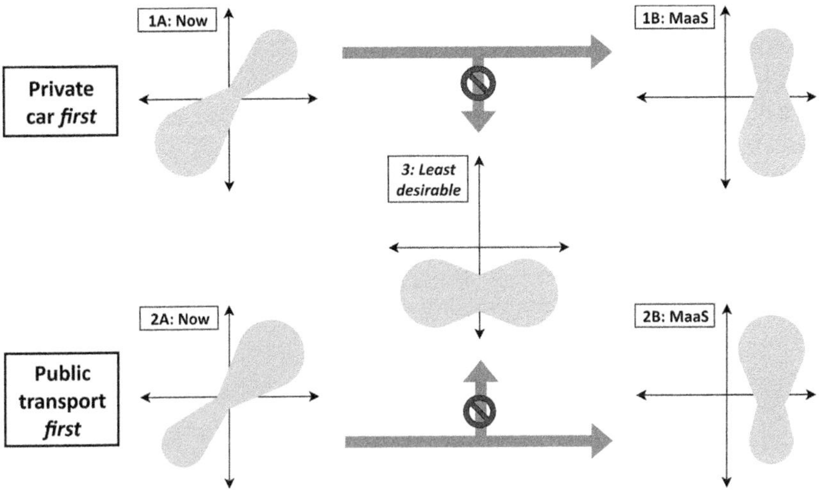


**FIG. 2.4** The modal development framework envisages how MaaS might look in terms of the centre of mass of modes (as defined by their respective spatial–temporal efficiencies) in both (1) private car *first* and (2) public transport *first* cities. A third (3) least desirable future should be avoided (Wong et al., 2020).

Australia, where the vast majority of travel is by private car (upwards of 80%). On the other extreme are public transport *first* cities (2A), such as in Asia and Europe, where public transport commands the leading mode share. These two settings and their specific MaaS modal mixes are illustrated diagrammatically in Fig. 2.4.

In auto-centric private car *first* cities, MaaS can help to make public transport more attractive to existing car users. The low density and low land use diversity of these cities means that public transport is unlikely to start taking centre stage. The aim, therefore, is to move point-to-point transport from private modes to shared modes, moving up the temporal efficiency dimension (from privately-owned to fleet-managed form). Early opportunities include targeting families' second cars and those who use their cars exclusively to access public transport (example market segments are studied in Chapter 5). The shared modes need to be deployed/accessed in a way which supports the increasing use of public transport (see Section 2.6). Fig. 2.4 (1B) shows the possible market share of public and shared modes in a private car *first* MaaS future.

In public transport *first* cities, it is important that MaaS does not replace the many significant high volume and high capacity services which already command a high market share. In such environments, the greatest risk as described in Section 2.4 is where more personalised shared modes displace existing public transport patronage. MaaS should therefore be designed as a supporting mobility tool to high volume systems. The mix of modes under MaaS is shown in Fig. 2.4 (2B). Another common question is how MaaS might work in high density urban environments, as compared with rural and regional environments where road space is more readily available. This may be analogised to the public transport (2B) and private car (1B) futures where the modal mix is a direct function of the urban environment. In either extreme, Fig. 2.4 (3) represents the least desirable outcome where public transport is displaced and MaaS products are comprised entirely of the least spatially efficient modes. The key focus of MaaS is on the temporally efficient two right quadrants—as it is a model based on access, not ownership. It is now important to consider at the strategic level exactly how MaaS in *bringing together all temporally efficient modes across a range of spatial efficiencies* may be deployed by integrating public and shared modes across spatial and temporal dimensions.

## 2.6 Improving modal efficiency through MaaS

There exists already an abundance of literature on the integration concept (Chowdhury and Ceder, 2016; Grotenhuis et al., 2007; Mulley and Moutou, 2015; Preston, 2010), but this has often been centred around public transport in isolation (often around infrastructure concerns), without regard for shared mobility modes or indeed private modes of transport. More recently, the rationale for integration has been clarified, with Veeneman (2019, p. 39) stating that "integration should put all modes in their strength and provide efficient integration between the different modes". The spatial and temporal efficiency dimensions outlined offers itself as a conceptual basis as a framework for this integration. This integration will ensure that the transport network is network-wide efficient, not just efficient within a single mode or operator (Chapter 3 offers additional contributions on the service integration objectives of MaaS). MaaS offers unique prospects to achieve this objective—and operationalising such ideals through MaaS is not often enough credited as the overarching objective for MaaS.

### 2.6.1 Spatial integration

Different modes offer different spatial performance, and ought to be deployed in a spatial (land use) setting most appropriate for the said mode. Denser environments naturally see greater demand on limited road space and so more spatially intensive mass transit options should be deployed wherever possible. The urban design and transport policies should also encourage active travel. In more suburban and rural environments with more sparse land use patterns and travel demands, point-to-point transportation can play a greater role. This delineation manifests itself not only between land use types but also between different types of travel or flow. High volume radial travel to and from the urban core or central business district are best suited for high capacity modes whilst orbital/circumferential travel see less volume and hence can be better served (for a given service level) by less spatially intensive modes. Mixed land use cities may see a hybrid state of play. Already, the trend towards tiered bus networks (e.g. rapid, suburban, local) consolidating services on frequent trunks (Nielsen et al., 2005; Walker, 2008) pay homage to this concept but further exacerbate the first and last mile challenge. Shared modes can play a perfect role under a trunk and feeder system to feed thriving arterials, but the institutional regime and contract design must be conducive and sufficiently incentivise such service offering (explored in Chapter 6).

One of the opportunities for MaaS is to offer end users choice for different market segments and journey types, but to do so in a way by nudging behaviour through pricing that is consistent with broader societal objectives (see Chapter 8). In a MaaS future, customers may choose between a cheaper transfer ride and a single-seat journey (as well as shared occupancy or sole occupancy), but this latter must be priced accordingly so as to trade off between the spatial–temporal characteristics of different modes—and to not let demand inundate the network. The underlying rationale relates to the scalability of each mode as demand grows. For public transport on dedicated corridors, crowding manifests and this reduces the road space per passenger but travel time remains generally consistent. In the case of private cars (and most shared modes), the converse occurs with road space per passenger held constant (often valued as 'comfort'), but journey time and reliability (temporal components) suffering. There is hence a trade-off between these spatial and temporal elements and the right policy settings (see Chapter 8) can help to ensure an adequate mix. Those who value space must pay for it and those who value time need to be afforded that certainty. Spatial integration is a key enabler for this MaaS vision of the future.

### 2.6.2 Temporal opportunities

The other component of integration which is rarely mentioned in the literature is integration in the temporal dimension. The very nature of travel is that it is 'peaked'; and the transport system across all modes seeks to meet this peak demand (Walker, 2012). Roads are less adaptive to demand, with the capacity generally static—much latent capacity in the off-peak but generally failing to meet peak demand (manifesting itself as congestion). Public transport also sees crowding, but service levels can be dialled up and down as per fluctuations in demand. However, the public transport system still sees elements of fixed peak demand 'costs'. For instance, peak demand defines the vehicle requirements, vehicle capacities as well as staffing levels (Vuchic, 2005). In fact, peak costs are the highest due to the vehicles procured and additional personnel employed to service peak periods exclusively (De Borger and Kerstens, 2007; Walker, 2012), all of which sit idle and unproductive at other times during the day. The temporal efficiency of public (and shared/fleet-managed) modes is hence a function of the peak-to-base ratio—the ratio of vehicle assets being used in the peak versus the base (often defined at midday). Temporal integration across public and shared modes offer the potential to develop synergies and better enhance temporal efficiency, by better utilising vehicle assets.

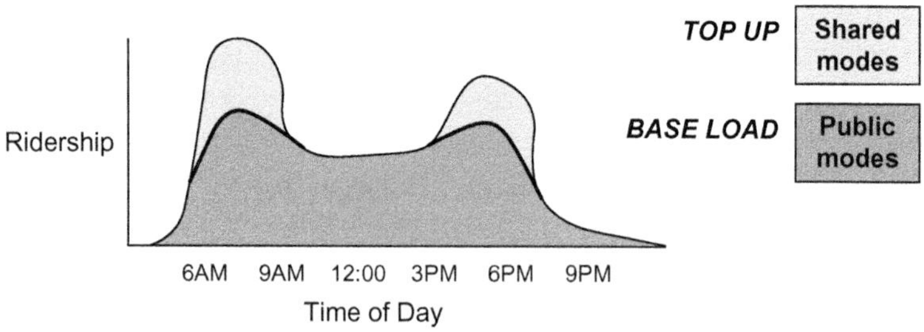


**FIG. 2.5** Potential model for temporal integration between public transport and shared modes (Wong et al., 2020).

The idea hence is to use digitally-enabled shared modes as a top-up service to conventional public transport as the base load, illustrated in Fig. 2.5. Therein lies the opportunity to reduce the peak-to-base ratio and save peak service costs for the public transport operator, by outsourcing the most expensive (peak) service to TNCs. The key to enabling this is also to ensure that vehicle occupancies on these shared modes can also be lifted during peak periods. The shared modes top-up might also provide a better (for instance, door-to-door) service so should be priced at a premium accordingly. In Wong (2015), the distance decay function for temporal variations in transit patronage was plotted, suggesting that there may be particular geographic contexts where this model of temporal integration may be best applied. Naturally, temporal variations also exist at other scales such as between winter/summer months and school term/holiday periods. Specific vehicle types might also help cater for specific trip purposes, such as a small pod for journey-to-work and a family vehicle for a road trip. The opportunity under MaaS is to better coordinate demand with the supply of services and vehicle assets. By enhancing the temporally efficient use of vehicles through the work of a centralised coordinating entity, this will permit a smaller total fleet pool.

## 2.7 Demographic change and the sharing culture: Niche or scalable?

As described in Sections 2.5 and 2.6, the key ideal of MaaS is to encourage private car users onto shared transport and shared transport users onto public transport (as well as private car users directly onto public transport). Doing so represents an upwards spiral with the greater use of modes which are more temporally efficient as well as spatially efficient (Fig. 2.3). Whilst integrative technology can help enable this move, a key precursor is also people's willingness-to-share.

Demographic change has been put forward as a key enabler of this paradigm, and already said to have enabled the acceptance of shared mobility services (ridehailing, bikesharing, carsharing, and microtransit). Demographic change is a major push factor for their uptake, encompassing youth driver licensing decline (Delbosc and Currie, 2013), drops in driving amongst millennials (McDonald, 2015), and attitudinal changes in cars no longer being held as a status symbol—at least in a growing number of developed economies. Millennials and young consumers also appear to be the driving force behind the growth of the access or collaborative economy—the idea of 'servitisation' in renting goods and services on demand rather than acquiring them permanently. Examples have proliferated across many sectors including media, hospitality, education, financing, the labour market and property. A comparison has been drawn (and the link questioned) between millennials' disposition to share on social media and their propensity to share personal space (Delbosc and Mokhtarian, 2018), especially given that shared mobility services might imply a higher level of personal intimacy than public transport—a psychological barrier for some users (Gardner and Abraham, 2007).

The idea of 'peak car' is closely related to these demographic and technological changes which are supposedly reducing the need to travel. The precursor to this concept is the idea of saturation. Metz (2013) offers an excellent synopsis of what is termed the 'fourth' era of travel, where average per capita growth in daily travel has ceased. Goodwin and Van Dender (2013) point to the importance of locational effects, including factors like settlement size, density or degree of urban development on car ownership and use measures, which are usually only considered in aggregate (by city or country). Indeed, there exists a view that the effects of an ageing population has a far greater effect on shaping car travel trends, over and above any attitudinal changes held by millennials (Kuhnimhof et al., 2013). As such, a number of authors have suggested that the notions of peak travel and peak car may be premature.

One major unknown is whether millennials will continue with their inner urban location choice and use of sustainable modes when they grow older, or will their travel patterns revert to car dependency as displayed by earlier generations (Delbosc et al., 2019; Delbosc and Nakanishi, 2017)—paying credence to the idea of life cycle stages and the fact that lifestyle preferences are not static but dynamic. McCarthy et al. (2019) offer reasons to be optimistic, by challenging the notion that all parents adopt car-oriented behaviour following parenthood. Another demographic factor relates to an ageing population, with increasing life expectancies leading to a greater proportion of dependents who can no longer drive (Shergold et al., 2015). This acts as a push factor towards the acceptability of shared transportation. Cultural attitudes towards sharing assets and space will be an important influencing factor going forward. As new vehicular technologies come online, there will be a greater emphasis on how vehicles are owned and used (e.g. autonomous vehicles and new 'repositioning' congestion). In the future, MaaS will also rely on people accepting a shift from vehicle ownership to access in terms of how they consume transportation.

One of the dominating themes used to support MaaS, as referenced earlier, is the claimed role of MaaS in contributing to reducing private car ownership.

The premise is that a subscription plan that gives one-stop (application-based) easy and convenient access to many modal transport services will encourage individuals to dispose of their private vehicles, be it all or the second car where a household has multiple private vehicles. If this is to eventuate, then it is suggested that individuals will be in a position, through their choice of a subscription plan, to use whatever mode suits a particular travel circumstance. The move or otherwise to a sharing culture is a pivotal topic in relation to how MaaS might add value to broad societal goals. The need to behaviourally change people from using a low marginal cost mode (with high fixed cost that is their private car) to a high marginal cost mode like MaaS enters the fray as another challenge for how scalable or niche MaaS might turn out to be (Mulley, 2017).

Some very strong behavioural assumptions are being made under this somewhat idealistic prospect about people's willingness-to-share mobility services. At one extreme, studies have suggested that individuals that still wish to use a car prefer to travel without a stranger or to travel alone and are not disposed to having to talk to others during a journey. At the other extreme, there exists arguments to suggest that sharing will appeal. Standing et al. (2019) provide a detailed assessment of the attraction and challenges in achieving a sharing culture, discussing the facilitators and barriers for sharing in transport. Facilitators include trust, adequate regulation, ease of use of technology platforms and a rethink of the value of ownership. Barriers include over-regulation, lack of trust until recommended by someone, trust in potential sharers, set-up costs and a lack of profit (for service suppliers), and long-held norms and values in relation to independence, private space and status.

There are, however, a number of different interpretations of sharing. They include using a car-based service with a driver but travelling by yourself, travelling with other members who are known to you as a point-to-point service, and travelling in a group of people who are strangers (e.g. in microtransit) where the origins and destinations are different. A useful way to think about this is to distinguish self-service, for hire or required membership. How might these different contexts potentially impact on the transport network's performance?

Another issue is the misrepresentations by TNCs concerning the use of the terminology 'sharing'. TNCs providing ridehailing have long associated their products with the misnomer 'ridesharing'—despite there being no coincidence of origin and destination between the driver/partner and passenger(s). With ridesharing (both casual carpooling and formalised liftsharing), both the driver and passenger(s) share the same (or similar) destination, thereby reducing the number of cars and hence net road space required. Ridesharing/carpooling drivers are usually not motivated by fare income but rather social benefits when they share a destination with the passenger—part of a regular journey-to-work trip, for instance. Ridesharing operates on a cost recovery basis (so it is not considered a commercial activity in the context of taxation), whilst ridehailing is for profit with drivers dispatched much like that of any taxi service. Clever branding and deceptive marketing have allowed TNCs to misappropriate language to convince their customers that by 'sharing' they are travelling more responsibly.

Indeed, Sigala (2019) finds that people who participate in the sharing economy are primarily motivated by financial reward. The shared services have simply "dress[ed] up our consumerist tendencies in a more palatable ideology". Bardhi and Eckhardt (2012) also concurs that the sharing economy model is commercial rather than social, so better defined as an 'access' economy. Whether sharing is niche or scalable hence remains open to be seen.

## 2.8 Conclusions

This chapter has sought to bring clarity to the underlying rationale for MaaS. A number of myths about the concept are dispelled and the underlying basis identified as a journey towards greater integration. The theoretical antecedents for MaaS are identified by offering a historic perspective to its development linked to earlier incarnation like the concept of mobility management. In doing so, the core, underlying principles of MaaS in shifting transportation based on asset ownership to transportation accessed on demand and consumed as a service are underscored.

The need for MaaS has been placed in the context of an emerging transport paradigm shaped by new mobility services, technologies and businesses, and what these could do to the transport network and urban realm. Two scenarios of modal displacement and modal convergence are suggested, along with the unintended consequences they might bring to our cities. Modal displacement concerns how TNCs are interacting with conventional public transport providers, and the impact of growing point-to-point transportation on road congestion, as passengers are drawn away from more spatially efficient but less personalised public transport modes. Modal convergence proposes a future where autonomous taxis become a dominating mode, bringing enormous risks around how they might affect people's location choice, and in the longer run, urban form of our cites.

The second half of this chapter offered a conceptual framework within which to evaluate future modal development scenarios. The modal efficiency framework situates all modes within spatial and temporal efficiency dimensions. The ideal scenario in bringing together all temporally efficient modes across a range of spatial efficiencies can usefully be described in a process called MaaS. Further discussion on how this could be operationalised spatially (via a hub-and-spoke model) and temporally (as a peak top-up) are envisaged. The chapter concluded with the need to encourage sharing and how demographic change might be an enabler or hindrance to this objective.

The key message in this chapter is that MaaS offers itself as a unique opportunity to enhance the efficiency of our transport networks and our cities. The integration of temporally efficient modes across a range of spatial efficiencies, aided by digital technologies and bundled subscription products offers up prospects that can help to reduce car ownership and car dependence. In the next chapter, a broader view of the global MaaS debate is explored, informed by this understanding of the MaaS vision.

Chapter 3

# Global debate and experience with MaaS

## Chapter outline



## 3.1 Introduction

The chapter sets the current debate and experience in the context of the early roots of MaaS. In the 1990s there was recognition that flexible transport schemes were at a turning point with better telematics (allowing dynamic dispatching and real-time updates to waiting passengers) and organisational frameworks (allowing multiple provision from a single dispatch centre) but the need for workable business models was a barrier to wider implementation (Ambrosino et al., 2004). Since then, the technological framework has developed beyond all expectations, providing ubiquitous coverage to smart applications and pervasive and persistent ownership of smart devices that can access the smart applications in real-time.

It is the technological developments which have spearheaded the new understanding of MaaS and differentiate it from its organisational predecessors. Whilst definitions vary, the concept of MaaS has several dimensions: in the form of an app and in real-time, it provides mobility services using multimodal options, through a journey planner that provides the user with multiple customised options and offers the opportunity for payment either at the point of use or with a pre-purchased mobility bundle and providing the ticket for travel. This single platform is envisaged to eventually be transferable around the world from city

Understanding Mobility as a Service (MaaS). https://doi.org/10.1016/B978-0-12-820044-5.00003-8
© 2020 Elsevier Inc. All rights reserved.

to city and region to region and also to remain pervasive to the user by working and monitoring the journey in real-time and providing options for recovery in the case of disruption. None of the offerings to date completely fulfil all the dimensions of MaaS described above but 'Whim' (from MaaS Global) offers the critical smart app, journey planning and payment functions. The chapter will chart the development of 'Whim' alongside the increasingly numerous MaaS operators working in single locations and map these against the characteristics of the application to provide a full understanding of the MaaS experience to date. This codification and classification of MaaS operations will be undertaken in close liaison with Chapter 4 where MaaS trials will be detailed.

This chapter next looks at the background to MaaS before reviewing the various definitions that have been proposed. The following section considers the representation of MaaS via 'levels of integration' and goes on to chart the development of MaaS by analysing a selection of existing and former MaaS Schemes in terms of their status and levels of integration as at December 2019. Finally, a series of reflections on the global debate are offered.

## 3.2 Background to mobility as a service

With the rise of personal motorisation over the past 50 years there has been a long-term deterioration in the operating conditions for conventional bus services. Across urban areas in particular, there remains a need for robust and efficient mobility solutions which are suitable to the urban form and are well integrated in the local planning system (Ambrosino et al., 2016). Innovative measures to increase the quality of conventional public transport services and strengthen the efficiency of the now established 'new' mobility schemes such as private and peer-to-peer ridesharing, car sharing, bike sharing (and more latterly e-scooters) are increasingly occurring. Operationally, the traditional contrast between collective and individual transport solutions is gradually blurring which in itself has helped to presage the development of MaaS, although this may not be the viewpoint of passengers.

Over the last 25 years a variety of flexible and demand responsive transport services applications have shown important advantages and benefits, particularly in several European cities. Flexible Transport Services (FTS) can be defined as a transport service which is adapted for meeting users' needs, typically on a trip-by-trip basis with a certain level of flexibility on three operational dimensions (routing, timing of the service, vehicle used) in order to enhance service offer and minimise costs in response to demand (Ambrosino et al., 2016).

Mulley (2017) explains how a step change in technology promises much to sponsor new transport paradigms. Technology enables change and often it is dramatic when the 'right' technologies come together at the right time. This is precisely what happened with FTS from the late 1990s when with the advent of transport telematics it became possible from an operational point of view to organise services around the concept of a TDC (Travel Dispatch Centre), as the key operational (and technological) resource supporting the operation (Ambrosino et al., 2016).

A further relevant argument in understanding the development of MaaS offered by Mulley (2017) is that while MaaS may be new, its predecessor, Mobility Management (the management and delivery of coordinated transport services to customers) is not. Indeed, Mobility Management as a concept has been an integral part of discussions in the FTS literature where the on-demand provision of services is characterised, for example, by the virtual agency concept linking customers and flexible transport suppliers. Such a concept has been trialled in both urban and rural pilots in Europe (Nelson et al., 2010). However, these projects have mostly remained trials or one-off initiatives, impeded by the inability of technology to enable the jump to mainstream delivery.

The coming of age of the required technology, and the developments in the service-sharing economy have enabled wide scale on-demand mobility services and the emergence of MaaS as a potentially concrete market option. As such, the family of FTS has now expanded to include collective taxi and demand responsive bus services, dynamic car-sharing schemes (such as ShareNow and Zipcar), dynamic ridesharing services (like BlaBlaCar and Flinc) and peer-to-peer transport arrangement schemes (such as Uber, UberPop, and Lyft), and more latterly e-bike sharing and e-scooter sharing. All of these can now be considered as integral components of a truly intermodal mobility offer which lends itself to management via the concept of MaaS.

## 3.3 What is meant now by mobility as a service?

Conceived in Finland, through work commissioned by the City of Helsinki and originally the subject of a Masters thesis at Aalto University in Finland, MaaS was described as "a system, in which a comprehensive range of mobility services are provided to customers by mobility operators" (Heikkilä, 2014: 8). Mobility operators were seen as companies which, as intermediaries (typically referred to as aggregators or brokers), acquire services from providers and sell them to consumers. From this beginning, the concept of MaaS has attracted significant attention from academics, peak bodies representing both operators and users (such as UITP,[a] Polis[b]) and also governments. MaaS has first been articulated in a practical way by MaaS Finland (now MaaS Global), and subsequently introduced in Helsinki, Finland, and in other places in Europe.

The definition of MaaS remains elusive in terms of finding a definition which is universally accepted. Table 3.1, adapted from Sochor et al. (2018) and

a. UITP (*Union Internationale des Transports Publics*) is the International Association of Public Transport, a worldwide network to bring together all public transport stakeholders and all sustainable transport modes (https://www.uitp.org).

b. Polis is a network of European cities and regions cooperating for innovative transport solutions (https://www.polisnetwork.eu/).

**TABLE 3.1 Definitions of mobility as a service.**

| | |
|---|---|
| Arthur D. Little (2018, p. 59) | "The concept of 'Mobility-as-a-Service' (MaaS) aims to provide consumers with integrated, flexible, efficient and user-oriented mobility services. It implies a shift away from the personal ownership of individual motorised transportation modes, and non-integrated means of transportation towards the use of integrated multimodal mobility solutions consumed as services. This shift is enabled by combining transportation services from public- and private-transportation providers through an 'integrated mobility platform' that creates and manages the journey and integrates planning and payment (based on mobility packages tailored to the needs of each customer segment) on a one-stop-shop principle." |
| Atkins (2015, p. 19) | "MaaS can be defined as: The provision of transport as a flexible, personalised on-demand service that integrates all types of mobility opportunities and presents them to the user in a completely integrated manner to enable them to get from A to B as easily as possible." |
| Docherty et al. (2018) drawing on Thakuriah et al. (2016) | "where individuals' ownership of vehicles is increasingly replaced by "usership", that is the ability to purchase access rights to an interoperable package of mobility services (car, taxi, bus, rail, bike share) owned by others, usually corporate, providers. This is facilitated by integrated aggregation and payment platforms, with intensive processing of 'big data' to match provision to demand in real time." |
| Ghanbari et al. (2015) | "MaaS, a multi-actor environment that provides seamless door-to-door services for end users by combining several modes of transportation." |
| Heikkilä (2014, p. 8) | MaaS is "a system, in which a comprehensive range of mobility services are provided by customers to mobility operators." |
| Hensher (2017) | MaaS "combines transport services from public and private transportation providers through a unified gateway that creates and manages the trip, which users can pay for with a single account." Hensher continues to suggest the design and implementation of MaaS can be related to the three Bs—bundles, budgets and brokers—whereby in MaaS, customers can purchase 'bundles of mobility' with 'budgets' referring to end user preferences and 'brokers' are the business models around which MaaS is delivered. |
| Hietanen (2014, pp. 1–2) | "MaaS is a mobility distribution model in which a customer's major transportation needs are met over one interface and are offered by a service provider. Typically, services are bundled into a package." |

**TABLE 3.1 Definitions of mobility as a service—cont'd**

| | |
|---|---|
| House of Commons Transport Committee (2018) | "An idea that is already being piloted abroad and in the UK is Mobility as a Service (MaaS). MaaS is the term for the digital platforms (often smartphone apps) through which people can access a range of public, shared and private transport, using a system that integrates the planning, booking and paying for travel." |
| K2 Swedish Knowledge Centre for Public Transport (2017) | "The term 'Mobility as a Service' stands for buying mobility services based on consumers' needs instead of buying the means of transport. Via 'Mobility as a Service' systems consumers can buy mobility services that are provided by the same or different operators by using just one platform and single payment." |
| Kamargianni and Matyas (2017, p. 3) | "Mobility as a Service is a user-centric, intelligent mobility distribution model in which all mobility service providers' offerings are aggregated by a sole mobility operator and supplied to users through a single digital platform." |
| König et al. (2016) | "Multimodal and sustainable mobility services addressing customers' transport needs by integrating planning and payment on a one-stop-shop principle." |
| MaaS Alliance (2018a,b) | "Mobility as a Service (MaaS) is the integration of various forms of transport services into a single mobility service accessible on demand."; "The key concept behind MaaS is to put the users, both travellers, and goods, at the core of transport services, offering them tailor-made mobility solutions based on their individual needs. This means that, for the first time, easy access to the most appropriate transport mode or service will be included in a bundle of flexible travel service options for end users." |
| MaaS Global (2018) | "MaaS, short for Mobility as a Service, brings all means of travel together. It combines options from different transport providers into a single mobile service, removing the hassle of planning and one-off payments." |
| MuConsult (2017, p. 4) | "MaaS is defined as the range of flexible, partly demand-driven, multimodal mobility services in which tailor-made integrated travel options are offered to travellers via a digital platform." (translated from Dutch) |
| Polis (2018) | "Mobility as a Service (MaaS) has been marketed as a new transport concept that may change or disrupt current models of transport provision, particularly in urban areas. The concept of MaaS claims to offer a personal mobility package based on lifestyle needs and delivered through a single interface and subscription. MaaS, driven partly by business and technology priorities, will have to have an impact on policy thinking, including at local, national and EU level." |

*Continued*

**TABLE 3.1 Definitions of mobility as a service—cont'd**

| | |
|---|---|
| Samtrafiken (2017, p. 4, 18) | (p. 18) A way of thinking where "mobility is something that can be purchased as a service and does not require owning a private car." (translated from Swedish)<br>(p. 4) Also, "services that facilitate travelling from A to B by different means of transport" ... "the services can be anything from a multimodal travel planner to a full mobility subscription. The services can also include transport of goods as a complement to personal mobility. The common starting point is that the services should inspire and attract travellers to more sustainable travel and to reducing private car dependency." (translated from Swedish) |
| Shaheen et al. (2017, p. 144) | "MaaS emphasises mobility aggregation, smartphone and app-based subscription access, and multimodal integration (infrastructure, information, and fare integration). MaaS tends to emphasise the integration and convergence of passenger mobility services, mobile devices, real-time information, and payment mechanisms." |
| Transport Systems Catapult (2016) | "manage the provision of a transport related service(s) which meets the mobility requirements of a customer." (p. 10)<br>"The [mobility] service model is associated with understanding the 'who?' and 'why?' of customers' mobility requirements and only then is the transport solution offered as a 'how?'" |
| UITP Policy Brief (2019, p. 2) | "Mobility as a Service (MaaS) is the integration of, and access to, different transport services (such as public transport, ride-sharing, car-sharing, bike-sharing, scooter-sharing, taxi, car rental, ride-hailing and so on) in one single digital mobility offer, with active mobility and an efficient public transport system as its basis. This tailor-made service suggests the most suitable solutions based on the user's travel needs. MaaS is available anytime and offers integrated planning, booking and payment, as well as en route information to provide easy mobility and enable life without having to own a car." |

**Source:** Adapted from Sochor, J., Arby, H., Karlsson, I.C.M., Sarasini, S., 2018. A topological approach to mobility as a service: a proposed tool for understanding requirements and effects, and for aiding the integration of societal goals. Res. Transp. Bus. Manag. 27, 3–14, and extended for this chapter.

updated for this chapter, provides a range of published definitions. Sochor et al. (2018) analyse these definitions to provide a topology of MaaS. The purpose in this chapter is different: this chapter examines the commonalities of the definitions with the intent of classifying the range of schemes or products that have been identified as MaaS.

Table 3.1 is not attempting to be exhaustive in the collection of the various definitions of MaaS. It is however indicative of the different stakeholder's views. Sochor et al. (2018) identify the pre-cursor to MaaS (Heikkilä, 2014;

Hietanen, 2014) as more concerned with the different types of mobility collaborating with public transport than the more modern interpretation of MaaS which has shifted the emphasis from the modes per se to the usage of the modes through a single aggregator. Importantly, from the perspective of this chapter, these definitions of MaaS have a number of crucial elements in common. To qualify for MaaS, the scheme or product first must offer a mobility service with the user at the centre of the offer; second the mobility options offered must be selected from a multimodal portfolio and finally, the offer must provide the integration of transport service starting from providing the information for travel, enabling a payment option (either at the point of use or with a pre-purchased mobility bundle) and providing the ticket for travel. Although, not part of a basic definition, the user centric nature of MaaS implies that a definition that includes feedback to users on the travel activities and advisories of opportunities to improve the travel experience and obtain positive health benefits and even reduce emissions would be helpful.

The integration of services has a number of dimensions and is described by MaaS topologies. Sochor et al. (2018) develop 4 stages: integrated information, for example providing a multimodal journey planner, integrated booking and payment using a smart card or some other form of payment such as a credit card, organisational integration where the different modal options are presented seamlessly to the user, irrespective of the ownership and bundling or subscription to a suite and quantity of mobility services for a time-related fee. Lyons et al. (2019) describe MaaS as an "evolutionary continuum in terms of integration" (Lyons et al., 2019, p. 23) and so, similarly to Sochor, see integration as a central focus in the developmental stages of MaaS. This is discussed in more detail below.

To date, MaaS as described above has been primarily a European concept (illustrated in Table 3.2). In Australia, MaaS has developed to have the same interpretation (Ho et al., 2018; Hensher, 2017; Mulley et al., 2020). In India, too, MaaS seems to be understood as a similar concept with at least academics considering its applicability. However, in the US, the underpinning of MaaS in terms of providing a service rather than the product of a transport asset which is personally owned is more captured by the growth of Transport Network Companies (TNCs) which, usually through apps, matches passengers with vehicles providing the mobility service. Transport as a Service is the phrase which characterises the US offers in this field. The US Department of Transportation has also promoted the term 'Mobility on Demand' with an emphasis on commodified transportation services, as well as system management (Shaheen et al., 2017; Cohen, 2018) and is thus quite different to MaaS. In the People's Republic of China (PRC), there are a proliferation of apps offering similar services to the TNCs yet in Hong Kong, which perhaps has the only public transport system not requiring subsidy, there is next to no interest in MaaS nor of its constituent mobility services such as bike share (which maybe more to do with local topology). More recently Zipster has been rolled out in Singapore.

**TABLE 3.2** MaaS schemes, their status, and levels of integration as at December 2019.

| Name | Place | Status: Pilot (P)/ Operational (O) | Dates | Urban (U)/ Rural (R) | Number of modes | Level of integration: Sochor et al. (2018) | Level of integration: Lyons et al. (2019) | Weblink |
|---|---|---|---|---|---|---|---|---|
| CityMapper Pass | London, UK | O | 2019–present | U | 3 | 3 | 4 | https://citymapper.com/pass?lang=en |
| Communauto | Canada and France | O | 2018 | U | 3 | 2 | 4 | https://www.communauto.com/index_en.html |
| Hannovermobil 2.0 | Hannover, Germany | O | 2016 | U | 5 | 2 | 4 | https://www.gvh.de/home/?L=1#/ |
| Foli | Turku | O | [b]–present | U | 4 | 2 | 4 | https://www.foli.fi/en/mobile-ticket |
| Jelbi | Berlin | O | 2019 | U | 6 | 2 | 4 | https://www.jelbi.de |
| MaaS Madrid | Madrid | P | 2019 | U | 5 | 3 | 4 | https://www.youtube.com/watch?v=x2lO4n4zg1c |
| Moovizy 2 | Saint-Etienne | O[c] | 2019 | U | 9 | 2 | 4 | https://www.transdev.com/en/solutions/moovizy-maas/ |
| myCicero | Italy | O | 2014[b] | U/R | 4 | 2 | 4 | http://www.mycicero.it/eng/tp_b/index.html |
| Smile | Wien, Austria | P | 2014–May 2015 | U | 7 | 2 | 4 | http://smile-einfachmobil.at/index_en.html |
| swa Augsburg | Augsburg, Germany | O | Nov 2019 | U | 4 | 3 | 4 | https://www.sw-augsburg.de/mobilitaet/emobilitaet/ |

| | | | | | | | | |
|---|---|---|---|---|---|---|---|---|
| TAC Mobilités | Annemasse, France, and Geneva, Switzerland | O | 2019–present | U | 3 | 2 | 4 | https://www.ratpdev.com/en/newsroom/news/ratp-group-launches-its-first-maas-app-annemasse |
| Tripi | Sydney, Australia | P | Nov 2019– | U | 7 | 3 | 4 | Closed scheme to an employee group. See Chapter 4 |
| UbiGo | Gothenburg, Sweden | P | 2013–2014 | U | 5 | 3 | 4 | https://ubigo.me/en/ |
| UbiGo 2.0 | Stockholm, Sweden | P | 2019–present | U | 4 | 3 | 4 | https://www.fluidtime.com/en/project/ubigo/ |
| Whim | Helsinki, Finland | O | 2016–present | U | 7 | 3 | 4 | https://whimapp.com |
| WienMobil | Wien, Austria | O | 2017–present | U | 7 | 2 | 4 | https://www.wienerlinien.at/eportal3/ep/channelView.do/pageTypeId/66533/channelId/-3600061 |
| Beeline | Singapore | O | August 2015– | U | 1 | 2 | 3 | https://www.beeline.sg |
| EC2B | Gothenburg, Sweden | P | 2019–present | U | 4 | 2 | 3 | https://ec2b.se/ |
| Choice/Queenstown | New Zealand | P | 2017–2018 | U | 5 | 2 | 3 | https://www.nzta.govt.nz/traffic-and-travel-information/mobile-apps/choice-app/ |
| Ghent University MaaS Pilot | Ghent, Belgium | P | April–June 2017 | U | 5 | 2 | 3 | http://www.idm.ugent.be/maas/ |

*Continued*

**TABLE 3.2** MaaS schemes, their status, and levels of integration as at December 2019—cont'd

| Name | Place | Status: Pilot (P)/ Operational (O) | Dates | Urban (U)/ Rural (R) | Number of modes | Level of integration: Sochor et al. (2018) | Level of integration: Lyons et al. (2019) | Weblink |
|---|---|---|---|---|---|---|---|---|
| Ridemate (Auckland) | New Zealand | P | 2017–2018 | U | 5 | 2 | 3 | https://nzta.govt.nz/traffic-and-travel-information/mobile-apps/ridemate-app/ |
| S'hail | Dubai | O | 2017–present | U | 5 | 2 | 3 | https://www.rta.ae/wps/portal/rta/ae/home/smart-apps |
| TRIPPS Beta | Leidsche Rijn | P | 2019–present | U | 4 | 2 | 3 | https://innovactory.com/en/2019/08/12/mobility-as-a-service/ |
| Tuup Turku | Oulu, Turku and Tampere, Finland | O | 2016–present | U | 9 | 2 | 3 | https://www.kyyti.com/ |
| Whim | Birmingham, UK | P | 2018–present | U | 3 | 2 | 3 | https://whimapp.com/uk/ |
| Zengo | Geneva/ Lausanne, Switzerland | O | 2019–present | U | 5 | 3 | 3 | https://www.zengo.ch |
| Zipster | Singapore | P (beta version) | March 2019–present | U | 4 | 2 | 3 | https://zipster.io/ |
| BRIDJ | Sydney, Australia | P | August 2018– | U | 1 | 2 | 2 | https://www.bridj.com/ |

| | | | | | | | | |
|---|---|---|---|---|---|---|---|---|
| Kätevä Seinäjoki | Finland | P | 2016–2017 | R | 3 | 2 | 2 | http://www.komialiikenne.fi/w/kateva--sovellus |
| MinRejseplan | Denmark | P | 2018 | U/R | 2 | 2 | 2 | https://www.nordjyllandstrafikselskab.dk/English/Bus-&-train |
| Mobility Mixx | Netherlands | O | 2014[b]–present | U and R | 7 | 2 | 2 | https://mobilitymixx.nl/en/home.html |
| Mobility.2. Services | Palma, Spain | P | 2013–2016[a] | U | ? | 2 | 2 | https://civitas.eu/content/mobility-20-services |
| NaviGoGo | Dundee, Scotland, UK | P | 2017–2018 | U | 4 | 2 | 2 | https://static1.squarespace.com/static/5cee5bd0687a1500015b5a9f/t/5d5c0a6c3e4b3a0001242602/1566313071168/NaviGoGo-Pilot-report.pdf |
| NS-Business Card | Netherlands | O | 2012[b]–present | U | 6 | 2 | 2 | https://www.ns.nl/en/business/ns-business-card |
| Postauto | Switzerland | O | April 2019[b]–present | R | 1 | 1 | 2 | https://www.postauto.ch/de/fahrplan-und-angebote |
| Sonnera Reissu Hämeenlinna | Hämeenlinna and Ylläs, Finland | P | 2016 | U/R | 3 | 2 | 2 | https://yhteiso.telia.fi/t5/Blogi/Sonera-Reissu-Alyliikennepalvelut-ovat-jo-taalla/ba-p/126052 |
| Switchh Hamburg | Hamburg, Germany | O | 2018 (at least)[b]–present | U | 2 | 2 | 2 | https://www.switchh.de/hochbahn/hamburg/switchh/homepage |
| TIM | Graz, Austria | O | September 2016 (at least)[b]–present | U | 4 | 2 | 2 | https://www.tim-graz.at/ |

*Continued*

**TABLE 3.2** MaaS schemes, their status, and levels of integration as at December 2019—cont'd

| Name | Place | Status: Pilot (P)/ Operational (O) | Dates | Urban (U)/ Rural (R) | Number of modes | Level of integration: Sochor et al. (2018) | Level of integration: Lyons et al. (2019) | Weblink |
|---|---|---|---|---|---|---|---|---|
| Trav.ly | UK | O | 2008–present | U/R | 2 | 2 | 2 | https://www.trav.ly/ |
| Utrect Region Pass | Utrecht, The Netherlands | O | 2016–present | U/R | 4 | 2 | 2 | https://utrechtregionpass.com/ |
| UESTRA | Hannover, Germany | O | [b]–present | U/R | 4 | 2 | 2 | https://shop.uestra.de/index.php/ |
| Door to gate | Munich, Germany | P | 2017–present | Airport | 5 | 1 | 1 | https://www.globalairrail.com/images/events/2017/Airport_Access_Ideas_Forum_2017/Case_Studies/AAIF2017%20-%20Case%20Studies-MaaS.pdf |
| TripGo | Global | O | 2012–present | U/R | Multi | 1 | 1 | https://tripgo.com |

[a] *End date not clear.*
[b] *Start date not clear.*
[c] *Launch date, end 2019.*

Japan, as with Singapore, has a very high public transport in its cities[c] and there are recent signs of possible MaaS implementation with MaaS Global announcing an extension of Whim in April 2019.[d] MaaS Global in Japan is spearheaded by connections with the Japanese railway companies, in particular with the Odakyu Electric Railway Co. Ltd. which appears to be the leader of a consortium of operators forming MaaS Japan. This is at an early stage of development (press release dated 30 October 2019[e]) but the plans for MaaS Japan include an extended journey planner with booking and payment for multimodal travel (rail, bus, taxi, on-demand shuttles, car sharing, and bike sharing). Interestingly the Odakyu company aims to establish the purchase of tickets from other MaaS apps (including Whim and Zipster if and when they are established in Japan), particularly those used by tourists. In Latin America, there is little evidence yet of the concept developing in any formal manner although there is a long history of informal shared, flexible transport solutions which could provide a useful basis for development taking account the widespread available of smartphones.

This chapter looks next at the global distribution of schemes described as MaaS in terms of their degree of integration in line with the discussions in Sochor et al. (2018) and Lyons et al. (2019). The section therefore begins by looking at typologies of integration before setting out schemes and discussing the current global state-of-the-art in mobility services.

## 3.4 Levels of integration and mobility as a service

Sochor et al. (2018) present a classification of MaaS, reproduced as part of Fig. 3.1. This proposes five stages of integration (including no integration). In discussing the different levels of integration, Sochor et al. (2018) point out that no one level may be considered better than another because this depends on what the user needs, although greater opportunities for meeting sustainability goals for cities would be achieved with greater integration. Their typology finishes with a level of integration of modal offerings which includes the integration of social and transport policies where its' added value is to reduce private car ownership and use at the city level. This level is interesting for the way it would require public authorities to act in providing the incentives for citizens to behave sustainably as well as providing rules for the use of infrastructure (these issues are discussed elsewhere in the book but it is important to note the way in which this classification includes this level of integration as a final step).

c. Japan has a mode share of 43% of the total passenger-kilometres travelled in 2016 as compared to about 2% in the US. In the bigger cities (Tokyo, Osaka) the mode share exceeds 50%. For further discussion of mobility in Japan, see 'Rebooting Japan's mobility market' at https://www.mckinsey.com/industries/automotive-and-assembly/our-insights/rebooting-japans-mobility-market (Accessed 5 November 2019).

d. https://www.goodnewsfinland.com/maas-global-brings-mobility-on-a-whim-to-japan/ (Accessed 5 November 2019).

e. https://www.odakyu.jp/news/o5oaa1000001necq-att/o5oaa1000001necx.pdf (Accessed 5 November 2019).

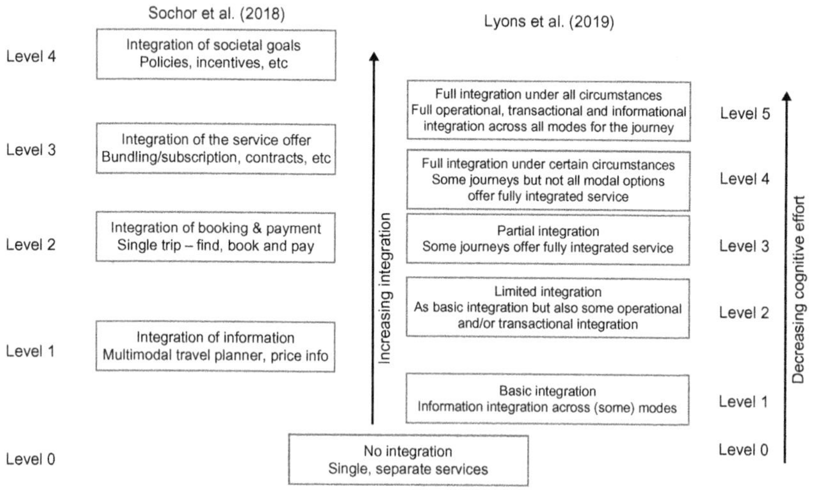


**FIG. 3.1** A classification of integration. *(Modified from Sochor, J., Arby, H., Karlsson, I.C.M., Sarasini, S., 2018. A topological approach to mobility as a service: a proposed tool for understanding requirements and effects, and for aiding the integration of societal goals. Res. Transp. Bus. Manag. 27, 3–14. https://doi.org/10.1016/j.rtbm.2018.12.003 and Lyons, G., Hammond, P., Mackay, K., 2019. The importance of user perspective in the evolution of MaaS. In: Hensher, D.A., Mulley, C. (Eds.), Transportation Research Part A: Policy and Practice. Special Issue on Developments in Mobility as a Service (MaaS) and Intelligent Mobility, vol. 121. pp. 22–36. https://doi.org/10.1016/j.tra.2018.12.010.)*

Fig. 3.1 also shows the taxonomy of Lyons et al. (2019). As expected, this is similar to Sochor et al. (2018), differing in levels which provide finer detail over the level of integration. The Lyons et al. (2019) classification is based on integration combined with cognitive effort on the part of the user with six levels, again starting from no integration and falling short of the final level of Sochor et al. (2018) shown in Fig. 3.1. However their final level, Level 5, is described as when MaaS provides a travel experience "on a par with the convenience of the private car overall" (Lyons et al., 2019, p. 30) although the degree of operational integration that this requires is such that it may not be attainable. Lyons et al. (2019) view integration from a specifically user perspective and include a discussion of the cognitive effort associated with travelling, arguing that greater integration reduces the cognitive load on travellers.

The remainder of this section looks at schemes which purport to have some element of MaaS and that were in the public domain during December 2019. Table 3.2 shows these, sorted by the level of integration classification proposed by Lyons et al. (2019) as this gives more finely graduated levels of integration. Additional information for the schemes are included in terms of location and number of modes involved which in turn are used to further differentiate the level of integration. Operational status and whether a scheme is urban or rural is also shown. The purpose of looking at the levels of integration in existing schemes is to identify experiences to date and to use this to frame the challenges for the future.

Whilst all the Level 2 schemes (on both classifications) have an element of payment integration, few of the schemes offered rebates as part of their pricing scheme with Beeline, Navigogo, Smile, Switchh Hamburg, TAC Mobilitiés, TIM, and UbiGo, Whim (Helsinki) and Zengo being exceptions. Even fewer schemes offered pricing bundles or subscriptions with UbiGo, Whim (Helsinki and elsewhere) and the new entrants such as swa Augsburg and Tripi being the exceptions. There was some variation in the number of services offered ranging from 9 (Tuup, Finland and Moovizy) to 7 (Mobility Mixx, The Netherlands, Smile in Vienna and Whim in Helsinki), and more commonly 3 or 4 modal offerings. It is, however, acknowledged that the number of services can be affected by whether public transport is broken down into its constituent modes or whether public transport is counted as a single mode. Rural applications are included in 11 of the 43 schemes identified, although in some cases these are schemes which traverse very wide operational areas that may be deemed both rural and urban such as Mobility Mixx in the Netherlands. Examples of dedicated rural MaaS schemes remain rare although arguably there are niche markets to be developed here (e.g. amongst tourists). Chronologically speaking, the earliest schemes date from 2012 with a surge in activity from 2016 onwards. The ephemeral nature of early MaaS schemes can also been seen in Table 3.2 with almost a quarter of the schemes documented no longer extant and of course, failed schemes which are not documented are excluded by default. One notable casualty is the New Zealand NZ Transport Agency pilots (Ridemate in Auckland and Choice in Queenstown), which have been subject to an independent review (Deloitte, 2019) which documented failings in the management, governance and functioning of the Transport Agency.

## 3.5 Beyond the definition—Charting the development of mobility as a service

This section charts the development of MaaS in three locations closely associated with the early development and growth of schemes. The experience of Finland is characterised by early technical development and implementation followed by sustained growth. In Sweden early development of UbiGo has been followed by a gap and then the re-establishment of UbiGo 2.0 schemes; while in the UK the on the ground implementation has been slow (and includes an attempt to transplant the Whim experience) but central government is now driving an agenda for MaaS.

### 3.5.1 The Finnish experience with MaaS

Finland has long been characterised by high levels of digital connectivity throughout the country. Digitalisation is helping the transport sector to find new solutions and bring greater efficiency and transparency to the transport system. The Finnish national government aims to promote the use of digitalisation in the transport sector, including via the development of an ambitious National MaaS Framework which is built around the 'Transport Code' introduced under The Act on Transport Services (2018)[f] and which is designed to encourage new digitally led business models as a precursor to MaaS-type services. Further impetus has been provided by a new public procurement law requiring the use of electronic channels.

The Act on Transport Services (2018) underpins Finland's development of a unique country level approach to the development of MaaS involving supporting legislation and a focus on new business models. Labelled the 'Transport Code' by the Ministry of Transport and Communications (MTC), the Act includes an obligation for transport operators to provide essential information and access to sales interfaces of ticket and payment systems. The Act facilitates entry of the taxi sector and increases the freedom of taxi operators to develop their services. All transport modes (road, shipping, rail transport, and aviation) are included to enable multi-modal travel chains. The development of the Transport Code has helped to place Finland at the forefront of MaaS. MaaS Global is one high profile example of a Finnish company promoting the MaaS concept through its Whim product. Finland is also home to the world's first Rural MaaS project.

MaaS Global[g] envisages a future environment where MaaS could offer an alternative to owning a car with personalised bundles or packages which offer the best option for every journey (e.g. a taxi, public transport, a rental car or a bike share). MaaS solutions can also offer value added services like deliveries for groceries or restaurant meals. In June 2016 MaaS Global test launched Whim in Helsinki. The app[h] became openly available in the Helsinki Region in May 2017. The experience of the Helsinki application for the period January–December 2018 has recently been published as Whimpact (Hartikainen et al., 2019). In 2017, MaaS Global raised additional venture capital, and has subsequently expanded to Antwerp and the West Midlands.

The Rural MaaS project was led by The Ministry of Agriculture and Forestry and aimed at creating a national vision for MaaS in rural and sparsely populated areas. It focused mainly on recognising emerging and potential business models for both commercial and publicly supported transport services. The project improved awareness of the MaaS concept in rural areas by sharing knowledge, and by providing measures and recommendations for developing mobility regulations and raising awareness related to the technical aspects of MaaS. The outcome is reported in Rural-MaaS (2017).

Smith et al. (2018b), see also Chapter 7, comment that the idea of creating multi-modal mobility packages was first promoted at an MTC think tank in 2012 (by Sampo Hietanen, then CEO of ITS Finland, who later became CEO of Maas Finland, subsequently MaaS Global).

f. https://www.lvm.fi/-/act-on-transport-services-to-cover-the-entire-transport-system-971134.
g. https://maas.global/.
h. https://whimapp.com.

In early 2015, MTC and the Finnish Funding Agency for Innovation (Tekes) launched a joint programme for the development of MaaS. Eight pre-studies were funded and several MaaS-related pilots were performed during 2015 and 2016. The more substantial examples are shown in Table 3.2 and included:

- The telecom company Telia Finland Oy developed a MaaS application called Reissu, and conducted two pilots, one for commuters in the city of Hämeenlinna and one for tourists travelling to the ski resort of Ylläs, before selling the brand to the Finnish company Semel Oy in December 2016.
- Tuup Oy, a start-up company, launched the first version of a MaaS application in 2016. It enables purchase of public transport tickets in Turku and taxi hailing in some areas, as well as exclusive access to Kyyti, a taxi-pooling service currently available in Oulu, Turku, and Tampere.
- Sito Oy, a Finnish consultancy firm, piloted a MaaS application, Kätevä, in Seinäjoki between November 2016 and April 2017. The service provided three types of mobility packages that combined local buses, DRT and taxis.

In addition to the MTC/Tekes joint MaaS programme, another public actor, Export Finland, has launched a growth programme for MaaS, aimed at helping Finnish MaaS-related ventures to attract international investors and to take advantage of global business opportunities.

The highest profile activities are those of MaaS Global (described above and in Table 3.2). Even in the strongly supportive environment of Finland, moving from pilots to established operations has not been without casualties with only MaaS Global (Whim) and Tuup (Kyyti) surviving from the early pilots. Tuup began with a shared single mode (taxi) and has moved to a multiple service offering. Interestingly, whereas Tuup started small in Turku MaaS global has targeted the entire Helsinki Metropolitan area.

Another relevant initiative is the rural transport and mobility national communication project 'Digiboksi'[i] which collects, processes, and spreads concrete information about the changes in the transport and mobility sector affecting rural areas. The initiative aims to show how digitalisation and changes in legislation (Transport Code) can enable more flexible organisation of transport and mobility services. It covers the whole of Finland with the main target group being rural SMEs.

### 3.5.2 The Swedish experience

The Go-smart project, financed by the Swedish Innovation Agency, allowed a MaaS product called UbiGo[j] to be trialled in Gothenburg in 2013/14 with encouraging results. UbiGo was positioned as 'a broker of everyday urban travel' and offers users one-stop access to a full range of collective mobility services

i. www.vtt.fi/sites/maasdigiboksi.
j. http://www.ubigo.se/.

(bicycle, public transport, car sharing, car rental, taxi). Sochor et al. (2016) describe encouraging findings from the six-month UbiGo trial in Gothenburg (2013/14) during which over 12,000 transactions (public transport day tickets, car or taxi reservations) were made. They noted that (at that time) the main obstacles to further dissemination of MaaS appeared to be found within and between service providing companies and organisations in terms of regulations and institutional barriers; one of the greatest challenges was integrating all aspects of mobility into a single service. The early UbiGo trials are one of the few anywhere that have been evaluated to any extent (see for example, Sochor et al., 2016; Sochor et al., 2015b) and are discussed in Chapter 4. Findings from the evaluation revealed that participants generally appreciated that UbiGo made multi-modal travelling cheaper, more convenient and helped them try out less familiar modes. Despite the limited duration of the trial there is evidence that it did promote changes in households travel patterns towards greater use of public transport and active modes.

A relaunch for Stockholm (UbiGo 2.0) occurred in May 2019 offering public transport, taxi, rental car, and car sharing options for subscription plans to residents in the participating neighbourhood. This service will be evaluated thoroughly.

A new service known as EC2B[k] has also begun in a specific residential area of Gothenburg from February 2019 offering the possibility of a subscription plan including public transport, car sharing, bike sharing and moped sharing. The trial is at Viva, a centrally located and newly built, tenant-owned apartment complex designed to demonstrate a reduced ecological footprint. Tenants have exclusive access to an app that enables them to book and pay for a pool of shared vehicles (electric bicycles and electric cargo bicycles) located within the complex. They can also purchase public transport tickets and book and pay for car sharing services. Tenants are also offered mobility consultations to discuss sustainable travel options.

### 3.5.3 The UK experience

The UK Parliament's Transport Select Committee enquiry on MaaS was published in December 2018 (UK Parliament Transport Select Committee, 2018) and represents an interesting *institutional* insight into the development of MaaS. The stated intention of the Report is to increase public awareness of what MaaS is; to show policy makers why it could be important and is worth investing time and effort to understand; and (significantly) to clarify the Department for Transport's (DfT) role in shaping its development in the UK. In respect of the latter, specific tasks identified for the DfT include encouragement to provide leadership; to provide practical support for the development of MaaS in the UK; and to review and update existing guidance and legislation and bring

k. https://ec2b.se/.

forward new legislative proposals where necessary to provide a suitable regulatory framework for MaaS. There is also a call for the Government to fund pilot programmes of MaaS applications across the country.

The *industry-led* developments in Scotland are also noteworthy. MaaS Scotland[1] was established by Technology Scotland (the independent body for the enabling technology sector) and ScotlandIS (the trade association for the digital technologies industry) in March 2017. It is a formal network for the MaaS ecosystem, facilitating initiatives that will deliver the benefits of MaaS to Scotland. In particular there was a desire to capitalise on the fact that Scotland is home to some 240 companies, public agencies, funders and universities all with the capability to contribute to the MaaS value chain. The mission of MaaS Scotland is to support the growth of a strong cluster of companies who can supply products and services along the MaaS value chain in partnership with the public sector. MaaS Scotland membership had reached 72 members at March 2019. MaaS Scotland has been hailed as the blueprint for similar clusters around the world.

There have been a small number of MaaS trials to date in the UK. 'NaviGoGo' is Scotland's first MaaS web application; co-designed by young people, for young people. The consortium's 'Pick & Mix' project was funded by Innovate UK and a consortium led by ESP Group. A 6-month Beta trial with 100 young people ran in Dundee and North East Fife (October 2017–March 2018). The application's key features included a personalised journey planner with fare calculator responsive to a user's profile and entitlements (trains, taxis, buses, and shared bikes); a journey payment platform; a taxi splitter tool for calculating the cost of a taxi journey with friends; a 'Discover a Destination' database containing local transport information and incentive points for positive/sustainable choices through Young Scot rewards.

During the 6-month trial (see ESP Group, 2019) more than 2000+ journeys were planned, 480+ journeys booked and paid for and 38% of participants travelled by bus after finding out the price. Overall, £3500+ NaviGoGo spend was reported. The trial ceased pending further funding and the development of a scalable business case which remains one of the challenges for effective and sustainable MaaS schemes.

The Whim App developed by MaaS Global was launched in April 2018 in the West Midlands. The app offered access to National Express buses and Midland Metro trams, a taxi operator (within a 3-mile radius) and a rental car operator, with the ability to book and purchase tickets. Bike share is expected to be included. Users were initially offered the options of paying one trip at a time (Pay as You Go—Whim to Go) or choosing a monthly package (Whim Everyday/Whim Unlimited). From January 2019 only Pay as You Go is available following an initial disappointing uptake prompting an official 'rethink' of the product.

1. https://maas-scotland.com/.

## 3.6 Reflections on the global debate

This section seeks to identify key questions from the global debate relating to the development of MaaS over the last 5 years, drawing on the experience to date and analysis of the schemes discussed earlier in the chapter. The ten questions posed in this section will be shown (unfortunately) to raise more questions than answers but will point to further chapters in this book where the debate is further elaborated and where some answers will come to light. Each of these questions are revisited in Chapter 9 (Future Challenges) to confirm the insights derived from the chapters and to identify further questions raised.

*Question 1: Who is MaaS most attractive to?*

This is a basic question that still has no conclusive answer.

A number of different contributions have been made in terms of stated preference/choice experiments, conducted in Sydney, Australia (e.g. Ho et al., 2018), London (e.g. Mayas and Kamargianni, 2017; Ho et al., 2020), and Zurich (e.g. Guidon et al., 2020). These all provide different insights, being based on different survey instruments. Ho et al. (2018) suggests that infrequent car users might be the most interested in a bundled approach of MaaS and that public transport offerings in Sydney were not at the core of respondent's MaaS plans with the main message being that those who were only private car or only public transport tend to have less interest at present than those already undertaking multimodal journeys. The study found, on average, about 47% of respondents ($n=252$) identifying they would 'consider' subscribing to a MaaS plan. Guidon et al. (2020) identify that a number of modes including public transport, car sharing and park and ride services exhibit a higher willingness to pay by respondents when in bundles as compared to when they are not.

One main finding of most stated preference/choice experiments is that customers may seek to purchase plans that best cater for their current mobility need, which corresponds with earlier evidence on habitual travel behaviour (e.g. Gärling and Axhausen, 2003). This raises the concept of 'relative attractiveness' of bundles depending on the target group. Reck and Axhausen (2020) explore revealed preference data to analyse the viability of different subscription plan components. They find that public transport season tickets form a viable core of a MaaS package for most respondents. In contrast to many current MaaS pilots (cf. Table 3.2), car-, bike-sharing, and taxi use remains too infrequent to include as recurring credit in MaaS plans. Rather, is the economically more sensible option for consumers.

There is only little evidence from real-life pilots with the sole well documented exception being the UbiGo pilot (Karlsson et al., 2016). Stated choice experiments are hypothetical and in settings where MaaS is unfamiliar and are no substitute for having pilots including multi-modal options for users to provide a better indication of who MaaS would be most attractive to. This is discussed more in Chapter 5.

*Question 2: How can more pilots be encouraged for learning?*

Table 3.2 shows that many of the identified MaaS schemes, albeit restricted to those MaaS schemes which have, or have had, 'wheels turning' on the ground, are pilots or operational at relatively low levels of integration. One of the better documented cases of 'mobility on demand' is 'Kutsuplus' in central Helsinki which had a subsidy per trip of around 20 Euros and was never likely to be a viable long-term solution, although not MaaS, it did show itself to be attractive to a wide user base (Weckström et al., 2018).

Too often, the pilots that have been introduced are looking at specific markets such as how MaaS could operate to include a first and last mile service, and whether MaaS can facilitate one-way trips. To provide answers to the many questions that remain, pilots must replicate—even if on a small area basis—the fuller suite of interoperable multi-modal services with payment and bundle opportunities for us to learn whether MaaS can transcend to the next level. The new UbiGo pilot in Stockholm maybe the first that offers this information. MaaS trials in Sydney 2019–20 and planned for Switzerland (2020) also have this intent.

The Sydney trial will enrol participants, who work, live and travel in the Sydney Greater Metropolitan area, to arrange their everyday travel needs through a MaaS app. The plans will give participants access to public transport (including train, tram, ferry, and bus) and a large portfolio of car-based transport services (e.g. taxi, car share, and car rental). The participants will be able to find, compare (e.g. in terms of cost, travel time, emissions and health benefits) and book these services through the app.

*Question 3: Will MaaS be too expensive to deliver beyond high density areas?*

The clear majority of the MaaS schemes in Table 3.2 are urban based which prompts the question as to whether MaaS will ever be able to grow beyond the urban areas? If MaaS is to become a predominantly urban phenomenon, will it be viable only in high density urban areas such as are seen in Europe? It is noteworthy that Kochai, India is thinking of introducing some sort of MaaS offering and here the densities are on a different scale from what is seen in Europe but also in the US and in Australia. Regional settings may offer a more simplified setting to test MaaS, although if the objective is to reduce car use (and ownership) which is the major contributor to traffic congestion, then the urban setting should be the main focus.

*Question 4: Who are the key stakeholders in the MaaS ecosystem?*

Influential work by the UK's Transport Systems Catapult (Transport Systems Catapult, 2016) identified a number of key stakeholders in the MaaS ecosystem: These were categorised as (a) the Customer who consumes the MaaS offer from the MaaS Provider (or Operator); (b) the MaaS Provider who designs and offers the MaaS value proposition to satisfy customer demand and which can be fulfilled by either public or private sector actors or, as Hensher (2017) suggests, an entrepreneur to broker new types of service, thus overcoming the traditional constraints of spatial boundaries in public transport contracting; (c) the Data Provider who acts as a data broker to service the data and information sharing requirements of the Transport Operators and MaaS Provider; and (d) the Transport Operator who provides the transport assets and services including public and private transport, highway capacity, urban-realm assets such as car parking, electric vehicle charging points, and digital assets such as ITS infrastructure. A further stakeholder could be added in the form of the MaaS Champion who can provide strong leadership. This is discussed more in Chapter 7.

*Question 5: What are the critical factors affecting the delivery of MaaS?*

MaaS Scotland (2018) characterise these as comprising: interoperability between ecosystems; digital connectivity; data and API sharing; regulation and legislation; and skills needs and opportunities. A further fundamental requirement (not always recognised at the pilot stage) is the sufficient availability of transport services for consumers to choose from. Incentives and financing are also important topics affecting market uptake (Chapter 5).

*Question 6: What are the potential problem areas for MaaS?*

The history of 'failed' schemes captured by Table 3.2 would suggest that there are problems to be overcome. The UK Parliament Transport Select Committee (2018), in identifying the prospects for further development of MaaS, have identified a number of potential problems or disadvantages of MaaS that should be overcome, principally: an increase in the use of taxis and PHVs (as with the arrival of ride-hailing aps) at the expense of other modes is not necessarily desirable and may contribute to worsening traffic congestion; MaaS may contribute to worsening digital and social exclusion, while recognising the possibility to encourage first and last mile services and one way trips; and MaaS solutions being available in some places and not others (i.e. boundary limitations). It is also possible that MaaS, instead of building public transport mode share may abstract from it, leaving public transport less well patronaged and requiring greater subsidy.

*Question 7: Is there too much hype? Is MaaS capable of making it to mainstream?*

One of the key questions for debate is whether MaaS is just hot air hype. Although a growing scientific literature has emerged, and continues to do so, there are still many unanswered questions as illustrated by the myriad of definitions discussed in this chapter. The major question is what underpins the concept of MaaS and whether or not it will make it beyond the pilot or limited operation to what might be regarded as mainstream. There is still limited clarity as to how MaaS will develop and whether or not maturity in MaaS will yield the benefits it promises and which are captured in the level 4 integration of the Sochor et al. (2018) vision of the integration of societal goals (see Chapter 4).

The coming of age in the digital world is advanced as motivating the MaaS premise. However, it is clear that more than technology will be required. How will the attitudes towards sharing and the move away from asset owning be accomplished? Will this begin with the younger generation and grow as this generation ages and is replaced by the next younger generation? Is a true multi-modal MaaS likely to appeal most in geographical jurisdictions where travellers are already using a mix of available modes? How will this impact on land use and the eventual shape of our cities—will they become more compact or will MaaS, in making mobility easier, lead to greater sprawl?

*Question 8: What does success look like for MaaS?*

It is still early in the development of MaaS. One of the limiting factors to date is the paucity of detailed evaluation studies of MaaS trials (with UbiGo being the exception) and Chapter 4 provides a synthesis of what has been learnt to date. The need to achieve critical mass for MaaS schemes is one obvious measure of success and learning from the ongoing experiences of Whim in Helsinki (and its relative lack of success in Birmingham) will be important in this respect. More widely in society there are changing attitudes towards sharing (Standing et al., 2019) and this provides an opportunity for transport (indeed sharing, along with electrification and automation have been referred to as the 'three revolutions' taking place in urban transportation). MaaS solutions require an environment where sharing feels natural. The MaaS operators (identified above under the key stakeholders) will also have a view on what constitutes a successful outcome for MaaS. In particular a positive outcome for public transport is likely to depend on getting the contracting issues under control. Creating circumstances where it is natural for public transport operators to seamlessly integrate with first and last mile services (perhaps even operating them themselves) will be a measure of success. Similarly, enabling the customer to have the opportunity to plan, pay for (by PAYG and/or subscription plan) and execute trips according to their personal preferences, as indicated by the definitions in Table 3.1, is the desired outcome.

*Question 9: Are the business models still too much in their infancy?*

Big questions and therefore debate surround how MaaS will be organised. The MaaS vision is predicated on public transport offerings being at the centre of the MaaS bundle. If this is the case, what are the organisational challenges for government in terms of legislation and governance? Public transport is subsidised—sometimes heavily—how will the governance be able to provide this subsidy in what is being promoted as primarily a market response to user demand? A fuller discussion of the governance issues relating to MaaS implementation is made in Arup

(2019). Questions about governance lead to the important further question as to how will the supply side emerge to provide what is demanded by users? Will it be existing transport providers that change their offering or will there be new brokers linking the demand and supply side? If there are brokers, will there be enough reward for the risk that they undertake? Will they always have transport experience or will they be non-mobility providers, for example, technology providers, vehicle manufacturers or perhaps financial enterprises? How does MaaS grow from the successful and commercially operated TNC operators to a multimodal system where the central plank of public transport will almost certainly need to be subsidised. This is discussed more in Chapter 6.

Finally, there is the issue of technology and autonomous vehicles—both separately discussed in this section. However, it must be recognised that, whilst technology has moved leaps and bounds, there are still few apps supporting full integration as shown by Table 3.2. A bigger unknown relates to the way in which autonomous vehicles will affect our landscape more generally and MaaS in particular—this is the focus of a question below (see Chapter 8).

*Question 10: Opportunity or threat from autonomous vehicles?*

The implications of AVs for the development and sustainability of MaaS has received less attention in the debate. It is widely expected that AVs will have the potential for greater door to door solutions which is something that can also be expected of MaaS. And yet much is still unknown about AVs, particularly around aspects of public adoption of AVs, including: what people are willing to pay for autonomous vehicles; what benefits people expect from AVs; what factors about AV concern the public and how AVs will impact on the environment. If AVs ultimately have negative consequences for public transport (e.g. through creating more traffic congestion by encouraging private use of AVs as is discussed in Chapter 8) then this will be bad for MaaS which is predicated on encouraging greater use of the available transport resource on a shared basis. However, MaaS could be a tool to facilitate integration of AVs with public transport, thus counteracting these potential negative consequences. A study conducted by Woldeamanuel and Nguyen (2018) to understand perceptions of millennials and non-millennials regarding AVs found that a greater number of millennials (41%) believe that traffic congestion reduction is likely to happen, informed or otherwise, compared to non-millennials (23%). This is the cohort that will determine the future role of AVs within MaaS schemes.

Chapter 4

# MaaS trials—What have we learnt?

## Chapter outline



## 4.1 Introduction

MaaS has become popularised since its introduction in 2014 (Heikkilä, 2014; Hietanen, 2014), and has generated great activity for public and private transport and technology actors around the world. Whilst concentrated in mainland Europe actors in Asia, North America, and Oceania have been interested. As showcased in Chapter 3, this widespread and growing interest in MaaS has generated many MaaS trials and interrelated activities. However, it has been argued that few of these trials thus far have been systematically and independently evaluated (Karlsson et al., 2017b). In general, little information on the outcome of most of the trials seems to be openly shared within the research community.

The shortage of detailed assessment reports is indeed striking, not least given the history of evaluation of intelligent transport systems applications over

Understanding Mobility as a Service (MaaS). https://doi.org/10.1016/B978-0-12-820044-5.00004-X
© 2020 Elsevier Inc. All rights reserved.

the past two decades (Mulley et al., 2019), opening up speculation on whether the motivation is lack of data, time, knowledge or interest, or something else. Primarily though, the lack of shared insights implies that the trials largely have failed to shed light on the promises (and perils) of MaaS, thus not substantiating policymakers' and practitioners' decisions on if, and if so how and when, they should engage in the development and diffusion of MaaS.

The main purpose of this chapter is to establish the practical experience of MaaS thus far in order to inform policymaking, entrepreneurial actions and research activities going forward. To do so, the chapter first complements the overview of past and present MaaS trials outlined in Chapter 3 by providing in-depth descriptions of the setups, processes and outcomes to date of five prominent examples of MaaS trials. This is followed by a discussion on key lessons learnt from these trials, as well as from the pool of MaaS trials in general. Lastly, based on the discussion on lessons learnt, the chapter pinpoints avenues for future MaaS experimentation and research.

## 4.2 MaaS trials

Chapter 3 set the current debate and experience in the context of the early roots of MaaS. The global development was charted by the identification of more than 30 current and recent MaaS or MaaS-like schemes, documenting their status and levels of integration following the taxonomies of Sochor et al. (2018) and Lyons et al. (2019). In this chapter, five specific trials are selected for detailed discussion: two from Sweden (UbiGo and EC2B in Gothenburg); one from Finland (Whim in Helsinki); one from Germany (Mobil-Flat in Augsburg); and one from Australia (Tripi in Sydney). In contrast to the bulk of MaaS trials, these are all trials which have been thoroughly documented, evaluated and disseminated to a wider audience, and in the case of Sweden and Australia are associated with on-going programmes of research. As such they lend themselves to a discussion on key lessons learnt which follows in Section 4.3.

### 4.2.1 UbiGo, Gothenburg 2013–2014

The concept of customised, multi-modal mobility packages was in a Swedish context initially proposed in 2011 within a government funded R&D project. The project, which examined business opportunities associated with multimodal services and sought to initiate processes for their realisation, concluded that the conditions were in place for services that provide metropolitan citizens with comprehensive, reliable, customised and usable mobility services that reduce costs, increase flexibility, and contribute to sustainable everyday travel (Boethius and Arby, 2011). The business concept was further developed between 2011 and 2014 in a two-phased collaborative R&D project named Go:Smart (Strömdahl et al., 2014). One of the aims of the Go:Smart project, which was cofunded by the Swedish Innovation Agency and the Region of Västra Götaland, was to explore a potential path towards reduced need for private car ownership by piloting a new business and partnership model that integrated transport modes and made use of new opportunities brought by information technologies. Accordingly, the project developed a MaaS service entitled UbiGo (although the term MaaS was yet to be introduced) and trialled it in the second largest city of Sweden, Gothenburg, with 71 households as paying customers over a trial period of 6 months, November 2013–April 2014 (Strömdahl et al., 2014). This trial is frequently referred to as the first comprehensive example of MaaS, and is also the first to be thoroughly documented.

The UbiGo service interlinked the regional public transport system with car- and bike-sharing schemes as well as with a rental car- and a taxi service. Customised and modifiable subscription plans were developed for each household, based on their preferences, which primarily were recorded via an introductory survey on their current travel behaviour. The customised subscription plans featured reduced prices for public transport tickets (including a daily ticket, unique to the trial), and free membership of the city's bicycle sharing system, among other things, but were in general designed to offer non-discounted pricing. The households only paid for the services that they used and unused credits were transferred to next month's subscription. Moreover, the households were given the possibility to set their car aside in the care of the project with some economic compensation, mainly for depreciation. Planning, booking, payment, and feedback was made possible through a responsive website, presented to the users as the UbiGo app.

In contrast to most other trials, the UbiGo experiment in Gothenburg has been thoroughly evaluated, and the results widely disseminated. Among other things, the evaluators concluded that the participating households in general appreciated the piloted service since UbiGo helped them try out unfamiliar transport modes (Strömberg et al., 2016) and made multi-modal travelling less expensive and more convenient (Sochor et al., 2015a). All in all, it seemed to promote changes in the households' transport patterns towards more use of public transport and active modes during the trial (Sochor et al., 2016), thus possibly contributing to policy objectives. Four categories of users that chose to sign up for the trial were identified through a qualitative analysis: *Car shedders* wanted to try to live without owning a car; *car accessors* wished to gain access to a car without having to purchase one; *simplifiers* saw UbiGo as a smarter way to handle their use of multiple services; and *economizers* identified that UbiGo could gain them cheaper access to public transport (Strömberg et al., 2018).

The participating transport providers, authorities, and agencies also cherished the promising outcome of the project, and a company was formed, aiming to refine and commercialise the trialled service. Notwithstanding these positive outcomes MaaS developments stalled after the trial. Almost 5 years after the UbiGo trial, the public transport authority that participated in the UbiGo trial is hosting and participating in multiple new MaaS trials (among them the EC2B trial outlined in Section 4.2.3) but is yet to graduate from the testing phase.

In parallel, a new company has been formed to refine the UbiGo concept, and to bring it to the open market. As of December 2019, they are testing their product via a trial in Stockholm.

A superficial understanding of how straightforward it is to implement MaaS may allude to the public transport authority intentionally halting the MaaS developments in order to seek how to place itself as the main benefactor of MaaS (Smith et al., 2019a). Rather, as discussed in Chapter 7, the "evaluation of UbiGo indicated that the main obstacles to further dissemination of MaaS may be found within and between service providing companies and organisations in terms of, e.g. regulations and institutional barriers" (Karlsson et al., 2016, p. 3265). In other words, MaaS does not fit well with the current institutional setting in Sweden, and the Go:Smart project was not setup in a way that made continuation of UbiGo after the project likely or even possible.

### 4.2.2 Whim, Helsinki 2016—Present

If the UbiGo trial in Gothenburg by many is recognised as the first mover, the trial of Whim in Helsinki (which eventually transmuted into a continuing business) is without a doubt the one that has received most widespread attention thus far. The MaaS label is said to initially have been introduced to Finnish authorities by the future cofounder and CEO of MaaS Global around 2011 (Mukhtar-Landgren and Smith, 2019). Still, even though it was not named as such yet, MaaS has been on the agenda for Finnish authorities since the early 2000s as part of a wider commitment to the development of intelligent transport systems (Audouin and Finger, 2018). Largely driven by a quest to streamline public spending on transport and the idea that economic growth will result from cross-industry collaborations and sound market competition, Finnish authorities have implemented multiple measures to facilitate MaaS developments in recent years (Smith et al., 2018b). A main measure has been to fund multiple MaaS trials via the Finnish Funding Agency for Innovation (now Business Finland), one of them being Whim—a service developed and managed by MaaS Global.

Following the founding of MaaS Global (at that point called MaaS Finland) in May 2015, Whim was offered to a limited number of beta testers in Helsinki in October 2016. In November 2017, it was commercially launched to the Helsinki public. Users could by then search and pay for regional public transport and search, book and pay for car rental and taxi via the Whim app. Three types of subscriptions were offered: *Pay-as-You-Go*, which featured regular prices and no subscription fee; *Whim Basic*, which cost €89 monthly and gave the subscriber unlimited public transport access within the city of Helsinki, as well as up to €39 to spend on car rental or taxis (within tightly prescribed geographical limits); and *Whim Go*, which for a monthly fee of €149 provided unlimited access to public transport within the city of Helsinki, and up to €124 to spend on car rental or taxis (Audouin and Finger, 2018). Subscribers of the two latter plans could also choose to pay more to extend the coverage of the included public transport. Since the initial launch of Whim, MaaS Global has introduced new modes (the city's bicycle sharing system and a car sharing scheme) as well as new and modified subscription plans (see whimapp.com/plans/).

MaaS Global has secured a reported €53.7 million in investments from a wide variety of companies from several industry sectors in four sets of funding rounds (MaaS Global, 2019b), won several industry awards, and expanded into the UK and Belgium (MaaS Global, 2019a). Moreover, the Finnish Ministry of Transport and Communication was praised by the intelligent transport system community for their work on enabling MaaS (ITS World Congress, 2017).

In terms of usage, MaaS Global announced that four million trips had been powered by the Whim app by February 2019 (Huhtala-Jenks, 2019). The dataset of trips that were booked in Helsinki during 2018 has been analysed by the consultancy firm Ramböll and published in a much discussed report entitled Whimpact (Hartikainen et al., 2019). Although the report suffers from overstatements and from failing to consider self-selection bias (cf. Wong, 2019c), it does suggest a few interesting things regarding user interest and behaviour. Firstly, the report mentions that Whim had 70,000 registered users at the end of 2018, signifying a high penetration rate (more than 10% of the population of Helsinki). Unfortunately, how many that actually used the app and how those who do are distributed across the different subscription plans is not reported. However, the number of subscribers to *MaaS Unlimited* (a plan that gives unlimited public transport and 2 hours of free car sharing per day) is too small to be included in the analysis, indicating that very few had subscribed to this plan. Secondly, actual numbers of trips or purchases are unfortunately not presented either, but the trips made possible by the app were distributed as follows: 95.2% public transport (2.15 trips per user per day on average), 3.75% taxi (0.07 trips per user per day on average), 1.02% city bicycle, 0.03% rental car (900 trips in total), and 0.001% car sharing (included only towards the end of 2018). These numbers suggest mild multi-modal travelling and showcase quite clearly how central public transport is to the Whim concept. Thirdly, the starting points of the trips were generally located in very central or quite central parts of Helsinki, insinuating that Whim primarily attracts urban dwellers, at least in Helsinki (Hartikainen et al., 2019).

### 4.2.3 EC2B, Gothenburg 2019—Present

To regain the momentum of MaaS developments following the cessation of the initial UbiGo trial, the regional public transport authority has engaged in a few new MaaS-related trial activities since 2017. One such trial, funded by the Swedish Innovation Agency (among others) is the EC2B ('easy to be') trial at Viva, a centrally located and newly built, tenant-owned apartment complex consisting of 132 apartments distributed across six blocks.

Branded as a demonstration of how the ecological footprint of housing and living can be reduced, the Viva apartment complex features novel approaches to for example apartment layouts, building materials, shared resources and energy supply (Riksbyggen, 2016). One of the most notable features of the complex, which provides a unique opportunity to promote and test MaaS solutions, is that there is no residential car parking for the tenants. Instead, Viva has a large-scale underground bicycle garage, including a bicycle ramp and a bicycle elevator, as well as e-mobility charging facilities and a room with repair stands and tools.

Since February 2019, the tenants also have exclusive access to the EC2B app. It enables them to book and pay for regional public transport, a pool of shared vehicles and a car sharing service. The vehicle pool includes six electric bicycles, two electric cargo bicycles, and a three-wheeled electric moped, while the car sharing service includes four electric cars parked outside Viva and several cars of different models within walking distance. Apart from booking and payment functionalities, the EC2B app features payment history and occasional discounts for public transport and can be used to access information and customer support. Furthermore, as part of the EC2B, the tenants are offered an advisory meeting with a mobility expert in connection with moving in, to discuss personalised information on sustainable travel options.

Based on observations, interviews and sale statistics, Smith et al. (2019c) scrutinised the tenants' processes of adopting MaaS. Three of their key findings are summarised here. Firstly, regarding who the users were, the interview results indicated that the group that has implemented EC2B as a tool for solving their travel needs in general had lived longer at Viva, were younger, and were less likely to own a private car, compared to those who did not own a car. Secondly, regarding how EC2B was used, the study found that the usage of the integrated transport services had increased gradually, and that the services had been used for a spectrum of reasons, such as trips related to shopping, hobbies and errands as well as pure leisure trips. Thirdly, regarding the impact, the study reported that many of the car-owning tenants at Viva were using their cars to a lesser degree compared to how they travelled prior to moving in. Although not the most important factor, the access to EC2B appeared to play a role in this shift, as it gave the tenants access to a range of alternative modes and a smooth way to trial them (cf. Strömberg et al., 2018; Strömberg et al., 2016). For the non-car-owning tenants, EC2B was found to reduce travel time and hassle, and to offer a sense of independence.

### 4.2.4 Mobil-flat, Augsburg 2018—Present

Stadtwerke Augsburg is a municipal utilities company whose portfolio includes operating the public transport system in Augsburg, Germany. Besides trams and buses, Stadtwerke Augsburg also operates the city's sole car sharing system (both free-floating and station-based) as well as a bicycle sharing scheme.[a]

a. Nextbike, a German white-label bikesharing company, provides the software backend.

This multi-modal portfolio of services assists Stadtwerke Augsburg in positioning itself as the city's public transport operator *and* mobility services broker (cf. Hensher, 2017) simultaneously.

Following their long-term multi-modal mobility strategy, Stadtwerke Augsburg started a MaaS project named Mobil-Flat in October 2017. About 50 Augsburg inhabitants were invited to subscribe to a mobility bundle in a year-long trial. While Stadtwerke Augsburg's overall goal of its MaaS journey is user retention, the goal of this first trial was to learn about travel behaviour under the influence of a bundle (Reck and Axhausen, 2019a). The trialled bundle contained a monthly budget of 30h of car sharing (any vehicle, unlimited driving distance), unrestrained number of 30min rides with the bicycle sharing scheme and a city-wide public transport pass. The bundle was priced at €75, which compares to a minimum price of €110.5 for stand-alone services (€52.5 for the public transport pass, €48 for car sharing without surcharges per kilometre and €10 for bicycle sharing). Trial participants were asked to complete a simple mobility diary for the entirety of the program to enable research and development of proceeding bundles.

Drawing on the analyses of the trial booking data, Stadtwerke Augsburg refined its subscription bundles and launched Germany's first two commercial multi-modal subscription bundles on the first of November 2019. The first bundle ('swa Mobil-Flat S') is a slightly smaller version of the trialled bundle: 15h of car sharing (half of the trialled version), and the same public transport and bicycle sharing budgets, priced at €79 per month. The second bundle ('swa Mobil-Flat M') essentially continues the trialled bundle at a price of €109 per month (after an initial 6 months discounted price at €79 per month). Initial uptake of these bundles has been promising with about 150 sign-ups in the first 2 weeks.

Stadtwerke Augsburg is collaborating with ETH Zurich to evaluate the first trial results as well as the uptake of the two commercially launched bundles. While the evaluation is still in progress, a few observations can be made already. Perhaps most interesting is the unusual order of developments. Many cities and regions approach to MaaS can be described as bottom-up, meaning that development of a multi-modal journey planner and a joint payment method precedes the introduction of multi-modal bundles. In contrast, Stadtwerke Augsburg jump-started to offering subscription bundles (cf. level three in Sochor et al., 2018) *before* offering a fully integrated mobility app (cf. level one and two in Sochor et al., 2018). Potentially, this approach has helped them to avoid/postpone some of the technology related barriers that many other MaaS developments have faced (see Chapter 7) and instead focus on the bundle design aspect of MaaS. Still, several technological developments are planned for 2020, including the introduction of a fully integrated mobility app (thus potentially transforming Mobil-Flat into a true MaaS solution according to the definition used in this chapter). Consequently, Mobil-Flat seems to be an increasingly interesting case to observe and learn from.

### 4.2.5 Tripi, Sydney 2019—Present

The Tripi trial project is Australia's first MaaS trial, funded by the iMOVE Cooperative Research Centre as a partnership between the Institute of Transport and Logistics Studies at the University of Sydney, Insurance Australia Group (IAG)—a major insurance business—and SkedGo—an App developer. It has the aim of advancing the understanding of the role that MaaS can play in both improving the travellers' experience of using multiple complementary transport services and in contributing to improvements in broader community benefits by providing a pertinent alternative to owning and using private vehicles.

The project draws on insights and experiences from the MaaS trials in Europe (see Chapter 3) and seeks to address significant knowledge gaps by investigating how different bundles of mode mixes and payment models affect MaaS uptake and travel behaviour. Experience to date shows that very little is known about what transport services MaaS should include and how these should be bundled into subscription plans, to reap the potential societal benefits of MaaS.

The trial is situated in the Sydney region, which has an appropriate institutional setting for several reasons. Sydney has an extensive public transport system and many private transport services providers are currently operating there, which enables the creation of comprehensive MaaS bundles. Furthermore, public sector actors in Sydney have shown interest in new ways to improve the public transport offering (e.g. Perera et al., 2019), and Sydney has an open data platform that will help in the process of aggregating numerous open and private data sources to provide insights and understanding of the travel behaviour and infrastructure utilisation within the region from the trial participants.

Using an app-based setting, the project has enrolled up to 150 employees of IAG to participate in a six-month trial commencing in November 2019. The first month of the trial will be Pay-as-You-Go followed by 5 months of incrementally reviewed and adjusted as appropriate subscription plan offers that are co-created and reviewed each month, with the option to stay with Pay-as-You-Go. Eligible participants, who work, live, and travel in the Sydney Greater Metropolitan area, will arrange their everyday travel needs through a MaaS app (a customised version of SkedGo's TripGo travel planner, known as Tripi) linked to subscription plans offered by a mobility broker (IAG). The plans will give participants access to public transport (including train, tram, ferry, and bus) and car-based transport services (traditional taxi, ridesourcing, and car sharing). The participants will be able to find, compare (e.g. in terms of cost, travel time, emissions, and health benefits) and book these services through the app. As such, the trial will enable the participants to perform multi-modal journeys seamlessly, and the sum of (either all or parts of) the transport services will offer the participant equal or better choice of mobility, compared to owning a private car and/or their previous modal options.

The participants will, at the outset, get to choose between a range of subscription plans, distinct in terms of both mixes of transport services and payment structures. In particular, the payment structure will vary in terms of whether the individual transport services are paid for upon usage or monthly. The design of the plans will be informed by research undertaken at the Institute of Transport and Logistic Studies at University of Sydney to identify the role of specific modal offerings over a subscribed period including the subscription price associated with various planned offerings (Ho et al., 2018).

Ultimately, it is intended that by generating real-world knowledge about how mode mixes and subscription plan types appeal to different segments of the population and how they impact their satisfaction and travel behaviours, the Tripi trial will substantially advance the understanding of how MaaS solutions can be designed to contribute to a transition towards an increasingly sustainable transport system centred around public transport and complementary transport services.

## 4.3 Lessons learnt

When analysing the outcomes and insights from the (limited) pool of MaaS trials, it is important to keep two fundamental limitations in mind. Firstly, most MaaS trials have thus far been small-scale in terms of geographical coverage, timeframe and numbers of users (Whim being the obvious exception). Hence, they have neither covered long-term effects nor potential scalability gains. For instance, among the better documented cases, both UbiGo and Tripi capped the user base, and were confined to six-months of operation. Consequently, we are unfortunately not able to draw any categorical conclusions on the long-term impacts or scalability of MaaS diffusion at this point in time.

Secondly, the conditions for the trials vary significantly. For the trials described in this chapter, this is particularly apparent in terms of local contexts, institutional environments, the setups of the trial projects, and the constellations of the project consortia. Since MaaS is seemingly *en route* to become a global phenomenon, this limitation is likely to remain. To make it even more complex, MaaS is a blanket term that comprises several different types of services. For instance, Tripi, Mobil-Flat, Whim, and UbiGo offered subscription plans to the users, whilst EC2B merely used a Pay-as-You-Go model. These services also exhibited vast differences in what transport services they integrated, how their apps were designed, and what market segments they targeted. Simply put, there seems to be no one MaaS solution. Therefore, one should be careful when generalising findings. However, despite these two important limitations, we have identified five important lessons from the trial activities undertaken, which we discuss next, and which could inform further MaaS experimentation and research, as described in Section 4.4.

### 4.3.1 Lesson 1: MaaS is more than an app and a subscription plan

The introduction of eye pleasing and user-friendly apps (whose significant development effort should be acknowledged), as well as upfront advertised and discounted fares did, without a doubt, contribute to ridesourcing firms' recent disruption of the traditional taxi industry. Yet, the relative contributions of introducing more efficient driver-passenger matching technologies, larger scales of operation, and more flexible labour supply models cannot be overlooked (Cramer and Krueger, 2016). Likewise, Whim has been widely praised for their app (at least within the industry), but it is arguably their subscription plans that have created most buzz (again, at least within the industry). Likewise, MobilFlat has received considerable media attention, despite the lack of new digital technology. Both the design of pricing models and of the main digital channels will indeed likely be very significant for users' experiences of MaaS for the foreseeable future. However, the MaaS trials have informed us about how several other demand-side aspects can be influential too.

Some of these aspects were closely linked to the provided apps—for instance, the first users of Tripi were more excited about the mobility wallet function than its subscription plans—while other aspects were linked to components of the MaaS solutions, such as the offered support functions. For example, in the UbiGo trial, UbiGo took responsibility for dealing with the administration associated with delays and trip failures experienced by users, including finding substitute services and applying for compensation. Although this support feature was rarely used during the trial, Sochor et al. (2015a) noted that it seemed to add value by creating a sense of security for the users. In the EC2B trial, the palette of face-to-face and online support offered by EC2B helped the users in trialling the service, and made them feel taken care of (Smith et al., 2019c).

Based on the UbiGo experience, Karlsson et al. (2016) emphasised the importance of an holistic understanding of the service of MaaS in order to cater for positive user experiences. Similarly, drawing on an analysis of a corporate-oriented MaaS trial in Stockholm, Hesselgren et al. (2019) concluded that "without the material elements, such as the service application and the different transport modes, there will be no system, but introducing the material elements is not enough to form new mobility practices" (pp. 8). In other words, to facilitate broad uptake, positive use experiences, and behaviour change, MaaS should deliver on its core functions—finding, booking, and paying for transport services—and address the user needs that lies beyond, or in between these. In the end, although the MaaS premise initially was motivated by digital developments, it is the users' perception of the sum of the service components that may set MaaS apart from pure information or payment technologies, such as travel planning devices and bank cards.

### 4.3.2 Lesson 2: MaaS can attract interest, but might not be for everyone

Whim has gained considerable attention in Helsinki and several million trips have been powered by the platform during its first years in operation. This indicates that MaaS can appeal to the masses and facilitate large numbers of trips. Despite targeting small and distinct groups of users, EC2B and Tripi have both also managed to spur significant attentiveness to their services, thus supporting the finding, substantiated by the Whim trial, that there is sufficient interest in MaaS products. However, the setups of the trials, and the outcomes of them, also suggest that MaaS might not be for everyone, at least not yet.

It must be accepted that the trial participants are hardly representative of the general population. For instance, one can assume that both the EC2B and UbiGo user groups were abnormally entranced by the opportunity to participate in sustainability branded research and development. The EC2B users had chosen to live at BRF Viva, which was advertised as "Sweden's most innovative plus energy district" (Riksbyggen, 2016, p. 1), while the UbiGo users signed up for a trial of "the future's travel service for urban households," which possibly "can reduce the Gothenburg citizens' need to own and use a car" (Chalmers, 2013, p. 1). Moreover, the users of EC2B and UbiGo seem to be unusually capable and willing to be flexible in order to try out new things, as both services exhibited quite complex on-boarding processes at the point of the trials. This self-selection bias probably holds true for most of the trial populations. As explained by Rogers (1995), most products and services are first adopted by people that have financial liquidity, hold opinion leadership and are willing to take risk. If the innovation diffusion continues, the more risk averse and demanding majority is likely to follow.

Still, there are other indications that MaaS might not be for all, even in the future. Whim has primarily focused on urban dwellers in Helsinki, and especially attracted people living along public transport trunk routes (Hartikainen et al., 2019). Similarly, UbiGo, EC2B, and Tripi were all targeted to populations either living or working in urban centres. The vast majority of existing MaaS trials have been set in urban contexts, although some exceptions exist, such as the Reissu trial in the Finnish ski resort Ylläs. Hence, MaaS seems to be an urban concept thus far. Furthermore, even though more or less all tenants at BRF Viva appeared to genuinely appreciate the overall idea of EC2B, older tenants and tenants who owned private cars were less likely to adopt EC2B into their daily practices (Smith et al., 2019c).[b] While the car owners were less motivated to test EC2B, the older tenants wanted to participate, but struggled with understanding apps and procedures, and were not as keen to use unfamiliar and active modes (Smith et al., 2019c). In general, MaaS trials have featured some generic boundary conditions that might exclude a large share of the population from the potential user base. Firstly, an app is generally the main communication channel, thus requiring access to, and skills in using, the Internet and a smart phone. Secondly, most payment methods have required access to a bank card, which many of the poor, as well as children, often do not have. Thirdly, several of the trials have featured car sharing and car rental schemes as one of the core transport modes. Thus, the users are prone to have a driver's licence

b. In contrast, Hartikainen et al. (2019) noted that early adopters of Whim were fairly evenly represented across most age-groups, although 57% of the users were below 40 years old.

and financial viability in order to make full use of the MaaS offering. All things considered, it seems unlikely that MaaS, at least in its current forms, will be a feasible transport solution for the entire populace.

### 4.3.3 Lesson 3: MaaS can influence travel behaviour, but not on its own

There is very limited empirical evidence on the effects on travel behaviour of introducing MaaS. Yet, drawing on self-reported travel patterns before and during the trials, the analyses of the UbiGo and EC2B trials both indicate that MaaS can influence travel behaviour towards less car use, although it is widely uncertain how transferable these results are to other services, contexts and timeframes.

Altogether, the UbiGo trial participants reported a net-effect of less private car use[c] more use of public transport, rental car, car sharing, and taxi, as well as more cycling and walking (Sochor et al., 2015b). As indicated by how much of their subscriptions they utilised, the participants used public transport, rental cars, and car sharing less frequently than they had planned, whilst taxi use overall was limited. Similar use patterns have been noted in the case of Mobil-Flat. While the bicycle sharing system hardly was used at all during the first trial, the car sharing consumption was often substantially lower than the budget size. This leads to the hypothesis of a flat-rate bias even for multimodal packages (Reck and Axhausen, 2019a). Moreover, the UbiGo participants seemed to change attitude to the different modes during the trial. They reported an increasingly negative attitude towards private car use, and more positive attitude towards public transport (Sochor et al., 2015b).

In the EC2B trial, many of the car-owners said that they were using their cars to a lesser degree compared to how they travelled prior to moving to Viva, and adopting the EC2B service (Smith et al., 2019c). The analysis concluded that the EC2B service appeared to play a role in this shift by offering the Viva tenants access to a range of alternative modes and a smooth way to trial them. Nonetheless, the analysis also found that the central location of the Viva apartment complex and the vicinity to public transport, as well as the longer distance to over-night parking due to the restrictive parking policy, seemed to be the most significant contributors, alongside the tenants' individual motivation to change their travel behaviour (Smith et al., 2019c). This finding suggests that the diffusion of MaaS might rest upon the fact that the target group is motivated to change away from their current practices, and that the introduction of MaaS is coupled with a decrease in the relative attractiveness of private car use. For example, in order to induce a shift to more sustainable travelling, the introduction of MaaS could be a tool to increase the relative attractiveness of transport services, whilst land-use policies, such as road space allocation, parking norms, and congestion pricing, could be used to lower the relative attractiveness of

c. 48% reported less private car use, 48% reported equal use, and 4% reported more use.

private car use. Drawing on a MaaS trial in Stockholm (separate from UbiGo) that gained little interest among prospective users and had limited impact on users' travel behaviour, Hesselgren et al. (2019) arrived at an analogous conclusion. Arguing that a switch to more sustainable travel behaviour requires more than adding a digital platform and a service application (cf. lesson 1), they called for more research into how the use of both carrots and sticks could promote the use of more sustainable modes of transport.

### 4.3.4 Lesson 4: MaaS trials are costly, and tricky to build on

Beyond the insights from actual trial results, and the lack of documenting thereof, the past and present processes of planning, negotiating, and implementing MaaS trials have generated a useful body of knowledge about MaaS. Especially, the convoluted development processes in Sweden and Finland (cf. Smith et al., 2018b) have showcased that the realisation of the MaaS concept is far from as easy as it first might appear (see the breakdown of institutional barriers in Chapter 7). In this section, we focus on two key challenges: high costs associated with preparing for, marketing and operating MaaS trials, and difficulties in transitioning from trial activities to business-as-usual operations. Both are associated with the need to establish more mature business models (Chapter 3).

In terms of preparation costs, the rollout of the UbiGo trial required many new developments from the participating organisations. Assisted by €925,000 in funding from the Swedish Innovation Agency, the preparation work included the development of a responsive website (i.e. the MaaS app), as well as business and organisation related developments, such as setting up the back-end organisation, designing a new type of daily public transport ticket, and making it possible to upgrade public transport zones on the fly (Strömdahl et al., 2014). From the perspective of the public transport authority, the EC2B trial represented yet another step closer to a viable long-term setup for MaaS, compared to the UbiGo trial. Thus, the trial required further investment on their side into developing the application programming interfaces for real-time data and digital tickets as well as into designing contracts and setting up an internal organisation and a business plan. Beyond preparation costs, both the UbiGo and the EC2B trial have been costly in terms of the operation as well, for instance regarding additional tier-one support, a more complex invoicing process and vehicle repairs.

Still, the biggest costs of MaaS trials are most likely associated with customer acquisition. The project partners have spent numerous man-hours into attracting and introducing users in all the studied trials, and monetary incentives might be needed as well. For example, the use of transport services in the EC2B trials started picking up after promotional discounts were introduced EC2B (Smith et al., 2019c). Other recent examples that point towards the difficulty of attracting users are MaaS Global's struggles with attracting Whim customers in West Midlands where the three initial plans at launch in April 2018 were replaced by Pay-as-You-Go only from January 2019. Similarly, UbiGo's expansion to Stockholm has been progressing slowly. Furthermore, after 2 years of offering external actors the opportunity to bundle public transport tickets into MaaS offerings, there are seven resellers active in the Flanders region. Their total sales of public transport tickets account for only 3% of De Lijn's digital sales (Kesteloot, 2019). In summary, it seems that significant costs are associated with attracting and retaining MaaS users.

Another big challenge is the transitioning from pilot to every-day operation, even when the trial is deemed as successful. Institutional barriers, including the public–private divide, make it difficult to set up a trial project so that continued operation is likely or even possible (Smith et al., 2019b). Simultaneously, long-term commitments from the public sector are important for the private sector's interest in investing in MaaS trials, as they often want to leverage the acquired user base and brand recognition. As a consequence, there is a risk of a falling out between public and private actors after MaaS trials, as exemplified in both Sweden and Finland (Smith et al., 2018b). Due to the difficulty in continuing services after the trials, there is also a risk of creating false hopes and expectations among the trial participants, which has ethical and reputational implications. Hence, a strong communication strategy that establishes a shared understanding of aims and goals among all stakeholders (including prospective users) prior to embarking on MaaS trials seems to be important.

### 4.3.5 Lesson 5: MaaS trials can create both direct and indirect returns

The goal of the UbiGo trial was to "develop the conditions for the implementation of an innovative service for sustainable personal transport", which in the long-run could "promote sustainable cities by offering a simple, flexible, reliable, and affordable service as an alternative to car ownership" (Strömdahl et al., 2014, p. 1). Arguably, the trial project did not deliver on this ambitious goal. Both UbiGo (the company) and the public transport authority are yet to advance from the trial stage. Nevertheless, the trial created manifold indirect returns for the development of MaaS in general, and for the participating actors in particular.

The UbiGo trial prompted industry awareness of, and activated interest in, the MaaS concept. As such, the trial was fundamental in kick-starting MaaS discussions and developments, in Sweden and abroad. For the public transport authority involved, the UbiGo trial also generated insight into the prospects of the unique daily public transport ticket that was tested through the trial, as well as a better understanding of the opportunities and challenges of integrating public transport with other types of transport services. Additionally, the UbiGo trial created numerous opportunities to leverage the acquired knowledge of MaaS for the private entrepreneur that initially proposed the project, as well as for the researchers involved in evaluating its outcome.

Indirect benefits have been reported from other trials as well. Based on their experiences with the seven active resellers of their digital tickets (i.e. MaaS trials), representatives of De Lijn reported that these activities had resulted in De Lijn becoming part of a wider ecosystem of actors. This gave De Lijn a chance to practice their skills in managing an ecosystem and improved the perception of De Lijn among the other actors in the ecosystem. These outcomes were deemed valuable for De Lijn's future developments in general. Furthermore, the MaaS trials generated practical insights into how De Lijn could develop their digital platforms, application programming interfaces and apps (Strömdahl et al., 2014). Likewise, Transport for New South Wales are hoping that their planned MaaS trials (cf. TfNSW, 2018), separate to the Tripi trial, will help them further develop their open data portal and contactless payment system—investments that they label as 'no-regret investments', basically since they foresee that they will be valuable no matter if MaaS prospers or not (Smith and Hensher, 2019). In Finland, the Whim trial is widely considered to have helped put Helsinki on the global map, to attract foreign investors and firms to Finland, and to create business opportunities for Finnish entrepreneurs (Mukhtar-Landgren and Smith, 2019). In Scotland, although there is only one MaaS trial to date (the NaviGoGo 'Pick & Mix' project, see ESP Group, 2019), an industry-led initiative led by the non-profit organisation MaaS Scotland is supporting the growth of a cluster of firms who can supply products and services along the MaaS value chain in partnership with the public sector. Hence, despite MaaS trials being costly, and tricky to build on, and even though we still know little about MaaS' potential impact on travel behaviour (although this is a key focus of the Tripi trial, which will be reported in due course), MaaS trials can be valuable to pursue, depending on the policy objectives.

## 4.4 Avenues for further experimentation and research

Three key messages to further experimentation and research emerge from the lessons depicted in the previous section. First, *we need better documentation of existing and future trials*. The global development of MaaS was charted in Chapter 3 by the identification of more than 30 current and recent schemes. Merely a few have arguably been thoroughly enough documented and evaluated to make them suitable for detailed scrutiny. Whilst additional grey material is rapidly emerging (e.g. Linton and Bray, 2019), it is essential that MaaS trials and evaluations are subjected to detailed analysis so that learning experiences, such as those identified in this chapter, can be maximised. In order to enable investigations into the transferability and generalizability of findings, it is important that the trials and implementations are evaluated and reported on in a comparable manner. Here, the Swedish MaaS roadmap is a nice example of what governments could do, as the roadmap dictates the development of an open MaaS database, and orders MaaS trials to be evaluated in a standardised way, if they are to receive funding from the Swedish Innovation Agency (cf. Pernestål Brenden et al., 2017).

Second, Whim in Helsinki is still the only long-term and large-scale implementation of MaaS. Among the cases considered in this chapter, both UbiGo and Tripi were confined to six-months of operation. Similarly, the NaviGoGo project comprised a six-month beta trial. When analysing behaviour change, six-months is arguably a (too) short time period. Additionally, user sample sizes have generally been small. The UbiGo trial comprised 71 households (83 if one counts participants that were involved in the project consortium) while EC2B targeted 132. Likewise, the Tripi trial engaged 150 IAG employees, and NaviGoGo worked with 100 young people. To better understand potential long-term effects of MaaS as well as the scalability of the diffusion of MaaS, *we need longer trials at scale*. There is an opportunity for governments to influence this agenda. In this respect it is encouraging that the UK Parliament's Transport Select Committee enquiry on MaaS (House of Commons Transport Committee, 2018) specifically tasks the Department for Transport with a leadership role and calls for the Government to fund pilot programmes of MaaS applications across the country. Similarly, the Scottish Government has established a MaaS Investment Fund in its 2018 Programme for Government.

Finally, *we need to study the impact (both short and long term) on wider user groups*. Most commentators agree that there is significant opportunity for developing MaaS solutions for specific market segments, although there is still no conclusive answer to basic questions such as: who is MaaS most attractive to (see Section 4.3.2)? What is the impact of MaaS (integration and/or subscription plans) on travel behaviour?. The experience with Whim in Helsinki (Hartikainen et al., 2019) confirms that the present MaaS environment is heavily driven by urban dwelling millennials whose travel behaviour appears to be less dominated by car ownership and more defined by their interest in technology. This partly explains the product placement to date. However, beyond the metropolitan focus, scholars as well as practitioners have lately started investigating rural applications of MaaS (e.g. Berg et al., 2019; Eckhardt et al., 2018). For instance, recent work (Mulley et al., 2018) has looked at a different but very specific segment of the population in Australia that have their accessibility provided by community transport, focusing specifically on New South Wales and Queensland. Community transport clients are predominantly (although not exclusively) older persons who do not have access to conventional public transport or are unable to use public transport easily. The 'MaaS community transport' study (Mulley et al., 2018) investigated the bundles of mobility services for which community transport clients would be willing to pay in the new era of person-centred funding where funding is placed directly with clients (rather than as a supply-side subsidy to the community transport provider) who then have a single budget to purchase mobility along with other services they require. More such initiatives are needed to understand the opportunities and limits of MaaS in terms of user groups and contexts.

In summary, this chapter concludes that in order to paint a fuller picture of how to realise MaaS, who MaaS is for, where MaaS has potential, and what MaaS leads to (etc.), more as well as longer and increasingly diverse MaaS trials and full-scale implementations, which are systematically evaluated, are needed.

Chapter 5

# What do we know about market interest and potential uptake?

## Chapter outline



## 5.1 Introduction

As MaaS continues to evolve, a key driver for its success will be the market demand and user's willingness to pay for mobility services. This chapter examines the demand for MaaS products where travellers can either pre-pay for their mobility services bundled into a MaaS plan or pay for each individual service via a Pay-as-you-Go (PAYG) option. The common feature between the two payment options is service integration, which is facilitated through a digital platform, usually in the form of a smartphone app that offers one-stop access to multiple modes of transport as well as providing journey planning, ticketing, and billing in real-time. The digital platform that powers MaaS better matches demand to supply than other uni-modal app (e.g. Uber, Public transport journey planners) by providing information about the availability of different transport options, with the potential of accounting for user preferences for time, cost, and the impact on the environment of these services (Guidon et al., 2020). Thus, MaaS is expected to facilitate multimodal journeys, hence reducing private vehicle use and its associated negative externalities such as congestion and pollution. MaaS is also expected to improve public health (through facilitating more active transport modes such as walk, bike, or car-share into multimodal journeys) and potentially lower public transport subsidy through an increased market share for public transport.

It is the potential societal benefits of MaaS that makes it in the best interest of the public since reducing the environmental burden and/or increasing the

Understanding Mobility as a Service (MaaS). https://doi.org/10.1016/B978-0-12-820044-5.00005-1
© 2020 Elsevier Inc. All rights reserved.

efficiency of the transport system have been articulated, for quite some time, as the priorities of most governments (see Chapter 8 for an in-depth discussion). In contrast, it is the value-added of MaaS achieved by integrating the existing transport services that decides whether MaaS will become a mainstream or a niche product. If the prospective users of MaaS do not see any added value of MaaS, or its realised value is not worth the membership fee, then the travelling public is unlikely to be willing to pay for these services. In this case, MaaS will be a niche product with very little potential for scalability. Only when the efficiency gains and the added value of MaaS clearly outweigh the coordination costs of providing MaaS might it be expected that MaaS could become a mainstream product since it would be profitable for mobility aggregators/brokers to offer MaaS (Guidon et al., 2020). Thus, one hint to the question as to whether MaaS will remain a niche or a mainstream product lies in the market demand for the MaaS platform, and (prospective) user's willingness to pay for various transport services, both separately as stand-alone services through a PAYG model and collectively through a subscription model in which a mix of transport services are bundled and priced as a monthly subscription plan.

Using state-of-the-art stated preference surveys conducted in Sydney, Australia and Tyneside, UK via face-to-face interviews, this chapter aims to shed light on several key unknowns including prospective users' preferences for various features of a MaaS platform, the potential uptake of MaaS, the mix of transport services potential users would like to be bundled, and the likely impact of MaaS on travel behaviour. The latter includes how MaaS adopters would access public transport services in the future (i.e. to what extent MaaS would address the first and last mile issue associated with public transport use), and how car drivers may question the necessity of their own cars in the presence of MaaS and vice versa. The discussion is enriched by cross-referencing to other studies on market demand for MaaS.

From the user perspective, this chapter draws implications for policy makers and MaaS innovators around the business model to follow, the level of discount required to obtain commercially viable products, the necessity of cross-subsidy in providing MaaS, and the likely market segments of MaaS offerings. Based on the user's willingness to pay estimates, this chapter also discuss issues around bundling such as how best to bundle, cost and market mobility plans to end users to obtain sustainable goals and a high take-up rate before exploring the ways in which MaaS might be introduced to the market in Chapter 6.

## 5.2 Research on MaaS demand: Market surveys and real-world trials

In order to assess the market demand for MaaS, most studies use a market research survey, usually in the form of a stated choice (SC) or stated preference (SP) survey (see Hensher et al., 2015). For segmentation analysis, these surveys often include background questions about the respondent's socio-demographics, travel patterns, attitudes towards different transport modes such as the private car, and attitudes towards the environment and healthy commuting. The stated choice survey method is deemed as the best approach for understanding market demand for MaaS because MaaS is not yet available on the market or it accounts for a very small market share at the time the research is conducted. This makes the revealed preference (RP) survey method infeasible. By contrast, MaaS components—including public transport, car-share, Uber/taxi, and bike-share all as stand-alone services—are quite familiar to the respondents. These facts make SP/SC surveys one of the most appropriate methods (in addition to a real-world trial method discussed below and in Chapter 3) to explore the market demand for MaaS, and business models that MaaS aggregators/brokers could pursue. The well-known issue of hypothetical bias associated with stated preference surveys is discussed later in the chapter (see also Hensher, 2010).

Apart from a handful of studies (ITS Australia, 2018; Fioreze et al., 2019; Guidon et al., 2020; Ho et al., 2018, 2020; Mayas and Kamargianni, 2017) that use the SP/SC method to investigate the market demand for MaaS, only a few MaaS trials have been conducted in different countries to test MaaS bundles in real markets and with real people. Kamargianni et al. (2016a,b) review several integrated and operational mobility schemes and offer introduce a further categorisation, over and above those discussed in Chapter 3, in the form of a ranking system based on the level of integration in terms of ticketing, payment, digital platform, and mobility bundle. Using this ranking system, they classified the UbiGo trial in Gothenburg, Sweden and Whim in Helsinki, Finland as highly integrated mobility schemes. The UbiGo scheme is documented in Chapter 4 (see also Sochor et al., 2014, 2016) whilst the Whim scheme is less well documented, apart from the Whimpact report (Chapter 4; Ramboll, 2019). Both schemes assess changes in travel behaviour (during the trial for UbiGo and during the first year of operations in the case of Whim) and report that trips undertaken by public transport modes, including traditional public transport and car-sharing, bike-sharing, increased whilst the share of trips by private car decreased (Ramboll, 2019; Sochor et al., 2016). These assessments provide the first indications that MaaS bundles could lower the environmental burden of the transport system; however, the extent to which MaaS bundles could reduce the environmental burden depends on the market size and the user willingness to pay for a MaaS bundle or its parts.

Market interest and potential uptake are the areas that these trials offer very little information about. The UbiGo trial, whilst enrolling a decent number of participants (71 households/customer subscriptions ~ 195 individuals) and offering customised combination of mobility services, has a non-representative sample with a majority of the participants (88%) living in apartments and more than half (54%) having no access to the private car. Thus, whilst this trial concluded that there is a demand for MaaS, the study cannot estimate how large the demand is and for what type of MaaS the market would strongly respond to (Sochor et al., 2016). Whim cannot answer this question either, since Whim currently only offers three tiers of service (see Chapter 4). Using RP data from the first year of operations, *Whimpact* (Ramboll, 2019) does not offer any insights into market demand for these different MaaS opportunities. The report points to "over 70,000 registered users" of Whim but it does not state how many of these are PAYG users vs monthly subscribers, and how many are active users vs in-active users (those who downloaded the Whim app but since then have not made any trip via this platform). The lack of detail may be due to commercial sensitivity for Whim but the lack of evaluation in the public domain, it does not help answer questions about MaaS usage. Thus, whilst there is active growing interest, MaaS is still in its infancy with much development, innovation, adaptation, and experimentation still to be undertaken (Ho et al., 2020). To date, UbiGo is the only trial that offers evaluation for further investigations of the market demand for MaaS bundles so that the increasing number of SP studies conducted in different countries by various research teams are very useful to understand the market demand and to inform the development of MaaS.

## 5.3 Market interest

The definition of MaaS, as discussed in Chapter 3, can be as basic as providing a digital platform that helps travellers plan their trips, but it can also be fully integrated services with many built-in features, including pre-payment options and financial discounts/incentives to alter travel behaviour as discussed in Chapters 1 and 7 (for example, by promoting more sustainable transport choices). This section summarises what is known about the market demand for these features (i.e. types of MaaS) by drawing from the literature on MaaS market research and real-world trials.

### 5.3.1 Digital platform (MaaS app)

Central to most types of MaaS is a digital platform that can facilitate information requests, match demand to supply, and finalise the service agreement (i.e. booking and payment). Thus, a MaaS app can be regarded as a pre-requisite of any MaaS offer. The critical questions are: (i) which features of the app the market demands, and (ii) whether the travelling public is willing to pay for use of such the app?

To date, only a handful of SP studies have examined these questions. Ho et al. (2018, 2020) conducted face-to-face interviews using experimental surveys in Sydney, Australia ($N$=252) and Newcastle Upon Tyne, UK ($N$=290) which hypothetically charge the prospective MaaS users (i.e. the respondents) a small subscription fee, ranging from AUD 10 to 20 a fortnight, for providing a fully integrated MaaS app that the PAYG user can use to plan their journeys, book tickets, access discounts (mainly for taxi mode) and manage payment per ride. They found that about 11% of Sydney respondents and about 13% in Newcastle are willing to pay the PAYG subscription fee for access to the MaaS app with the features described above. Both studies, however, were not be able to estimate the average user willingness to pay for the MaaS app due to the statistical insignificance of the PAYG subscription fee.

Also using an SP experiment, Guidon et al. (2020) conducted an online survey of 1000 respondents in the canton of Zurich, Switzerland. In their experiment, each respondent was presented with 18 choice tasks in which a smartphone app is one of the attributes that define the service bundles, comprising various transport services, each with a defined metric of entitlement per month such as kms, hours, days, minutes included in the bundle. They estimated that the average willingness to pay for the smartphone app is well over CHF 100 (~$US100) per month. The authors commented that "[t]he willingness to pay for the smartphone app is comparatively high, even for the Swiss price level" (p. 12) and offered two possible explanations. First, the respondents may attach too much weight to the MaaS app which was described, for the purpose of the experiment, to offer "ICT and price integration of all services, ticket integration, a comprehensive multimodal journey planner and the analysis of travel behaviour in the background to provide suggestions to optimize personal travel (e.g. in terms of cost)." (p. 12). The second possibility for the high willingness to pay for the smartphone app, according to the authors, relates to missing variables (such as user experience) that are correlated with the effect of the MaaS app.

Another SP study that offers insights into the demand of MaaS app and its features is that of Caiati et al. (2020). They recruited 1078 participants in the Amsterdam and Eindhoven areas of the Netherlands to participate in an online survey, which amongst other things, asked the respondents to indicate a set of advanced features they would want for the MaaS app in addition to its basic functionalities (travel planning, booking, ticketing, payment and invoicing). The advanced features include the ability to alert users in real-time about travel events, to synchronise with a personal agenda and to provide information about $CO_2$ produced and calories (Kcal) consumed for each journey. At the time of writing this chapter, the authors have not reported the results of the market demand for these advanced features of the MaaS app.

An on-going MaaS trial in Sydney (described further in Chapter 3) conducted a pre-trial survey to identify potential interest in different features of a MaaS app. The participants to the pre-trial survey were asked to indicate, on a scale from 1 to 5, how appealing are each of the following features:

(i) Route your journey according to what matters to you (e.g. multiple modes, cheapest journey, quickest time, lowest carbon emissions—it's all your choice).
(ii) The ability to book across multiple modes of transport (e.g. imagine stepping off the train and having your Uber waiting and ready).
(iii) A single payment portal for all transport modes, whether you choose a subscription plan or Pay-as-you-Go (PAYG).
(iv) The freedom to choose between payment models (i.e. pay per ride for different transport modes used vs subscription to monthly bundles to access multiple modes of your choice, at discounted rates)

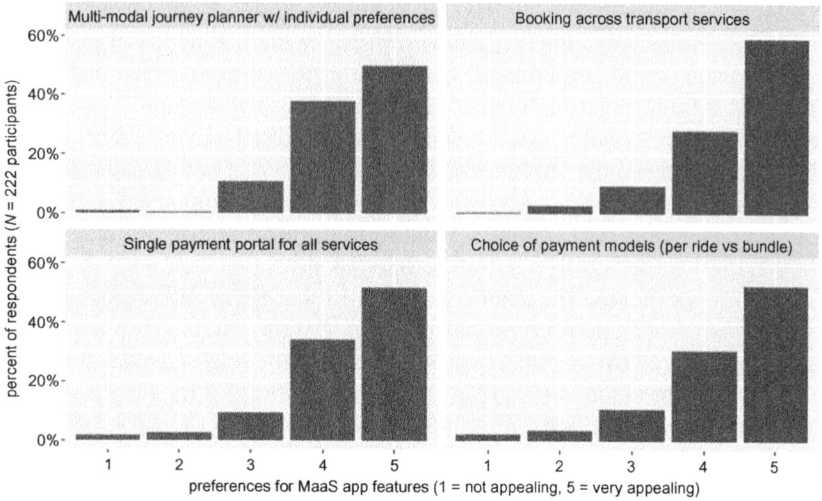


**FIG. 5.1** The appeal of different MaaS app features: preferences of prospective MaaS users.

Fig. 5.1 shows the preferences of the participants for each of these four features. As can be seen, all features are highly appealing to the prospective users of MaaS (note that the participants to the Sydney MaaS trial are recruited from the pre-trial respondents), with the ability to book across multiple transport modes being most attractive (nearly 60% of the respondents rated this feature as very appealing). The equivalent statistic for the other three features is slightly lower, at about 50%, but these features have a higher percentage of respondents who give a rating of 4/5. Overall, about 90% of the respondents said that these four MaaS app features are quite appealing or very appealing to them. The pre-trial survey, however, does not ask the respondent's willingness to pay for these features, directly or indirectly. This remains a subject of interest for the main trial in Sydney during the 6 month period from November 2019.

### 5.3.2 Mix of transport modes offer

Research evidence suggests that prospective users of MaaS highly rate a digital platform that can finalise the booking and payments across transport services, as shown in Fig. 5.1. A MaaS integrator/broker would need to integrate as many as possible of the transport modes available in a current market to widen the choice set of the users, and hence the market size; however, significant effort is required to add any mobility service into the digital platform that powers MaaS. One of the greatest challenges for the broker in integrating multiple transport services into a MaaS platform relates to their negotiations with transport providers so as to give users the ability to request information (i.e. search integration), book the services (i.e. booking integration) and pay for the mobility services they use (i.e. payment integration)—all within the same app. Given the effort required, MaaS integrators would naturally want to know which transport services are a 'must have' and which services are a 'nice to have' in order to make MaaS offerings appealing to the market that it aims to disrupt—specifically the personal car. This section summarises the published findings to date on the combinations of mobility services that travellers want to have access to, either through a mobility bundle or PAYG.

Guidon et al. (2020) report the results of a study on transport service bundling in which the user willingness to pay for stand-alone and bundled services are estimated and compared against each other. They found that the willingness to pay for public transport, car-sharing and park-and-ride services were higher when these modes are offered in bundles than when they are offered individually as stand-alone services. By contrast, bike-sharing, ebike-sharing and taxi services were valued lower in the bundles, compared to the stand-alone services. The authors suggest that it may be better to bundle public transport with car-sharing and park-and-ride into a periodical mobility plan whilst offering bike-sharing and taxi services on a pay per ride basis. They explain that the low-share modes (i.e. taxi, bike-sharing and ebike-sharing) may not be perceived directly as complementary to public transport (Guidon et al., 2020). However, the findings may also suggest a connection between current travel patterns of users and the MaaS bundles offered to them. Current users of low-share modes would be small in their sample which is representative of the population in the canton of Zurich in terms of age, gender, education and public transport season ticket ownership. Thus, offering a bundle that includes these low-share modes would be attractive to only a small subset of the sample, whilst many more respondents who are not current users of these modes might see the low-share modes more negatively when assuming that a cost for these modes, for which they have little interest in using in the present or in the future, contributes to the monthly subscription fee. As a result, the average willingness to pay for these low-share modes would be lower in the bundles than when they are offered on a pay-per-ride basis. This raises important questions on the relationship between a monthly subscription fee and the availability of specific modes regardless of whether these modes are available at a capped nor uncapped discount price of available under PAYG arrangement.

Caiati et al. (2020) examine the individual intention to subscribe to MaaS and preferences for bundle configurations using a portfolio survey in the Netherlands, where bicycle is a very popular mode of transport. By asking the respondents to pick up to four of the seven modes of transport to include in their mobility bundle, the authors were able to identify the substitution and complementarity effects amongst different mobility services. They found that public transport is most preferred amongst the modes on offer, followed by bike-share and car-share, whilst taxi and car rental is least preferred. In addition, they found that substitution effects between transport modes were very limited, except for e-bike sharing and car rental vs on-demand bus services where the respondents are less likely to bundle these modes together, although the effect is not statistically significant. The authors also found that the preferences for a mix of transport modes to be included in a monthly bundle depends on the pricing scheme. Specifically, the respondents generally prefer a flat rate (i.e. unlimited use) or a 2-part plan in which access to a transport service through the monthly plan is capped at a certain value (e.g. 2 days, 20 km included) which when exceeded will switch the users back to pay per ride. This finding is in line with the results found in Australia and the UK (Ho et al., 2018; Matyas and Kamargianni, 2018) in the sense that, all else being equal, the respondent prefers unlimited access to public transport services.

### 5.3.3 Population segment and MaaS niche market

One of the key questions for any new technology relates to early adopters. What segment of the population will be the early adopters of MaaS? There are a few studies that shed light on this issue.

In analysing a survey conducted prior to the UbiGo trial in Sweden, Strömberg et al. (2018) and Sochor et al. (2014) found that early adopters are initially motivated by curiosity (about 63% of the participants), with other motives including convenience, flexibility, environment, having access to car without the need to own one being much less important. Based on the attitudes and values the respondents perceived they would derive from UbiGo MaaS trial, the authors segment respondents into four subgroups/clusters: Car Shedders, Car Accessors, Simplifiers, and Economisers (Strömberg et al., 2018). The Car Shedders account for the smallest proportion (19/151 participants) amongst the four subgroups, whilst the Economisers (52/151) and Car Assessors (46/151) account for the majority of the participants. The first two subgroups (Car Shedders and Car Accessors) share the same motivation for joining UbiGo: they want to give up their private car for economic reasons. The latter two subgroups (Simplifiers and Economisers) already use public transport more often, but they seek the convenience of a one-stop access to a mix of transport services, and a novel and less expensive public transport ticket type. The four subgroups also differed significantly by their current travel patterns (level of car use, seasonal public transport card and use), and to a lesser extent, by social and environmental settings such as household size, household income and type of dwelling they reside in (apartment vs house).

The studies by Ho et al. (2018, 2020) suggest that people who are currently not using a car at all or using them very frequently (5–7 days per week) are less likely than average to choose a MaaS plan. Conversely, infrequent car users (1 or 2 days per week) and frequent car users (3–4 days per week) are more likely to take up a MaaS plan. With respect to socio-demographics, these studies found that there are some age effects on the likelihood of MaaS uptake, but the marginal difference in the likelihood of subscription between age groups is small. Caiati et al. (2020) also found that there are many socio-demographics that have a statistically significant effect on the decision of subscribing to MaaS or not. These include age, gender, income, education level, work status and individual income, driving licence, and household structure. This latter study, however, did not estimate the marginal effect of these socio-demographics on the decision to choose a MaaS subscription.

Fioreze et al. (2019) found that current travel patterns and individual attitudes are linked to the potential of MaaS adoption but socio-demographics are not. In particular, the authors found that there are four clusters of participants with different levels of MaaS adoption, but the average age is similar across the clusters. What distinguishes these clusters are the level of car ownership, frequency of car use, multimodal behaviour, and curiosity (i.e. attitudes towards various modes of transport, including emerging mobility services). These findings are largely in line with previous studies (Ho et al., 2018; Sochor et al., 2016) which found that those who presently use the car very often have the lowest intention to use MaaS. From this finding, Fioreze et al. suggest that "the sole idea of MaaS as a carfree, environmentally sound alternative to make car ownership superfluos may potentially be inefficient against avid car users" (p. 7). Indeed, a few studies have found the same effect of car dependency on the low potential of MaaS adoption (see studies cited above). Of these, perhaps the most informative study is Sochor et al. (2016) who emphasise the importance of a quality service design that addresses not only mobility needs but also opportunities for behavioural changes. The former requires a type of MaaS that provides added-value to the customers via a thorough understanding of different customer's needs and requirements. "An important part of the process is therefore to analyse the market and determine which market segments have or are perceived to have common needs so that the business can develop and promote a customized offer" (Sochor et al., 2016, p. 63).

## 5.4 Willingness to pay and potential uptake

Evidence from both SP studies and real world trials of MaaS, notably the UbiGo trial and the Whim products in Helsinki, suggests that there is interest in MaaS products. What is less clear is the type of MaaS the market demands and is willing to pay for.

As discussed above, MaaS can be as simple as the overlaying of a smartphone app on the existing mobility service to facilitate multimodal journeys and reduce the cost of transaction (what is called Light level MaaS in Chapter 1); however, MaaS is often understood as more than multimodality with fully integrated services. Thus, it is important to understand the type of MaaS offer when estimating its potential uptake and willingness to pay. Each MaaS product, be it hypothetical in a stated preference setting or real in a field trial setting, is designed with some specific goals. The goals often differ across the studies (see Chapters 3, 4, and 7), and thus a direct comparison of potential uptake and/or willingness to pay is not very meaningful.

One way to compare MaaS studies is through service development dimensions such as customisation, bundling and the range of the offer (Nordin, 2011). In the field of MaaS, *customisation* can be achieved through the provision a tailor-made service that meets each customer's needs and requirements. Examples are the UbiGo trial (a flexible subscription for the entire household) and the SP studies by Ho et al. (2018, 2020) which offered customised MaaS plans according to the respondent's current travel patterns and needs. MaaS can be seen as a special case of *service bundling* (Stremersch and Tellis, 2002) in the sense that two or more separate products are offered in one package (i.e. product bundling through a MaaS app) with the option of layering price bundling on top. Without price bundling, MaaS is offered under a PAYG option which provides more flexibility and less lock-in effect. With price bundling (i.e. a price tag attached to the entire MaaS plan instead of each of the included services), MaaS is operated under a subscription model where subscribers pre-pay for their monthly mobility needs (less flexibility and more lock-in effect). There exists a hybrid model where unused credits are rolled over to the next subscription period to have more flexibility in the subscription model. Finally, the range of mobility services included in the MaaS offers differ from one study to another, with SP experiments to date having more transport services in the bundle than those offered in the real world trials where the latter often faces the challenges of obtaining an agreement with service providers and platform integration.

Ho et al. (2018) estimated that the potential uptake of MaaS in Sydney metropolitan area is 47%, with 36% of the respondents indicating they would subscribe to pre-defined MaaS plans *tailored* to their current travel patterns and a further 11% would use MaaS as PAYG. A similar potential uptake was found in Tyneside, UK in a different study conducted by the same authors (Ho et al., 2020). In both Sydney and Tyneside, the estimated willingness to pay for 1 day unlimited use of public transport service was found to be significantly lower than the fare, whilst the willingness to pay for access to taxi discount and car-sharing was found to be the same as the market prices. By contrast, Guidon et al. (2020) estimated that the willingness to pay for public transport, car sharing and park and ride services in Zurich, Switzerland was much higher when these services were bundled into a mobility plan, compared to stand-alone services. The authors suspected that a flat-fare bias could be one of the reasons for the high evaluation of the bundled services, in addition to the positive valuation of service integration and the digital platform. Guidon et al., however, did not report the potential uptake of MaaS plans.

Caiati et al. (2020) reported a much lower uptake level in the Amsterdam and Eindhoven areas, with only 17% of the choices the respondents were offered being a MaaS subscription (no PAYG option was offered). The authors offered two possible explanations for this low level of uptake. First, it may be linked to the complexity of the choice experiment with many attributes, followed by a burden of constructing their own monthly bundle should the respondent state that they would be interested in subscribing. The second reason relates to the fact that many respondents, if not all, would have little experience with MaaS due to its innovative nature. Apart from the issues that pertain to SP design and the respondent's lack of experience, the possibility that the Dutch may currently have a low level of interest in MaaS cannot be excluded since Fioreze et al. (2019), using an ex-ante evaluation data, reported that about 20% of Paleiskwartier residents (a district in the city of 's-Hertogenbosch, the Netherlands) would take up MaaS. Interestingly, Whim previously launched in Amsterdam but now there is no trace of that on https://whimapp.com.

The Whim experience could offer important insights into the potential uptake and the types of MaaS the market demands (for example monthly subscription vs PAYG). The *Whimpact* report (Ramboll, 2019), whilst pointing out that Whim currently has over 70,000 registered users in Helsinki, did not say how many of these are PAYG users vs monthly subscribers, nor define the meaning of a registered user: Does downloading the *Whim* app constitute a registered user or at least one trip must be made via the Whim app for the traveller to be classified as a registered user? Even more intriguing is that this report shows an increase in the uptake level, approximated by the number of *Whim* users per day, between its first launch in January 2018 and January 2019; however, it offers no means (either statistic or scale on the vertical axis) to suggest the general uptake and the extent to which this has increased over the course of 1 year after its launch. Although user preferences for payment options (PAYG vs subscription) will likely depend on the service design, especially the discounts built in as part of the MaaS offering in return for less flexibility and more lock-in effects, it remains one of the unknowns regarding MaaS uptake. The MaaS trial in Sydney launched in 2019, using the Tripi app, aims to address some of these unknowns. This trial will advance the understanding of MaaS, particularly the role that it can play in improving both the travellers' experience of using multiple complementary transport services (in terms of cost, travel time, convenience, health benefits and perceived safety) and broader community benefits (air quality, reduced congestion); further details are provided in Chapter 8.

## 5.5 Conclusions

So, what is known about the market demand for various MaaS products? The answer at this juncture is limited, mainly because the number of studies on intelligent mobility are few, although fast-growing.

- To date, it is known that travellers are demanding a platform or app that can facilitate information requests, better match demand to supply, and finalise the booking and payment across transport services. What is not known yet is how much they would be willing to pay for such an app. A handful of studies looked at this, including the two surveys that the Institute of Transport and Logistics Studies at the University of Sydney conducted in Sydney Australia and Tyneside, the UK. These surveys found that whilst users value

the smart-app, their willingness to pay for it is not statistically different from zero. In contrast, the study conducted in Zurich estimated that the willingness to pay for a smartphone app that integrates all mobility services into a journey planner and acts as the ticketing and payment system was valued at well above USD $100 per month (Guidon et al., 2020). These conflicting results suggest that more research is required before a consensus, if there is one, can be reached.
- The travelling public also want to have a choice of payment method. That is, some want a pay per ride (or PAYG) and some want to prepay for a mobility plan that comes with discounts. It is interesting to note that a heterogeneous preference for payment method exists within the same market/country and also within the same organisation/entity. For example, in the Helsinki market, Whim offers both PAYG and monthly subscription models but in other markets such as West Midlands, the UK Whim only offers a PAYG option (with a failed attempt at introducing a subscription plan). In Australia, Vij et al. (2018) found that PAYG is more attractive but in our own research, subscription models were preferred (37% subscribers vs 11% PAYG).
- With respect to service design, research evidence to date suggests that some modes of transport such as public transport and car-sharing are preferred by the subscribers, whilst other modes such as taxis and Uber are welcome by only a smaller segment of population, with the effect of car-rental and bike-share on bundle uptake still debatable amongst the research community (ITS Australia, 2018; Guidon et al., 2020; Ho et al., 2020; Matyas and Kamargianni, 2018).
- Who are more likely to be early adopters of MaaS? A few studies point to the same characteristics of early adopters. They exhibit multi-modal behaviour, are concerned with the environment and a healthy commuting lifestyle, do not see car ownership important, and do not use a car often. A deeper understanding of the current behaviour and the characteristics of early adopters would help to better place intelligent mobility in the suite of transport options available to future travel markets.

There are many more questions that do not have an answer yet such as how intelligent mobility will change the way people live, work and travel and its values in relation to sustainability objectives. Whilst controversial, the early evidence suggests that uniting the existing transport services under the umbrella of MaaS may not be a game changer. Much more than just a smart-phone app is needed. More innovations that are profitable and sustainable are needed, both environmentally (such as alternative fuels) and politically (such as alternative to the current fuel excise) and need further appreciation of social and cultural attitudes towards sharing in a transport context. Without innovations beyond the concepts, MaaS is likely to be operated under the PAYG model, and this raises a question as to what is the value add for the customer beyond a better journey planner? The scepticism of using MaaS as PAYG has already been floated amongst MaaS respondents (Fioreze et al., 2019). This is understandable because the main purpose of the MaaS app is to provide information embedded in journey planning capability, plus other capabilities such as ticketing, booking, and billing management. Information changes the choice sets of travellers, usually by adding more options to it (Lyons et al., 2019). This results in an increase in the maximum expected utility. Whether the marginal increase in utility results in users paying for a MaaS app will largely depend on the user's circumstances. This may explain the belief that early adopters of MaaS may be tourists who demand more information in an unfamiliar environment with many irregular trips.

Chapter 6

# How might MaaS be best introduced to the market?

## Chapter outline



## 6.1 Introduction

This chapter complements Chapter 5 by turning the focus from the demander to the supplier interface.

Supply-side issues have to date received far less attention than demand-side issues in the mobility as a service (MaaS) literature. This is due to the genesis of MaaS which has its roots in promising better service for the customer, as well as the difficulty in conducting empirical research on business and government. Much of the present research on the supplier interface have been confined to exploratory work examining the desire for business and government to collaborate (Sarasini et al., 2017; Kamargianni and Matyas, 2017), partnerships between incumbent public transport operators and transportation network companies (TNCs) (Boone et al., 2018), barriers to greater collaboration and innovation in business (Smith et al., 2019b), as well as the role of government in MaaS business structures (Jittrapirom et al., 2018a). In particular, there has been limited empirical research on the design and structure of MaaS business models. However, the literature on this is growing with Polydoropoulou et al. (2020) providing a qualitative approach to identifying the basis of a business model that will allow operators to create, deliver and capture value, and Smith et al. (2020) looking at the role of what Sweden calls Intermediary MaaS Integrators (IMI)—the entity that brings together different providers of transport services

Understanding Mobility as a Service (MaaS). https://doi.org/10.1016/B978-0-12-820044-5.00006-3
© 2020 Elsevier Inc. All rights reserved.

and distributes these amongst customer-facing MaaS operators. The motivation for better understanding supply side issues is to provide another step towards successful implementation.

Another major unknown relates to the service delivery ecosystem for the MaaS proposition. The majority of existing research has focused on understanding demander/customer preferences, either by way of stated choice studies in the case of surveys or revealed preference through the many (albeit limited) real world pilots and trials. However, very little attention has been placed on understanding government and the business community's desire to provide MaaS services, beyond conceptual contributions prescribing a possible future ecosystem. Important questions, therefore, remain unanswered. Who takes the lead—will it be the public or private sector? What might be the role of subsidies and what sort of financial return might prospective MaaS businesses expect? Furthermore, how might firm characteristics like market sector, risk attitude and company size affect their buy-in? This is a fundamental oversight which necessitates quantitative and empirical evidence to establish the supply side interface for MaaS. Closely linked to this issue is the need to determine a market equilibrium for this future. There is little benefit in identifying end user desires in isolation if the business community is not willing to provide such services. Equally so, there exists limited value in exploring potential MaaS business models if they are disconnected from the demander interface and what government is willing to accept. For this reason, any proposed supply side research must be brought back to an initial understanding of demander preferences, as well as the societal value and purpose of MaaS to offer an integrated and holistic perspective for the future of this innovative transport model.

This chapter begins with an overview of how governments procure transportation, including the trend towards greater private-sector initiative and partnerships amongst public and private-sector entities. Next, the idea of delivering MaaS via a broker/aggregator interface is introduced, presenting a range of models capturing both economically deregulated and competitively tendered approaches and the benefits and challenges associated with each. Empirical findings based on a stated choice study of these MaaS business models reveals the potential interest from candidate actors and are presented in the context of how best to introduce MaaS to the market. A final discussion concludes the chapter, with links to the institutional and governance challenges to be explored in Chapter 7.

## 6.2 How do governments procure transportation?

Through offering a brief history of institutional reform in the transportation sector across developed economies, this section identifies the present trends in procurement including the growth of mobility partnerships; and suggests how these developments might be applied in the context of delivering MaaS.

The historical progression of reforms in contracting (specifically for urban public transport), shows how the developments have influenced and become a starting point for future contract reform in the move towards a MaaS setting. Since the late 1980s, most developed economies have been interested in developing a competitive environment so as to improve public transport services and grow patronage, whilst reducing the amount of subsidy and reliance on the taxpayer (Hensher, 2018a). An overarching desire has been to increase competitive tension between the client/purchaser (regulator/authority) and contractor/provider (operator). To do so, traditionally government-owned assets (not only in public transport but also airports and other utilities) have been divested over time as governments realise that they may be far more cost effectively run by the private-sector (typically delivering windfall gains of 30% or more upon privatisation). Alongside this, the rights to provide service have been allocated through contracting-out via competitive tender or negotiation as the procurement mechanism with the notable exceptions of the UK outside London and in New Zealand where economic deregulation was selected as the way in which public transport services were provided for the travelling public.

The early reform process was motivated by a need to improve cost efficiency and reduce commitments to upward spiralling network subsidies which were empirically shown to leak into wages (Bly et al., 1980; Pucher et al., 1983). Whilst the early reform process was heavily motivated by the need to improve cost efficiency, this was subsequently replaced by the more holistic desire to place contracted services within the context of land use, wellbeing and wider economic benefits (Wong and Hensher, 2018). Economic deregulation was associated with competition likened to that seen in the 1920s with 'chasing, nursing and hanging back' emerging on highly populated routes in many UK towns (outside London) (Foster and Golay, 1986). More recently, this on-road competition *in* the market (Dodgson and Preston, 1991; Preston, 1992b) has been subtly changed with a movement by New Zealand and many regional cities in the UK moving to a competition framework more *for* the market model which can enable greater network effectiveness and system integration. In contracted markets, however, the trend has been very different. Early contracts were often awarded on the basis of the lowest cost but after multiple rounds this has tended to have an adverse effect on service quality (Veeneman and Smith, 2016). More recently, there has been increasing recognition of the transition/transaction costs associated with the disruption of changing operators (Hensher et al., 2016). Together and with the intention of improving quality, governments have taken on a greater role in network planning and other strategic-level objectives, with the remit of private operators becoming more operationally focused. The pendulum swing between varying levels of public and private initiative is a concept often described as a 'regulatory cycle' (Gwilliam, 2008), as the inadequacies of one regime are quickly replaced by the shortcomings of another.

Indeed, recent years have seen a move back towards greater private sector initiative. One of the key drivers towards greater private sector input in contract design stems from the increasing recognition of constraints and rigidities in existing contract specifications. Although there is much heterogeneity around the world, in a lot of advanced economy settings like Australia, developed Asia and most of Europe (barring the UK and Scandinavia), contracts are based on a gross cost model (where government keeps the fare revenue) with limited patronage incentives and often even the government ownership of assets like vehicles and depots. Singapore is one extreme case of a 'management contract' (Goh and Swee, 2017), where even scheduling functions and driver training are handled by government. These private-sector bus/rail operators run as a business-to-government model in an almost monopsonistic setting where the only source of external revenue is from (usually limited) charter activities. In many ways, the operator is stripped of many responsibilities apart from being asset managers and as organisers of labour, to deliver 'kilometres' procured by the government. Whilst such a model is hailed for lowering the barriers to entry and hence enhancing competition, it is also argued to stifle innovation. Not only is there little to no incentive for the operator to innovate, the contractual model also poses as a regulatory barrier for operators who may wish to explore new service opportunities. This exacerbates problems created by the institutional framework which may prescribe vehicles for specific modes (*buses can only be buses, taxis can only be taxis; a bus cannot behave like a taxi and* vice versa). For instance, the mode-specific nature of many contracts defines the vehicle type (often, full sized buses) and prevents the switch to smaller vehicles like taxis or minibuses, which may potentially offer more flexible services for lower cost.

Alongside operators wanting to diversify and innovate, there are an equal number of operators, if not more, who are quite content in generating a reasonable rate of return under the present model. However, contentment with the status quo does not imply that it is a model which is delivering value for the taxpayer. This is one motivation for the interest in a new approach to procuring operators and transport service such as is seen under MaaS. The desire to shift towards greater flexibility in contract design may be broadly described as a move from an output-based model to a more outcome-based method of procurement, an important design principle for MaaS settings. This means reimagining what have traditionally been intermediate objectives like service quantity and performance indicators such as on time running to the ultimate objectives of mobility and accessibility for the people. This means transcending the specification of contract boundaries, defined vehicle types and operating format to end-user related metrics of performance. The influx of new market entrants that are transportation network companies (TNCs) operating outside of the contracted environment is another major challenge and associated with a much more fluid set of actors in transport and blurring sector boundaries (see Chapter 2). It requires a rethink of the institutional and regulatory landscape and how transport services are procured in the future (Merkert and Wong, Forthcoming; Mulley and Kronsell, 2018).

Whilst multimodal contracts are often the norm in many mainland European settings, these generally place little onus on the operator in the contract design and specification phase. However, multimodal offerings do make it easier for the operator to internally cross-subsidise amongst/between their different services/modes, as well as to ensure that these services/modes operate complementarily to each other. Future contracts are likely to be far more market-driven, led by a co-design process between public and private sector enterprise (though the risk of regulatory capture must not be neglected). Leveraging external ideas and capabilities by inviting the private sector on board as equal partners rather than mere suppliers recognises that government does not necessarily know best. This collaborative innovation moves away from a traditional bureaucratic hierarchy and more by the availability of innovation assets (Smith and Hensher, 2019), and further exhibits itself in governments' approach to regulating and facilitating the introduction of new transportation technologies and business models. In Australia, multimodal offerings have been let in Newcastle, New South Wales (NSW) and Sydney, whilst access contracts (covering first/last mile travel to railway stations) have garnered interest in Melbourne showing a movement away from prescribing vehicles, technologies and business models to focusing on the mobility/accessibility outcomes for the end user or customer. These reforms will help enable the adoption of new technologies and business models, including the introduction of MaaS to the market. The Point-to-Point reforms in NSW (Australia) are a case in point—these have moved the responsibility for the vetting of drivers of small vehicles to the transport operator. Another example from NSW is the Regulatory Sandbox programme—a time-limited testing environment to remove regulatory barriers on a trial basis to test autonomous vehicles and electric scooters, amongst other things.

### 6.2.1 Partnerships in mobility provision

Central to MaaS is the establishment of a new business model which is built on the integration of distinct and detached services including commercially-driven shared mobility services (TNCs) and public transport which are either very low margin or financed through public subsidies. A common recommendation is for greater collaboration between TNCs and government agencies (including public transport providers). In the US, the number of cases of local governments and public transport operators cooperating have proliferated, with TNCs being tasked to provide services that integrate with public transport, particularly as first/last mile connections to railway stations (Boone et al., 2018). Recent evidence, however, suggests that disutilities of transfers and additional costs for the first/last mile service are major barriers to uptake (Reck and Axhausen, 2019b), which further suggests the importance of the integration of fare systems between the TNC and the public transport provider. Such models are far rarer in Australia, although government-contracted microtransit (demand responsive transport) have garnered particular interest of late especially in NSW in the form of on demand public transport (microtransit) trials.

An interesting series of insights drawn from the National Academy of Sciences (2019) concerns why different stakeholders choose to collaborate. For public transport agencies/operators, there is a desire to demonstrate innovation, improve mobility outcomes, improve cost efficiency and to avoid major capital expenditure such as commuter carparks (in the case of TNC-provided first/last mile services). Reducing taxpayer subsidy is often an underlying root motivation and studies like Boone et al. (2018) have sought to quantify the direct and indirect costs of providing or subsidising TNC services under supplementary and substitutive partnership arrangements. In a case study of Antonio, US, Boone et al. (2018) found per-trip subsidy savings by replacing low performing fixed route buses with subsidised ridehailing services. The case of Innisfil, Canada, on the contrary, has shown that TNC subsidies might exceed previous outlays for public transport provision if the service becomes too popular. According to National Academy of Sciences (2019), TNCs are motivated to collaborate with public transport by the opportunity to attract new customers, demonstrate good faith with their communities, and addressing shared challenges with the authority such as pick-up/drop-off efficiency and safety. This is an interesting finding and runs in contrary to other evidence which includes elements of suspicion, mistrust and territorialism amongst public transport operators' view of TNCs (reluctance to share data certainly does not help) and TNCs' views of government/incumbent operators. Issues in power dynamics remain, however, particularly around the control of branding, the customer and data—not well suited to private industry who also hold these dearly. Alliances between suppliers are another form of collaboration, and particularly important in the delivery of MaaS. Meurs et al. (2020) investigate the potential for alliance formation by suppliers as part of a MaaS pilot finding shared goals, risk limitation and trust (unsurprisingly) important in alliance formation but knowledge acquisition crucial. These issues have also been important in the context of on demand trials in NSW, where incumbent bus operators have partnered with specialised businesses in the form of a technology/platform provider to deliver services. This constitutes an elementary implementation of a broker/aggregator model (to be established in Section 6.3), by bringing two agents together.

The dynamics behind this relationship is of special interest as a precursor to establishing a multi-agent MaaS broker model. The on demand experience in NSW revealed a number of key lessons and considerations in terms of stakeholder support for innovation and collaborative approaches in the delivery of these services. Bus operators were required to select their technology/platform provider and to deliver joint proposals. These were understandably built on pre-existing relationships and the selected partners were small to medium sized (white-label) providers like Via, Routematch, TaxiCaller and Liftango (note Via has a substantial shareholding by Keolis and Liftango by Transdev). Internationally, Via has a track record of partnering with public transport providers to deliver white-label microtransit solutions (though in the US they operate a business-to-consumer service). Larger players like Uber, however, although initially active in discussions with bus operators, were reluctant to relinquish their brand—something seen as non-negotiable for bus operators who are increasingly dependent on their brand as a means to differentiate themselves from other operators. Furthermore, the larger TNC players were better accustomed to operating in their business-to-consumer (B2C) space as opposed to a business-to-business (B2B) or business-to-government (B2G) model. For the customer, the NSW approach has led to less integration as the information, ticketing and fare structures are bound up in the individual bus operator providers.

A question of great significance is who the new market players will be and what role incumbent market players will take up in a future MaaS ecosystem (as outlined in Chapter 3 as '*Who are the key stakeholders in the MaaS ecosystem?*'). Will the actors be dominated by mode-specific operators as incumbent suppliers of passenger service, or new non-mobility provider entrants interested in a new business opportunity? The preceding discussion focused on existing bus operators, some of whom might prefer to narrow their focus and be mere subcontractors to a broader, all-encompassing mobility broker. Alternatively, bus operators may see value in providing MaaS, and take up the broker role, subcontracting out part of their service to smaller vehicles using other providers like TNCs. Ultimately, this will depend on skills (especially in software development) and profit potential, and operators may play strategic games to maintain the status quo where income from government subsidies are already guaranteed. Issues of bias in terms of how an operator's existing service offering might influence the design of their product under MaaS is also a key concern (and explored in Section 6.5). To answer these many unknowns around service provision, it is necessary to draw up a future business model for delivering MaaS, often described as a mobility broker/aggregator.

## 6.3 Establishing a MaaS broker/aggregator

The previous section posits that identifying a suitable MaaS business model is perhaps the single most critical supply-side issue. Indeed, business models are identified in Smith and Hensher (2019) as one of nine essential areas of innovation for MaaS (the others being terminology, objectives, rules, technologies, modes, alternatives, partnerships and diffusion. See also Chapter 8). Business model innovation is required to deliver MaaS since it requires a design which will work outside the exclusive control of traditional firm boundaries (De Reuver et al., 2013). Whilst the previous section brought up partnership and collaboration issues, it highlighted the often-neglected dimension of internal processes such as anchoring and reorganisation, as well as intangible aspects like how best to foster a culture of innovation and responsible risk-taking by reference to the on demand trials in NSW. The example of on demand in NSW is also useful as a representation of a primitive model of a *broker* interface—hailed in Hensher (2017) as the *third B* (the other two being *bundles* and *budget*) central to the design and implementation of MaaS.

The mobility broker, also known as an aggregator or intermediary, functions as a new agent which brings together specialised businesses like mode-specific operators and non-mobility providers required to deliver an integrated MaaS offering for the customer. Kamargianni and Matyas (2017) propose that the mobility broker will need to bring together a business ecosystem of seven actors—transport operators (including mobility service providers like parking operators), data providers, technology/platform providers, information/communication technology infrastructure, insurance companies, regulatory organisations and universities/research institutions. Whilst integrating such an extensive network of actors would be ideal in helping to deliver fully-fledged MaaS (i.e. Level 4 in the Sochor et al., 2018 typology—see Chapter 3), it is likely that only a subset of these will be required as part of a MaaS business, and indeed might be necessary for a successful (swift) implementation. For instance, some actors like research institutions will advise rather than being directly involved in the broker business. The most critical actors (or functions) required in the broker model are transport operators, as providers of the physical transportation services; a financial enterprise, as a funder of the business (although this function could also be supported by government); and a platform provider, who offers up their technology (Wong et al., 2018). In effect, what is described is an agent that brokers travel (Hensher, 2018b), with its core value-add being the integration of actors, information and services. There exists a parallel with the civil aviation and hospitality sectors where intermediary brokers (travel agents and booking aggregators) have become a standard part of the ecosystem (Merkert et al., 2020). The broker forms the conduit for connecting the end users (as demanders) and the suppliers of the transport asset/capacity. Section 6.5 will situate the role of a MaaS broker/aggregator within a full framework of actors including demanders (customers), government (regulator) and downstream suppliers (transport operators).

The MaaS broker model brings many benefits but also issues and challenges for stakeholders within the transport ecosystem. Firstly, the MaaS broker permits multilateral relationships between agents as opposed to partnerships and collaborations which are usually bilateral. One of the concerns, however, is bias (or the perception of bias) amongst brokers who are also involved with service provision (in effect being both broker *and* supplier). For instance, Uber is expanding its platform beyond its own services to enable public transport operators and other TNC providers to 'plug in', and in effect becoming a multimodal, one-stop travel solution. The concern here is that Uber might be incentivised to promote its own services at the expense of others (competitors). This might be less of an issue if a public entity takes up this dual role as in the case of Stadtwerke Augsburg (c.f., Chapter 4). Another issue arising from the broker model concerns the relationship between incumbent suppliers and their customers. The addition of a third-party broker 'agent' will mean that a supplier loses direct access and ownership of their customer—including access to their data and with implications for the supplier's brand. Whilst proponents will argue that the future is based on 'shared customers', the loss of branding and access to customers is a genuine concern for many companies, particularly present-day market leaders (hence their desire to subsume the broker; thereby maintaining their brand and customer access). Smith et al. (2020) addresses these issues in the context of a failed integrator in Sweden. The final issue concerns what role government ought to play in the broker model. This question will be explored next.

### 6.3.1 Who takes the lead? Government or private sector

One major question concerning candidate actors is the role of government in an emerging MaaS future (see Chapter 8). The public sector plays a key enabling role in urban governance (Kronsell and Mukhtar-Landgren, 2018), and government policies including the activities of all public agencies can influence significantly the pace and trajectory of MaaS development (Smith and Hensher, 2019) – as has been particularly acute in the Scandinavian region (see Chapter 3). The *Finnish Transport Code*, for instance, which demands that all transport providers release single journey tickets for third-party resale (Smith et al., 2018b), was an instrumental enabler of MaaS. This sort of mode-agnostic regulation, where all modes are treated on a 'level' playing field regardless of vehicle type, ownership structure or how services are funded is a key reform for facilitating MaaS implementation. Such regulations have been the norm for some time in other utility markets like electricity, telecommunications and water. This homes in on one of the key contentions around whether government or a private sector entity ought to take up this broker/aggregator role.

There are many schools of thought on this question. Kamargianni and Matyas (2017) call for a government agency or quasi-government entity (including a public transport authority) to assume the MaaS broker role. The International Association of Public Transport (UITP) is also a keen advocate for a government broker, though this must be viewed in the context of their large membership base of government authorities/operators. On the other hand, Jittrapirom et al. (2018b), in a Delphi study of 46 experts found transport operators (which, depending on local context, can be public or private entities) as the preferred service integrator, followed by a third-party mobility provider and then local authorities. There is a strong argument that a government broker would be best placed to integrate services, given that they already procure public transport and authorise the operation of intermediate modes like taxis and ridehailing. Concerns exist, however, that government might not only lack the incentive to innovate but also cause a potential conflict of interest, especially where both public and private operators exist as is the case in many economies. For instance, a government broker might favour its own contracted modes over commercially-competing TNCs – though one may argue there is a societal prerogative for favouring public transport. A more fundamental question lies in whether governments see themselves playing the role of a transport intermediary. Across the West, there is an increasing trend of governments distancing themselves from service provision and leaving as much as it can to the private sector (as explained in Section 6.2). If private enterprise *will* function as a broker, then why should government?

The public sector does, of course, have an important role to play in encouraging innovation in the market and indeed contributing where appropriate itself, there remains strong support from the private sector to rely on private equity with appropriate regulations in place to encourage private sector activity. Government is better positioned playing a regulatory function to ensure a 'level' playing field (including setting common standards) for different MaaS operators to compete. For this reason, the model proposed in this chapter for the MaaS ecosystem assumes a private entity broker. Notwithstanding this, the mobility broker may also take the form of a public-private partnership—this may well be the initial model in many jurisdictions as government invests to catalyse the development of MaaS (including through seed funding and grants). There may also exist circumstances that call for government to take a more hands-on approach. In low volume rural communities, for instance, solely market-based solutions may not be suitable due to a shortage of services and competition. This is the justification for considering the market framework without government interference initially to determine what may be extracted before adding an institutional overlay to reflect that the market may not be the only (or best) arbiter of a successful MaaS model.

## 6.4 A structured ecosystem for delivering MaaS[a]

Having introduced relevant demand (Chapter 5) and supply side issues, as well as a brief review of transport contracting history which places the interface between suppliers and government in the spotlight, this chapter turns to situate these actors within a framework to conduct further investigation of a potential future MaaS ecosystem. Different alternatives are available depending on the role of public and private sector actors, with the extremes presented in Fig. 6.1, together with the status quo for how public transport has traditionally been procured by government. Model A represents the status quo, where the government (regulator) contracts suppliers (operators) to deliver public transport services for demanders (end users or customers). This model is premised on suppliers competing *for* the market (either through a competitive tender or negotiation) to win service contracts from the government. An economically

---

a. This section has been adapted from Wong et al. (2020).

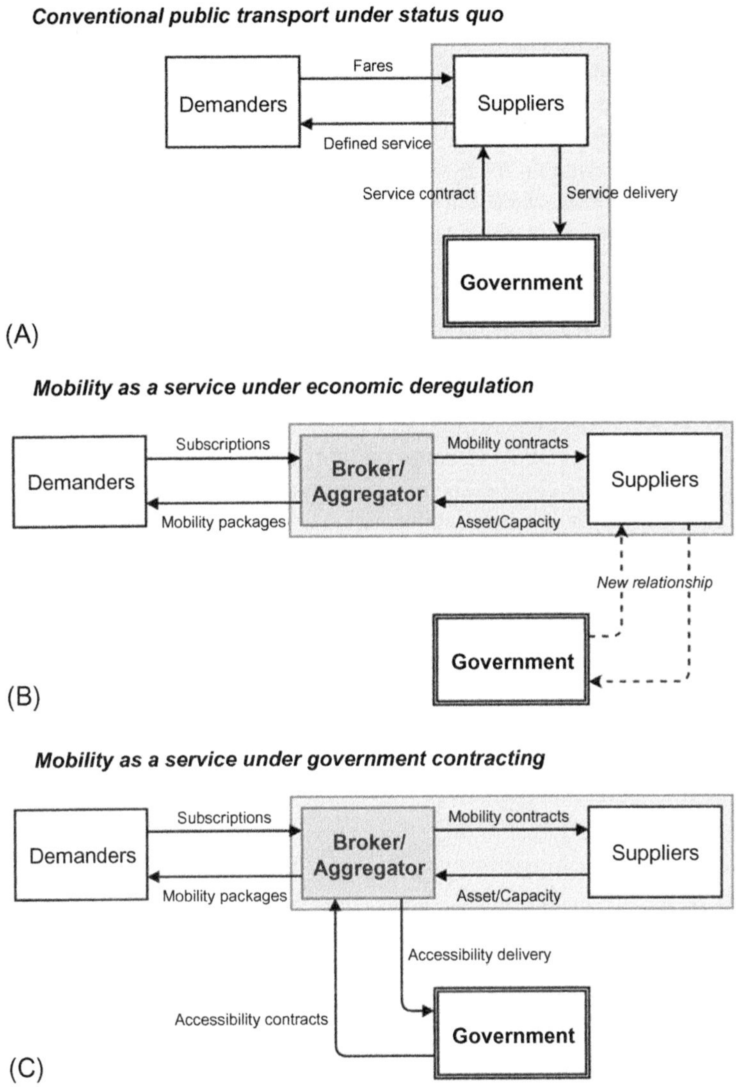


**FIG. 6.1** The present service delivery model for (A) conventional public transport under the status quo, and proposed framework for the MaaS ecosystem, comprising the new function for a mobility broker/aggregator, operating under (B) economic deregulation and (C) a government-contracted scenario (Wong et al., 2020).

deregulated (competition *in* the market) case, as exists for the bus sector in the UK outside London and New Zealand is not illustrated in the diagram. The diagram shows the supplier receiving fares from demanders whilst also meeting key performance indicators as stipulated in their contract to government. There is a blue overlay so as to include the situations where public transport services are delivered by a government operator (either a government department or agency), as remains the case in most US cities and many continental European economies.

As established in Section 6.3, delivering MaaS requires bringing together a range of complex stakeholders. Whilst authors like Kamargianni and Matyas (2017) have suggested up to seven relevant actors, many of these might be external to the broker interface. Potential actors as brokers include **mode-specific operators** or incumbent providers of passenger transport service (bus, rail, TNCs, etc.) and **non-mobility providers**, covering financial enterprises and technology providers (as suggested in Section 6.3), plus any other new market entrants (Wong et al., 2018). In Models B and C (Fig. 6.1), the MaaS **broker/aggregator** is shown where the blue overlay allows for the way in which existing mode-specific operators could also take on this broker role. The role of the mobility broker is to acquire transport asset/capacity from a number of suppliers (both mode-specific and non-mobility suppliers) and offer mobility services through a single channel (bundled or not) to demanders. The MaaS broker value-adds by integrating actors, information and services as part of their MaaS offering. The relationship of this broker situated amongst other actors including government is explored in the following two proposed models (designed as extreme ends of a spectrum) for MaaS. There may also be situations where the public transport services are delivered by a government operator (blue overlay in Model A), and this actor also then becomes the MaaS operator (as in the case of Augsburg, Germany), and hence the blue overlay in Models B/C would include government.

### 6.4.1 Free market operation

The market proliferation of TNC services like ridesharing, carsharing and bikesharing (see Chapter 2) occurs in what is essentially an economically deregulated market which may be the starting point for MaaS (Fig. 6.1 Model B). This sort of entry also underpins the majority of trials and pilots underway as tabled in Chapter 3 and discussed in Chapter 4. Under this scenario, government can only influence MaaS operators at the margin—for instance, by specifying the conditions and barriers (or lack thereof) for market entry. Model B constitutes a market driven scenario, with associated market impacts on modal shift, congestion, data sharing and exchange. As a policy 'vacuum', MaaS actors will be motivated by the commercial imperative which may or may not align with government's societal objectives for the transport ecosystem. Under Model B, the government will need to create a new relationship with existing transport operators, including reforming the present mode-specific, contracts—as has already been occurring in many markets (Hensher, 2017). Existing mode-specific operators active in a tendered environment might no longer be captive to one single customer (the government authority; as a monopsony at present), but rather, operate in a more competitive and dynamic landscape with a more fluid set of actors and revenue opportunities—the idea of transforming them into 'total' transport providers (Stanley et al., 2019).

An economically deregulated MaaS market might bring with it a number of risks. For instance, this might relate to possible monopolistic and predatory behaviour from larger brokers/suppliers. Analogous to this in the deregulated British bus market is the way in which larger bus operators were able to push out smaller players (Dodgson and Preston, 1991; Preston, 1992a). Closed, proprietary platforms are symptomatic of this development and industry associations like MaaS Alliance are working to create common standards of operations available to all operators. Initiatives like this will be critical for allowing the roaming of MaaS products across different geographic jurisdictions. Indeed, the greatest hurdle in any partnership is often linked to data sharing (National Academy of Sciences, 2019). In the main, public transport operators are either directly operated by government or run by a private operator (under contract to government) who are in effect an 'extended' public servant with a protected area monopoly for a defined period. The sharing of data is a given in contracted environments where it is stipulated as part of an agreement, and the data essential to determining the remuneration of the operator and to implement actionable benchmarking, including the administration of incentives and penalties linked to operator performance. For TNCs who operate in an economically deregulated market (and MaaS under Model B) and compete commercially, data sharing has been (and will be) a far more challenging proposition. TNCs have been hesitant to share data due to concerns about privacy, public records requests and competition. Indeed, for many TNCs and technology players in other sectors, their entire business model is predicated on collecting, mining and selling users' data (Wong, 2019a,b). In this case, why should they be expected to share their 'golden goose'? A further complication is that MaaS may be predicated on sharing user data which may be considered 'personal' under new legislation and subject to tight privacy controls (Cottrill, 2020).

A second challenge relates to modal mix (raised in Chapter 2), given that TNC-provided services (including personalised taxi modes) are usually more lucrative and operate with higher margins (profits) than public transport operators who are heavily subsidised with rates of return very marginal (tested empirically in Section 6.5). Under a free market entry, realities like this will likely affect the modal mix in terms of the mix of modes sold to the public as part of MaaS bundles (and how they are priced). A major risk is the possible financially-driven impetus to substitute customers away from public transport towards less spatially efficient modes (already the stated desire of many TNCs). Such commercial and strategically-driven decision-making will contravene the urban efficiency ideals of cities as set out in Chapter 2. The challenge, therefore, is to identify what kind of outcome emerges and then to approach with a critical eye as to what governance interventions might be necessary to control for any unintended consequences. Models in other utility markets like the work conducted by the Office of Rail and Road (ORR) and the Water Services Regulation

Authority (Ofwat) in the UK have been touted as one 'light touch' approach to move free-entry modes from self-regulation towards government acting as an independent regulator defining the conditions around safety and fair competition. An alternative to this is a government-contracted MaaS model (Model C) where the authority or regulator has wholescale control over the parameters of operations to ensure consistency with societal objectives. The challenge here is to maintain strong regulatory control and oversight whilst delivering on autonomous market freedoms.

### 6.4.2 Government-contracted model

A next generation service delivery ecosystem can bring many benefits including combining the best elements of competitive tendering and economic deregulation (see also Chapter 8). Fig. 6.1 Model C details a government-contracted MaaS model and its design is motivated by the ever increasing desire to welcome greater market initiative as has been a growing trend across many advanced economies over past decades (see Section 6.3). A central feature of this future is the shift in public transport contract design from their present output-based format in delivering kilometres on defined modes or vehicle types to outcome-based models which seek to deliver *accessibility* using any mode of an operator's choosing (Hensher, 2017). The move to mode-agnosticism will require the definition of more complex performance measures (e.g. related to customer accessibility rather than vehicle kilometres) but developments in technology is quickly making this possible. As an example of an accessibility-based measure, government might specify that a MaaS provider delivers $X$ percentage of residents services within $Y$ minutes at \$$Z$ price, for a given period of the day (e.g. higher service levels during daylight hours and less in the evenings) using any vehicle type and operating format. Rather than specifying particular modes of operation (and intermediate objectives like vehicle kilometres), the flexibility will allow the broker to operate or subcontract TNCs in lower density areas. These could feed seamlessly into high capacity mass transit to the urban core, itself topped up with direct, point-to-point services priced at such a premium that demand will not inundate the network. These spatial and temporal integration opportunities were detailed in Chapter 2.

In terms of MaaS broker/aggregator selection, this can be procured through a competitive tender initially, with the opportunity for negotiated contract renewal (with actionable benchmarking) at subsequent rounds once the market has matured. Tendering is a form of market-test which allows for the efficient selection of an operator, and is critical in the context of any government subsidies outlaid. The role of subsidies is further explored in Chapter 8, along with the related opportunity to incorporate a road user charge or network price as an input into the MaaS package price under a Model C governance regime.

As a summary to this section, Fig. 6.1 presents Model A as the status quo in which Model B as an economically deregulated model of delivering MaaS is positioned. An understanding of the market equilibrium which arises from Model B informs the nature of institutional overlay necessary for Model C as a government-contracted MaaS model. The focus of the next section is on developing Model B, relative to Model A and as a precursor to a Model C future.

## 6.5 Business preference for a MaaS mobility model

This section brings the views of the business community (broadly defined) to the different possibilities for MaaS business models. The evidence comes from a stated choice empirical study of business leaders representing 202 organisations across 28 countries (covering most developed economies). The interface between prospective suppliers and the MaaS broker/aggregator may be quantified through ***mode-agnostic mobility contracts***, based on the Model B framework presented in Fig. 6.1 in the previous section.

Fig. 6.2 as a screenshot of the stated choice study reveals the included components of the mobility contracts (and explains each attribute in detail), gathering insights around the modal mix, government support, return on investment, branding and equity contribution settings most likely to garner support from candidate businesses participating in a MaaS mobility model. Wong et al. (2018) describe the creation of these mobility contracts (based on stakeholder interviews) and design of the experiment in more detail. The results of the study are explored further in Wong et al. (2019).

The survey identified different ways in which businesses could potentially participate in the MaaS model—namely by ***investing in*** or ***supplying*** to the new MaaS business. The difference herein lies between contributing physical assets and assets in-kind, or becoming solely a financial shareholder in the broker/aggregator. It is generally more intuitive for mode-specific operators to supply (given their existing assets) and non-mobility providers to invest (since they do not operate transport services). Supplying physical assets was about 25% more popular than investing (note the sample was a roughly even mix of mode-specific and non-mobility respondents). Segmenting by organisation type, non-mobility providers overwhelmingly desired to supply technology assets, representing 73% of instances. For mode-specific operators, the most popular asset types with which to supply were vehicles (87%), personnel (77%), and bricks and mortar assets (62%). Bricks and mortar assets refer to infrastructure assets like depots, stabling facilities, as well as public transport stops and stations.

In terms of **modal mix**, public transport was revealed to be an important component amongst MaaS businesses which garnered the highest level of support. On average, public transport accounted for 45–55% of the revenue share in the mobility contracts chosen. Fixed route public transport was particularly important and accounted for the largest single revenue share amongst all respondent segments. This being said, there was some variability in terms of the role of fixed route versus on demand. Clearly, mode-specific operators (dominated by public transport operators) were more likely to support a MaaS business in

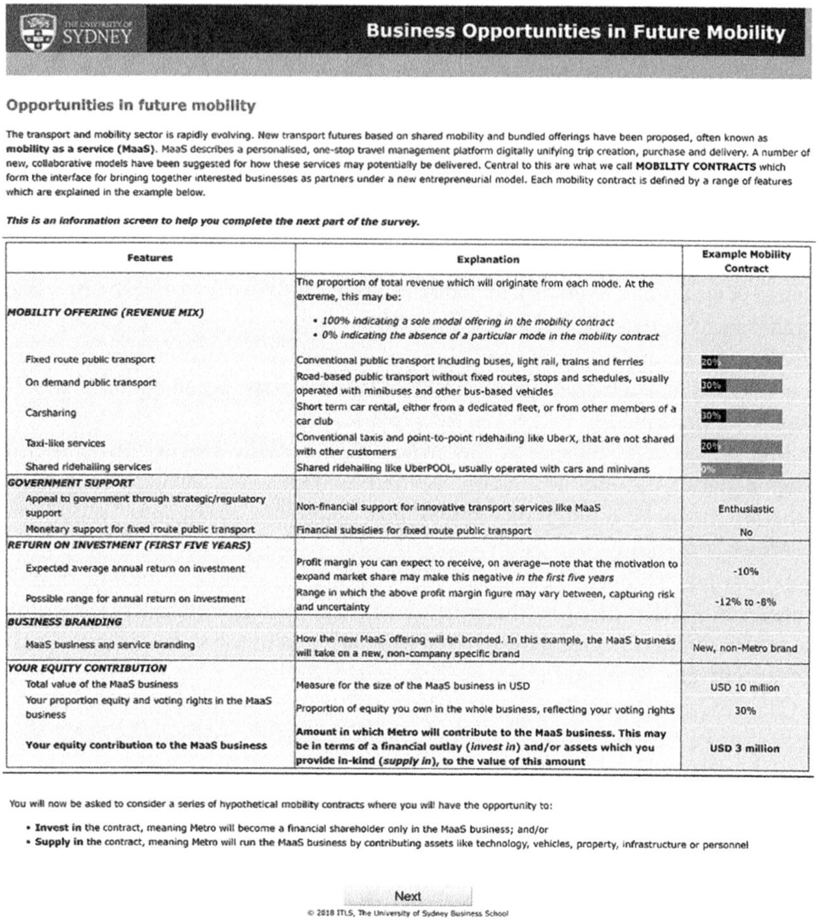

THE UNIVERSITY OF SYDNEY

**Business Opportunities in Future Mobility**

**Opportunities in future mobility**

The transport and mobility sector is rapidly evolving. New transport futures based on shared mobility and bundled offerings have been proposed, often known as **mobility as a service (MaaS)**. MaaS describes a personalised, one-stop travel management platform digitally unifying trip creation, purchase and delivery. A number of new, collaborative models have been suggested for how these services may potentially be delivered. Central to this are what we call **MOBILITY CONTRACTS** which form the interface for bringing together interested businesses as partners under a new entrepreneurial model. Each mobility contract is defined by a range of features which are explained in the example below.

***This is an information screen to help you complete the next part of the survey.***

| Features | Explanation | Example Mobility Contract |
|---|---|---|
| ***MOBILITY OFFERING (REVENUE MIX)*** | The proportion of total revenue which will originate from each mode. At the extreme, this may be:<br>• *100% indicating a sole modal offering in the mobility contract*<br>• *0% indicating the absence of a particular mode in the mobility contract* | |
| Fixed route public transport | Conventional public transport including buses, light rail, trains and ferries | 20% |
| On demand public transport | Road-based public transport without fixed routes, stops and schedules, usually operated with minibuses and other bus-based vehicles | 30% |
| Carsharing | Short term car rental, either from a dedicated fleet, or from other members of a car club | 30% |
| Taxi-like services | Conventional taxis and point-to-point ridehailing like UberX, that are not shared with other customers | 20% |
| Shared ridehailing services | Shared ridehailing like UberPOOL, usually operated with cars and minivans | 0% |
| ***GOVERNMENT SUPPORT*** | | |
| Appeal to government through strategic/regulatory support | Non-financial support for innovative transport services like MaaS | Enthusiastic |
| Monetary support for fixed route public transport | Financial subsidies for fixed route public transport | No |
| ***RETURN ON INVESTMENT (FIRST FIVE YEARS)*** | | |
| Expected average annual return on investment | Profit margin you can expect to receive, on average—note that the motivation to expand market share may make this negative *in the first five years* | -10% |
| Possible range for annual return on investment | Range in which the above profit margin figure may vary between, capturing risk and uncertainty | -12% to -8% |
| ***BUSINESS BRANDING*** | | |
| MaaS business and service branding | How the new MaaS offering will be branded. In this example, the MaaS business will take on a new, non-company specific brand | New, non-Metro brand |
| ***YOUR EQUITY CONTRIBUTION*** | | |
| Total value of the MaaS business | Measure for the size of the MaaS business in USD | USD 10 million |
| Your proportion equity and voting rights in the MaaS business | Proportion of equity you own in the whole business, reflecting your voting rights | 30% |
| **Your equity contribution to the MaaS business** | **Amount in which Metro will contribute to the MaaS business. This may be in terms of a financial outlay (*invest in*) and/or assets which you provide in-kind (*supply in*), to the value of this amount** | **USD 3 million** |

You will now be asked to consider a series of hypothetical mobility contracts where you will have the opportunity to:

- **Invest in** the contract, meaning Metro will become a financial shareholder only in the MaaS business; and/or
- **Supply in** the contract, meaning Metro will run the MaaS business by contributing assets like technology, vehicles, property, infrastructure or personnel

Next

© 2018 ITLS, The University of Sydney Business School

**FIG. 6.2** Explanation of attributes offered to respondents as part of the choice task introduction in the survey instrument, for a hypothetical medium-sized mode-specific operator Metro (Wong et al., 2019).

both invest and supply cases where there was a higher value being extracted from fixed route public transport. In contrast, the desired revenue share from on demand public transport was lower relative to their non-mobility peers. Carsharing and shared ridehailing played a far more subdued role in mode-specific preferred MaaS businesses than non-mobility preferred ones. This is consistent with the work of many non-mobility players who might play an enabling role for TNCs and shared mobility services. It also captures a range of technology-driven businesses and consultancies whose work is based on disrupting traditional transport players and offering personalised, application-enabled services. The support for taxi-like services amongst mode-specific investors (but not providers) is more puzzling—but evidently, the mode-specific sample saw opportunities in this space, potentially because many incumbent players are now struggling (with the advent of TNCs) and so the opportunity is ripe for potential acquisitions.

For the **government support** attributes, strategic/regulatory support was valued far higher than any specific financial support in the form of subsidies. Enthusiastic appeal to government was consistently preferred to lukewarm appeal. The presence of subsidies was even valued negatively in the case of non-mobility providers. For the mode-specific sample, many public transport operators are already dependent on government subsidies to provide their services. These results go to show a preference for government involvement at arm's length only, without the possibility of undue interference. The research has found empirically that the business community prefers a stable regulatory environment, with the legitimacy to operate and compete, as opposed to any financial support (i.e. subsidies) per se. As an aside, peak industry bodies like MaaS-Alliance and MaaS Scotland are already advocating for these policy reforms. This is especially true for the non-mobility providers who are accustomed to operating in an open market with little government intervention. The mode-specific sample showed greater relative reception towards subsidies, probably because many have usually operated in a highly subsidised contracted market in the past.

**Return on investment** is perhaps the most critical (but not sole) criteria governing business decisions. For this attribute, return expectations varied between 6.8% and 9.2% per annum, a range confirmed to be reasonable in post-survey interviews. A higher return expectation is evident when respondents were asked to invest rather than supply, across both organisation types. Clearly, respondents believed taking on an equity stake to be a riskier endeavour than providing in-kind contributions by supplying assets. This may be because, in the case of assets, respondent organisations are limited in terms of different revenue-generating activities they could undertake, so were hence willing to accept a lower return for their productive use. Interestingly, a substantially higher return requirement was evident for mode-specific over non-mobility investors. The interpretation here may be that non-mobility providers are accustomed to investing whilst for mode-specific operators, barring a select few multinationals, equity-only investments are a foreign concept and thus command a higher risk. What is most revealing is how the returns for investing were higher than for supplying. This may be because companies with existing assets were more willing to compromise in the selection of business activities as they are constrained as to what may be done with their assets. The returns for mode-specific operators were also slightly higher than for non-mobility providers in the case of investing in MaaS, potentially because mode-specific operators are not accustomed to being equity investors, and so required a higher potential rate of return in order to accept such risk.

The preference of the sample for the **branding** attribute was far less clear cut. Whilst constituent suppliers maintaining their brand emerged as critical in the stakeholder interviews (and supported by experiences like the NSW on demand trials), the results of the stated choice study was more mixed with many companies happy to leverage on a partner business' brand or alternatively venture into MaaS under a new brand as a way to manage risk (should the business be unsuccessful, for instance). In terms of **business size**, larger business propositions were preferred by non-mobility providers—more than double the size of those selected by mode-specific operators. The choice to invest or supply made little difference, however, although for mode-specific operators slightly larger businesses were preferred in the case of supplying—linked to the earlier comment about the risk of investing for mode-specific operators. The average preferred **equity stake** in the broker business is around 35%, with implied voting rights to the same extent. This shows that respondents did not seek to monopolise (unlike the largest TNCs), but were happy to partner with other businesses in the provision of MaaS. Again, there was little difference in equity share between investors and suppliers although mode-specific suppliers shares were slightly larger, demonstrating a slight desire to take on a leading role within the broker business.

The stated choice study devised willingness-to-pay estimates for each type of mobility contract attribute. These in turn can be used as inputs to determine the value of different MaaS business propositions. Table 6.1 shows the composition of these business and contract values based on mean preferred contracts (for

**TABLE 6.1** Example mobility contracts (based on mean values selected by the sample) and an estimate of the value proposition for each mobility business.

| Selected attributes | Full sample | Mode-specific | Non-mobility |
|---|---|---|---|
| Fixed route public transport (%) | 29.16 | 33.65 | 25.09 |
| On demand public transport (%) | 19.70 | 18.74 | 20.58 |
| Carsharing (%) | 16.41 | 14.98 | 17.71 |
| Taxi-like services (%) | 16.88 | 17.66 | 16.17 |
| Shared ridehailing services (%) | 17.86 | 14.99 | 20.46 |
| Expected average annual ROI (%) | 7.78 | 8.00 | 7.58 |
| **Contract value to invest (USD millions)** | **492.29** | **1036.23** | **371.40** |
| **Contract value to supply (USD millions)** | **1392.21** | **724.51** | **383.96** |

the full sample and segmented by mode-specific operators and non-mobility providers), given the preference function of the sample. On the whole, the MaaS business proposition is more attractive to mode-specific operators than non-mobility providers by an order of magnitude of around two. This may be linked to other (non-mobility type) business opportunities that non-mobility providers are also able to invest or supply in. For mode-specific operators there is a clear preference for investing as opposed to supplying—related to the earlier observation that perhaps the assets for these companies are tied up (e.g. by providing contracted services), with little excess capacity to move to MaaS-type business opportunities. For non-mobility providers there is little difference between the preference for investing and supplying. For the entire sample as a whole, there is a clear preference towards supplying, although this tendency is not evident when considering respondent segments individually.

The absolute values for these business propositions are illustrative and must be interpreted with some degree of caution – like for any (especially supply-side) stated choice study. Firstly, they are highly aggregated and as average figures are determined by the respondent sample (what is called a pivot design in how the mobility contracts were tested). The value propositions devised are also lifetime figures so depending on discount values, actual investments per year could differ immensely. The full lifetime values range between USD 400–1000 million, and so for a period (as an example) of 10 years, this would amount to USD 40–100 million in value per year (by straight line discount method). For an average 35% equity stake, this would imply USD 14–35 million in equity injection per annum. Follow up interviews and stakeholder meetings have confirmed these figures to be quite acceptable to the business community.

## 6.6 Conclusions

This section concludes the chapter by reflecting on responses to the global debate identified in the introduction in terms of the supply-side discussions, informed by the empirical study and the synthesis of global experiences.

In terms of the key stakeholders, this chapter identifies the three key stakeholders for delivering MaaS: the broker/aggregator, mode-specific operators and non-mobility operators and categorises constituent businesses in each of these categories. The chapter discusses the merits of government acting as the broker/aggregator as well as the role of government as a regulator/purchaser of the entire MaaS ecosystem. The role of government turns out to be a continuing point of contention in the future of MaaS. This chapter acknowledges that how government interacts in the MaaS ecosystem might be spatially contextual both country-wise and in urban/rural contexts. A look back to the past shows the different ways in which jurisdictions have moved from the public monopoly delivery of public transport services in the 1980s to a position which involves exposure to greater market forces, the growth in private operators (through privatisation), to mixtures of economic deregulation and competitive tendering.

The transition to greater competitive environments has not always been successful and the lessons learnt will be appreciated in the evolution of the MaaS model over time. Already, a difference in jurisdictional approaches towards the introduction of new mobility services can be seen with Australia, for example, appearing to be keen to encourage start-ups and existing businesses to take the role of broker in a test of a potential MaaS delivery model. Other jurisdictions, particularly those where public transport is still a public sector offering, are taking a less laissez-faire approach with government leading and controlling the delivery of multimodal MaaS services (partnering with private sector TNCs such as Uber). It is still too early to tell which model might provide the more successful outcome and how public and private agencies should co-ordinate and how the avoidance of anti-competitive behaviour can be secured in the MaaS modal mix. The latter is especially problematic where traditional public transport remains in the hands of the public sector.

Whilst government has a role to step in and regulate in the case of externalities and unintended consequences, this chapter also argues that it must 'get out of the way' and hold back from regulating too early. Government's role should be to enable innovation and allow a new MaaS ecosystem to emerge. To do so requires 'light touch' regulation to guide the market but also a 'firm' treatment to push for action and to regulate for any undesirable consequences, like anti-competitive behaviour (including the emergence of monopolies or oligopolies). Examples of actions that government could do to help enable a MaaS-ready environment include

- Ensure regulatory harmony (between modes and between jurisdictions)
- Develop the appetite for contractual reform and private-sector input
- Ensure private enterprise can partner and collaborate by providing a 'level' playing field
- Encourage innovation by supporting risk-takers such that they do generate a 'reasonable' rate of return

Finally, the chapter explores the question as to whether there is any certainty in a MaaS business model that will work by providing both quantitative and empirical evidence on business preferences as informed by a stated choice study. This supply-side study uniquely investigates the preferences of the different stakeholders (mode-specific and non-mobility stakeholders) and identifies possible contracts in terms of their modal mixes, equity stake and potential value proposition of the business (amongst other contract attributes).

In the next chapter, institutional and governance challenges linked to what has been identified in this chapter are discussed.

Chapter 7

# Institutional barriers and governance

## Chapter outline



## 7.1 Introduction

The Swedish roadmap for MaaS was drafted in late 2016 and endorsed by the Ministry of Enterprise and Innovation in spring 2017. The roadmap asserts that the diffusion of MaaS in Sweden should lower the negative externalities of the passenger transport system, and contribute to better utilisation of road space, more attractive urban environments and increased accessibility in non-urban settings (Pernestål Brenden et al., 2017). The roadmap also sets tangible impact targets for 2027. By then, the diffusion of MaaS should have resulted in a quarter of the Swedish population making regular use of shared mobility services and in a 15% reduction of the climate impact from passenger transports (Pernestål Brenden et al., 2017). According to the roadmap, the first step towards realising these targets is that the public transport tickets for Sweden's three metropolitan regions by 2019 are made available for digital third-party resale. When this chapter was being written, the end of 2019 was fast approaching. Still, all three public transport authorities in question were yet to open their tickets for third-party resale. Consequently, the type of MaaS trials and implementations that the roadmap envisioned has thus far not been possible, and following the constraints of annual budgets, much of the funding set aside to facilitate such activities has been forfeited.

Understanding Mobility as a Service (MaaS). https://doi.org/10.1016/B978-0-12-820044-5.00007-5
© 2020 Elsevier Inc. All rights reserved.

The overly optimistic timeline of the roadmap suggests that the complexity of realising MaaS was underestimated. Other examples that point towards an inadequate understanding of what the realisation process entails in Sweden include the disagreements that followed after the first MaaS trial in 2014 (see Section 4.2.1), and the failed attempt to establish a national MaaS integrator in 2017 (Smith et al., 2020).

Why the MaaS concept might be difficult to realise is an on-going debate within the emerging MaaS literature. At the concept level, 'the new freedom of mobility' has frequently been used as a catch phrase by vocal MaaS proponents (e.g. MaaS Alliance, 2017; MaaS Global, 2019c). Transport scholars have criticised this proposed promise of MaaS, arguing that it fails to acknowledge that the transport network is finite, and that network problems arise from the aggregate impact of individual activities (Pangbourne et al., 2018). Conceptualising MaaS as a multi-sided market, scholars have also recognised a chicken-and-egg type of dilemma, making it difficult for MaaS providers to allure both transport providers and users, at least initially (Li and Voege, 2017). On the user side, it has moreover been hypothesised that the perceived added value of MaaS might be fairly low, since many potential users are used to, and content with, operating multiple apps to satisfy their mobility needs (Jittrapirom et al., 2017). From the perspective of involved actors, the models for collaboration and business have been identified as the main issues. Passenger transport is a low margin business sector, and MaaS differs from current practices in that it is an intrinsically collaborative venture (Mukhtar-Landgren and Smith, 2019). Therefore, new approaches to distributing responsibilities, revenues and customer relations are needed. At the societal level, cultural practices and norms have been suggested to be the largest obstacles. In particular, it has been noted that current attitudes to ownership need to change in order to pave the way for MaaS diffusion (e.g. Hensher, 2017; Mulley, 2017).

Drawing on the convoluted development processes in Sweden, this chapter sets out to map, and make sense of, the key institutional barriers to the development and diffusion of MaaS. The objective is to better understand why the MaaS concept is difficult, but perhaps not impossible, to realise. The institutional framework that is utilised to organise the identified barriers is presented next. Findings are then reported, after which some recommendations on how to best address the identified barriers are proposed.

## 7.2 Institutional framework

The institutional framework for integrated mobility services (IRIMS) is a framework that aims to cater for institutional analyses of MaaS. It was first introduced in a working paper in 2016 (Mukhtar-Landgren et al., 2016), and has subsequently been applied and refined in several papers (e.g. Karlsson et al., 2017a, 2020). Broadly understanding institutions as "a relatively stable collection of rules and practices, embedded in structures of resources that make action possible" (Goodin et al., 2013, p. 480), the IRIMS framework recognises that institutions can be formal or informal (cf. Scott, 2014), and arise on different societal levels.

The IRIMS framework categorises institutional factors into three interrelated analytical levels: macro, meso, and micro. The macro-level focuses on larger social scales beyond the reach of most operational actors. It encompasses international and national regulations and policies as well as cultural, religious and political norms, amongst other things. The meso-level refers to the interactions within and between networks of operational actors, such as private entrepreneurs, public transport authorities and trade unions. Here, the culture of collaboration, and how international and national legal frameworks are implemented regionally and locally come into play. The micro level centres on citizens. Foremost, it focuses on their prospective and evolving roles in MaaS as customers and users. Thus, this level encompasses individual consumer aspects such as current travel patterns, household budgets and social activities.

## 7.3 Institutional barriers to Mobility-as-a-Service

Smith et al. (2018b) applied the IRIMS framework to an analysis of MaaS developments in Sweden and Finland. Drawing on this experience, they noted that the framework was lopsided, focusing too much on institutional structures. In order to cater for better policy advice on MaaS, they argued that studies utilising the IRIMS framework should be more attentive to the practice-based elements that, coupled with structural changes, can bring about institutional change (cf. Meyer, 1994). Examples of such practice-based elements include routines, procedures and conventions (March and Olsen, 1989). Following this advice, our analysis of the key institutional barriers that hamper the development and diffusion of MaaS in Sweden covers both institutionalised structures and material realms of practice. In line with the IRIMS framework, the identified barriers are categorised as formal or informal, and sorted upon whether they relate to the macro-, meso-, or micro-level, see Table 7.1.

### 7.3.1 Macro-level barriers

At the macro-level, MaaS related developments in Sweden have most notably been hampered by the perceived implications of international and national legislation and policies. This includes laws that are professed to limit the action spaces of public transport authorities and taxation schemes that create lock-in effects for private car use. However, as outlined below, a lack of a shared understanding of vision and targets for MaaS has seemingly also favoured inaction rather than action.

The European Union defines public transport as "passenger transport services of general economic interest provided to the public on a non-discriminatory and continuous basis" (EC 1370/2007, p. 6). With reference to this definition, the Swedish public transport act (SFS, 2010:1065) regulates what regional

**TABLE 7.1 Key institutional barriers to MaaS developments in Sweden.**

| | Formal barriers | Informal barriers |
|---|---|---|
| Macro-level<br>i.e. *the larger social scale and the state* | B1. Laws, regulations and reforms that limit the perceived action spaces of public transport authorities<br>B2. No explicit sectorial responsibility for national public transport developments<br>B3. Taxation schemes that create lock-in effects for private car use | B4. Lack of shared understanding of vision and targets for MaaS |
| Meso-level<br>i.e. *the operational actors and the interactions between them* | B5. Lack of tools and processes for public-private collaboration<br>B6. Separation of land-use- and public transport planning<br>B7. High levels of bureaucracy and political control within public transport authorities | B8. Low levels of trust and understanding across public and private sectors<br>B9. Risk averseness amongst both public and private actors<br>B10. Ambiguities regarding prioritisation and lack of innovation culture within public transport authorities |
| Micro-level<br>i.e. *the individuals as users and citizens* | B11. Miss-matches between MaaS offering and perceived mobility needs/problems<br>B12. Tedious on-boarding processes and complex systems to learn | B13. Current travel habits and vested interest, especially in private car use<br>B14. Low awareness of current transport related costs, especially related to private car use |

public transport authorities can and should do. Although it is not obvious from the exact wording of the definition, many public authorities in Sweden interpret the public transport act to not encompass non-traditional uses of public transport vehicles, such as for tourism- or event related transport (e.g. Swedish Transport Agency, 2019). Moreover, new types of sharing services are deemed to be excluded by the definition (Transport Analysis, 2016). In a study of an attempt to procure MaaS in West Sweden in 2016 (Smith et al., 2017, 2019b), three additional laws were identified as hampering to MaaS developments: the local government act (SFS, 2017:725), the law on state aid rules (SFS, 2013:388), and the competition act (SFS, 2008:579). Representatives of the actors involved in the studied procurement attempt generally perceived that these laws meant that the public transport authority could not take the role as MaaS provider/operator in the emerging MaaS ecosystem (cf. Smith et al., 2018a), thus limiting its action space.

In Sweden, the national government has thus far taken a relatively passive role. Even though several key public authorities at the national level have endorsed the MaaS roadmap, the vision, targets and tactics that the roadmap declares have arguably not been approved by many of the important stakeholders. For instance, the debate on whether public transport authorities should permit third-party resale of their tickets is far from settled (Smith et al., 2018a). Furthermore, the Swedish Transport Administration used to hold a sectorial responsibility for national public transport developments. It has been argued that the national governments removal of this responsibility in 2010 (Swedish Agency for Public Management, 2014) has left a vacuum. For example, in an analysis of the attempt to develop a national MaaS integrator, some interviewees noted that few of the involved actors were inclined to invest in national scale MaaS developments (Smith et al., 2020).

In contrast to the Swedish government, the national governments in Finland and Denmark have both commenced structural changes in the form of law reforms in order to push the development of MaaS (Isaksson et al., 2019). Moreover, both these governments have been quite active and vocal in promoting MaaS, especially the Finnish government, which has managed to establish an informal but strong national vision for how MaaS is to develop in Finland (Smith et al., 2018b). Although these structural and practical activities at the national level might be more successful in spurring initial action than the Swedish approach, there is arguably also a risk that the tactic could increase the not-invented-here syndrome at public transport authorities (cf. Antons and Piller, 2015). An analysis of the Finnish developments found that the Finnish government's activities effectively had limited the perceived action spaces of public transport authorities, forcing them to reactively adapt to the on-going changes and to primarily focusing on protecting their interests (Mukhtar-Landgren and Smith, 2019).

Beyond regulation and policies that hamper MaaS developments directly, several structural arrangements do so indirectly by encumbering the potential future uptake of MaaS. In Sweden, prominent examples in this space include tax deductions for costs associated with having company cars and for commuting by car (Holmberg et al., 2016). In general, the success of MaaS largely rests upon its relative attractiveness compared to private car use (Smith and Hensher, 2019). Thus, all direct and indirect subsidies associated with owning and using private cars negatively influence the potential uptake of MaaS and remains a major challenge for the MaaS ecosystem.

### 7.3.2 Meso-level barriers

At the meso-level, the actors aiming for operative roles in the emerging MaaS ecosystem have struggled with understanding and trusting each other, and thus with finding ways to collaborate on, and making business out of MaaS. Basically, a fundamental barrier to MaaS developments is that the concept entails new forms of collaboration between a complex network of actors that are inherently different and stem from separate industry sectors.

For example, consider Whim—the crown jewel of MaaS according to the industry press. MaaS Global is a Helsinki-based start-up firm. Their operation of Whim in Helsinki is enabled by investments from an array of national and international backers and by agreements with the regional public transport authority as well as with both global and local transport service providers. Moreover, MaaS Global has collaborated tightly with the Finnish Funding Agency for Innovation, the Ministry for Transport and Communication, the non-profit association ITS Finland, the City of Helsinki and an Australian platform developer in the development and marketing of Whim, amongst others.

The MaaS trials in Sweden have frequently featured similar constellations of actors, but have mostly not had the same level of success as MaaS Global has in Helsinki. Rather, multiple types of collaboration barriers have hindered the development processes, including incongruent views on how responsibilities should be distributed, a lack of clear leadership, insufficient models for innovation collaboration, and a prominent worry of being dominated by other actors and of losing control over the trajectory of the development (Smith et al., 2019b). Public-private innovation collaboration studies have found that the inherent differences across the sectors make it particularly challenging to establish inter-organisational trust in such networks (cf. Smith and Akram, 2017). The contested, cancelled and slow-moving MaaS developments in Sweden reiterates this notion, and suggest that the trust and collaboration problems in this case are closely linked to perceived uncertainties surrounding roles, mandates, business models, customer relations and proof of concept (Karlsson et al., 2020). Furthermore, the structural separation of the responsibility for spatial and public transport planning in Sweden make it particularly cumbersome to align MaaS activities with land-use policies and strategies. Likewise, the weak structural links between regional and national public transport systems impede MaaS developments on the national scale (Smith et al., 2020).

Despite all the trust and collaboration related issues outline above, many public transport authority representatives in Sweden believe that their internal barriers to MaaS developments are even harder to overcome. In particular, they find it difficult to convince the entire organisation of the promises of MaaS, and to prioritise MaaS over other development activities (Smith et al., 2020). Essentially, why should they invest time and money in a highly uncertain and challenging concept, when they have hundreds of other burning issues on the table? On top of that, the public transport authority that attempted to procure MaaS in 2016 seems to suffer from a lack of an innovation culture and of a systematised approach to handling inter-organisational innovation projects. Their organisational structures and targets are largely designed to manage the existing public transport system, whilst the mission to improve the network through collaborative innovation projects only appeared on their agendas quite recently (Smith et al., 2019b).

It has been noted that fairly high levels of bureaucracy and political control seem to make the public transport authorities slower and less flexible than private enterprises, which in turn makes them unattractive and difficult to collaborate with (Smith et al., 2019b). Red tape, and political control has also, alongside weak reward systems, been identified to harbour a risk averse culture (Bozeman and Kingsley, 1998). The public transport authorities protectionism and risk aversion have indeed frequently been called out as major barriers to MaaS developments, in Sweden and in general (e.g. Sochor et al., 2018). However, a low willingness to participate and invest in MaaS related activities has been noticed amongst private actors too (Smith et al., 2020). Similar to the public transport authorities, a few incumbent private transport service providers, whose participation the MaaS development is more or less dependent on (e.g. the largest car sharing firm in Sweden), have monopoly like positions to protect. Moreover, a frequent reasoning amongst commentators is that because the public transport authorities have not been clear about their long-term plans, the perceived risk for MaaS entrepreneurs and backers of investing in MaaS is high, especially since the viability of MaaS business models is unknown (Sarasini et al., 2017).

The private sector's reluctance to invest in uncertain and high-risk innovation projects is not unique to MaaS in Sweden. In the seminal book "The Entrepreneurial State," Mazzucato (2015) argues that the image of venture capitalists as the main entrepreneurs and risk takers in innovation is both fabricated and frankly far from the truth. Primarily focusing on short-term return of investment and on maximising shareholder value, private actors are generally not keen to enter innovation projects in the high-risk phases according to her (Mazzucato, 2015). Rather, Mazzucato holds that "nearly all the technological revolutions in the past—from the Internet to today's green tech revolution—required a massive push by the state" (p. 6). She concludes that the biased and simplified storyline of private actors as the risk takers, and public actors as merely wealth extractors, is hurting possibilities to build dynamic public-private collaborations. The Swedish experiences show that this issue can deter MaaS developments.

### 7.3.3 Micro-level barriers

Due to the small-scale and lack of systematic evaluation of most of the undertaken MaaS trials (see Chapter 3), the micro-level is arguably the most uncharted analytical level of the IRIMS framework at present. Still, a number of stated preference studies focusing on prospective MaaS users (e.g. Ho et al., 2018; Kamargianni et al., 2018a; Ratilainen, 2017) have generated insights on what might hinder MaaS adoption. For example, these hypothetical experiments have indicated that car owners are financially and habitually inclined to continue using their private cars, and suggested that it will be difficult to design and deliver a MaaS offering that can compete with the perceived flexibility and efficacy of owning and using a private car. The undertaken MaaS trials in Sweden, which this section will focus on, have confirmed these issues, and shed light on more hands-on structural problems such as miss-matches between MaaS offerings and perceived mobility needs, and tedious on-boarding processes and complex systems to learn.

The difficulty of breaking existing transport habits (i.e. non-deliberate choices), for instance in terms of mode selection, has been widely discussed in the travel behaviour literature (e.g. Gärling and Axhausen, 2003). Two key barriers to a transition away from habitual private car use on the user side have been identified: vested interests in car use, particularly in terms of large up-front costs, and the norm in many western societies that depicts car ownership as a vital component of the good life (Urry, 2004).

Both these barriers have been identified in the Swedish MaaS trials. Prospective users of EC2B that had not adopted the service, frequently mentioned that they already had a car and thus had no or limited need of a MaaS service (Smith et al., 2019c). If they had been car owners for many years, and were surrounded by other car owners, the hesitancy to test living without owning one seemed to grow larger. However, even though habits and norms certainly influenced the choice of buying/keeping a car, many car owners did so for a rational reason, such as having a long commute to work, or a summer house that they wished to visit at weekends. A perceived need for either long or frequent car trips led to a mis-match between the EC2B offering, since neither of the integrated transport services were targeted at such trips (Smith et al., 2019c). The UbiGo trial witnessed a similar problem. Approached prospective users who ended up declining to participate in the trial often mentioned that the offering did not 'fit' their mobility needs (Karlsson et al., 2020).

Another frequent explanation amongst the group of potential participants that declined the UbiGo trial was that they felt it would have required too much effort to learn how to use UbiGo and the integrated transport services (Karlsson et al., 2020). The tiresomeness of the multi-phased on-boarding process, and the perceived complexitivity of the system—including the app, the vehicles, the actor constellation and processes such as for picking up and returning vehicles—also hindered many, especially the elderly and less tech savy, from adopting the service in the EC2B trial (Smith et al., 2019c).

Beyond demanding trial participants to go through a lengthy on-boarding process and to learn about the service and how to use it, the UbiGo trial (see Section 4.2.1) also required the participants to pay for their travelling in advance by purchasing a subscription. For several prospective users, this was not acceptable (Karlsson et al., 2020). Furthermore, a few argued that the cost of the subscription would be higher than their present cost for travel. Although these might be perfectly true for some, it seems probable that the comparison in some cases was influenced by an underestimation of the costs associated with owning a private car (cf. Beirão and Sarsfield Cabral, 2007).

## 7.4 Implications for governance

The discussion of institutional barriers presented in the previous section suggests that MaaS is more incongruent with current practices within the transport sector than the MaaS literature tends to recognise (cf. Smith and Hensher, 2019).

In fact, the broad spectrum of the identified barriers implies that the process of realising MaaS will require both significant intervention from public as well as private actors on different institutional scales. This poses a governance challenge, at least if the diffusion of MaaS is to contribute to policy objectives. We draw on two strands of literature—transition management (Loorbach, 2007) and collaborative innovation (Torfing, 2016)—in order to outline five general tasks that public actors could undertake in order to lower the identified barriers. These tasks do not address barriers 7, 12, and 14 in Table 7.1, and the list is in general far from all-encompassing. For a more comprehensive view of the authors' policy recommendations, see Chapter 9.[a]

### 7.4.1 Establish a vision and a principal strategy for MaaS, based on policy objectives

*Addressing barriers 4, 6, 8, 9, and 10*

A central and immediate task when approaching the challenge of governing MaaS developments is to align operational and tactical MaaS activities with an overarching vision and a principal strategy. Basically, in one way or another, internal as well as external MaaS related activities should preferably contribute to the long-term objective. To be able to align tactical and operational activities, the vision and strategy must be established first. The vision should set the envisioned role of MaaS in the future transport system, whilst the strategy should indicate the principal approach in terms of how the vision will be fulfilled. This work includes specifying the sought societal effect, be that reduced emissions, improved accessibility, or something else. The vision and strategy must also be synchronised with other important and related planning documents, most notably plans for infrastructure development and land-use (as well as other visions of MaaS). Thus, the development of these documents is a collaborative endeavour that should engage a broad set of strategic and operational public actors that have the mandate and discretion to govern MaaS within and beyond their own organisations (Smith et al., 2018b). Moreover, to facilitate practical action, new entrants and incumbent transport providers should be invited to the discussion too.

To facilitate internal actions, the strategy should specify the priority of MaaS investments versus other activities. Here, introducing a level of slack for short-term key performance indicators—such as annual patronage growth in the case of public transport authorities—could cater for risk-taking and long-term thinking. To facilitate external actions, it is important that the vision is inspiring (cf. the moonshot) and that the strategy is relevant, shared and allows for experimentation.

The Swedish MaaS roadmap is arguably a good example of a national strategy based on local conditions and policy objectives. However, although less

a. See also Smith and Hensher (2019) and Smith et al. (2019a,b).

formalised, the market-oriented Finnish vision for MaaS has been much more successful in generating interest and spurring action (see Section 3.5.1). It is arguably also more entangled with, and supported by, structural changes to the transport sector, compared to its Swedish counterpart (Mukhtar-Landgren and Smith, 2019).

### 7.4.2 Explore mode-agnostic organisations, missions, and contracts

#### *Addressing barriers 1 and 2*

MaaS promises to integrate multiple transport services and modes from the perspective of users. Despite this, the planning of, and responsibility for, the modes are frequently separated. To overcome the problem of modal separation, Wong et al. (2018) brought forward the idea of mode-agnostic mobility contracts (see also Hensher, 2017). In other words, public transport authorities should refrain from stating what modes an operator should utilise to deliver mobility. Approaching the same issue, Smith et al. (2019b) argued that lawmakers should consider missions that give more flexibility in the means public actors are allowed to pursue in order to achieve policy goals, for instance by enlarging the definition of public transport to encompass more means of shared travelling (i.e. mode-agnostic missions). In a Swedish context, this could, for example, mean that public transport authorities would be allowed to plan for and procure car-sharing services.

Taking it a few steps further, we propose that it could be relevant to explore how to improve the alignments between the planning of all modes of transport, as well as between transport planning and spatial planning. One, perhaps radical and unpractical, measure would be to establish new public authorities with a sectorial responsibility for both transport in general (cf. Transport for London) and land-use planning within a given geographical area. The formation of such mode-agnostic and united authorities would strengthen structural links between transport and land-use planning, and possibly facilitate the implementation of integrated visions and targets, legislative frameworks, planning processes and policy programmes (cf. Schoeman and Schoeman, 2017).

### 7.4.3 Scrap excessive subsidisation of car ownership and use

#### *Addressing barriers 3 and 13*

MaaS developments are arguably caught between two regimes—the personal transport service regime and the private car regime—and contingent upon transforming the structures and practices that maintain both (Smith and Hensher, 2019). The rapidly growing body of grey literature on MaaS focuses almost exclusively on how to make it more appealing to travel via personal transport services. Still, from a transport policy perspective, it is in theory much easier and much more relevant to make it less appealing to travel by private car. A first step in this direction would be to scrap excessive subsidisation of car ownership and use, such as the tax deduction schemes in Sweden that favour commuting by car and to own, rent and lease company cars (although the Stockholm and Gothenburg congestion pricing schemes are positive initiatives in locations where multi-modal travel has great appeal). This could also include road pricing reform (see Chapter 8). However, such measures require a lot of political bravery and slickness, as the yellow vest movement in France have made very clear recently.

### 7.4.4 Implement more collaborative models for public-private innovation

*Addressing barriers 5 and 8*

The attempts to procure MaaS and to establish a national MaaS integrator were both targeted to ignite (and govern) MaaS developments in Sweden, in order to transform the delivery of public transport, and in the long run produce public good. However, both initiatives failed, arguably (at least partly) due to lack of inter-organisational trust and understanding. Drawing on an analysis of the procurement attempt in West Sweden, Smith et al. (2019b) proposed the use of less hierarchical and more flexible procurement processes, such as the pre-commercial procurement process (Edler and Georghiou, 2007) or virtual networks (Bakker et al., 2006), as well as contract forms that allow for intermediate steps that bridge the current gap between ‘no standard rules apply’ trials and ‘all rules apply’ standard contracts. Regardless if procurement models and contractual offers are used or not, we suggest that the implementation of new, more collaborative, models for public innovation are needed in order to build trust and understanding, and to create better opportunities for long-term, joint value creation across the public and private sectors when the level of uncertainty is high (cf. Smith et al., 2017). Here, we can learn from the broader literature on competitive tendering and contract design in the provision of mainstream public transport (see Wong and Hensher, 2018).

### 7.4.5 Target urban and sub-urban multi-modalists initially

*Addressing barrier 11*

Lastly, the varied outcomes of MaaS trials indicate that MaaS can attract interest, but might not be for everyone, at least in its current forms (see Section 4.3.2). In order to facilitate initial take up, we suggest policymakers to not try to develop universal MaaS solutions, but instead firstly target those who are more capable and willing to adopt MaaS, that is less likely to experience a mis-matches between the MaaS offering and their perceived mobility needs. Drawing on the UbiGo and EC2B trials, this group seems to include people that are interested in innovation and sustainability, are motivated to change their current travel behaviour, live in urban or sub-urban settings, and do not commute far or frequently by car, but perceive a need for car access every so often (Smith et al., 2019c; Sochor et al., 2016). Moreover, based on the takeup of Whim in Helsinki, this candidate group seems to be travelling multi-modaly already, but mostly by public transport (Hartikainen et al., 2019). Naturally, such a targeted approach raises equity concerns. Hence, MaaS investments should be flanked by investments benefiting those who do not benefit from MaaS developments.

## 7.5 Concluding remarks

The chapter finds that the development and diffusion of MaaS in Sweden faces manifold barriers at several institutional levels. At the macro-level, laws, regulations and reforms limit the perceived actions paces of public transport authorities, whilst taxation schemes create lock-in effects for private car use. At the meso-level, tools and processes for, as well as experience of, public-private collaborations remain painfully absent. Moreover, ambiguities around prioritisation and risk averseness act as internal barriers for involved actors. At the micro-level current travel habits, vested interests and a low awareness of current transport related costs contribute to a miss-matches between trialled MaaS offerings and perceived mobility needs.

Although one might expect that several of the identified barriers apply to other contexts and cases as well, exactly how they translate needs further examination. In particular, to establish generalisability, further investigations into barriers to MaaS developments in countries or regions with dissimilar socioeconomic circumstances, less developed public transport systems, and differently organised governments, as well as further studies that comprise later stages of MaaS developments, in both similar and dissimilar settings, are needed (Smith et al., 2019a).

Nonetheless, the long list of identified barriers suggests that the process of realising MaaS will require comprehensive actions from public and private actors. Given that the overarching aim is that the diffusion of MaaS should contribute to policy objectives, this poses an immense governance challenge on the public sector. The chapter proposes five tactics that could be implemented by public authorities to address the identified institutional barriers: (i) establish a vision and a principal strategy for MaaS, based on policy objectives; (ii) explore mode-agnostic organisations, missions and contracts; (iii) scrap excessive subsidisation of car ownership and use; (iv) implement more collaborative models for public-private innovation; and (v) target urban and sub-urban multi-modalists initially. Whilst perhaps theoretically sound, we recognise that these suggestions remain unproven. Hence, we hope that future research will look into the effectiveness of these, and other, governance tactics designed to facilitate the development and diffusion of MaaS.

Chapter 8

# MaaS and issues impacting on broader transport and societal goals

## Chapter outline



## 8.1 Introduction

> *Advocates suggest that, if the concept is successful, the pool of customers will grow as cars are abandoned in favour of MaaS. Hence most companies will want to participate in one or more MaaS platforms.*
>
> (Sipe and Pojani, 2018)

The focus of this chapter is on the externality impacts of MaaS. This is a difficult topic since there are so many unknowns, and the great majority of commentary to date has been somewhat speculative with 'what if' scenarios clouded by a sizeable amount of hype and rhetoric and a very liberal use of the term MaaS (see Chapters 1 and 3). Pangbourne et al. (2020) comment that "Whilst the rhetoric of MaaS is to promise efficiency to cities, freedom to citizens and profit to service providers…those promises do not guarantee efficiency or equity (and by extension are not ethical)."

Understanding Mobility as a Service (MaaS). https://doi.org/10.1016/B978-0-12-820044-5.00008-7
© 2020 Elsevier Inc. All rights reserved.

While we do not deny the real possibility of MaaS increasing the mobility choice set for (at least some segments of) travellers which in itself has potential societal benefits, in this chapter we want to go beyond identification of the appeal to consumers who take up MaaS offerings (detailed in Chapter 5) and speculate on how specific MaaS product offerings may or may not result in changes in key transport (and land use) performance indicators. Can MaaS deliver multi-modal mobility services that contribute to a range of societal aspirations (especially decreasing car ownership rates and lowering the environmental burden of the transport system) that are often articulated as part of the priorities and goals of government? These priorities and goals include the great potential to deliver new transport services, improve road safety, alleviate congestion, improve health benefits, reduce social exclusion, influence government subsidy of public transport, increase accessibility of existing public transport services, and increase economic productivity.

A related theme is whether, through MaaS, we can reappraise how road and public transport use is priced, using it as an opportunity to introduce more efficient modal prices (and subsidy levels that are deemed closer to optimal) that can be embedded (or disguised) in subscription packages, and which will be returned via a broker/aggregator to a modal operator and distributed to government or a private entity, as the owners of the key infrastructure.

MaaS, as one popular interpretation of future collaborative and connected mobility services, must also be considered under the presence and absence of autonomous vehicles (AVs—car and bus) since the inclusion of AVs has specific implications on the impact that the modal mix, offered in particular through a MaaS subscription plan, has on the performance of the transport network. An integral behavioural challenge is the extent to which we can change societal values to adopt a growing sharing culture (see Chapter 2) as a necessary but not sufficient pre-condition to reduce private vehicle use.

In summary, this chapter is on the role that government might or should play in the evolving MaaS market to ensure that societal outcomes are supported. It links into question 4 raised in Chapter 13: Who are the key stakeholders in the MaaS ecosystem? Whereas institutional and governance issues (including possible contracting models ranging from a laissez-faire arms-length approach (competition in the market) to a more regulated model based on competition for the market) are addressed in previous chapters, this chapter focusses on a number of costs and benefits that define the contribution to efficiency and equity of transport services within a network (i.e. accessibility, social exclusion, traffic flow and subsidy implications). Some overlap with other chapters may be expected as we discuss the broader societal challenges.

There are far more questions than answers at this stage in the MaaS journey, and hence this chapter is often speculative, if not controversial, in its commentary. This is necessary to encourage ongoing inquiry through research and real world applications (the latter hopefully well documented and transparent, as argued in Chapter 3).

## 8.2 Smart transition and societal impacts

The transition to smarter mobility, often referred to as Smart Transition, typically hopes for greater car sharing (facilitated by apps) and less owning of cars by private individuals, as well as the future role of (green electric) autonomous vehicles. It has an underlying mandate to redefine and commit to a Collaborative and Connected Society (CCS), a phrase increasingly used in many jurisdictions (e.g. Transport for NSW) whereby the mode is far less important than the service levels that satisfy customer needs. While we will always need reflective and effective governance frameworks to ensure delivery of CCS (see Chapter 7), we have an opportunity through MaaS to break the stranglehold that outmoded mode-specific regulatory models have had on the provision of transport services.[a] MaaS platforms encompass every aspect of daily travel, from payment systems to route planning with efficient and affordable first and last mile options. Why should we continue with mode-specific contracts, often associated in the public transport sphere with public monopolies or provided by competition for the market (i.e. competitive tendering—see Hensher, 2017), all supported with provider-side subsidies? This includes the limitations imposed on the over-specification of network service levels (and the predominance of timetables for conventional public transport). The car-based systems associated with taxis are now being broken by the arrival of new service models such as Uber, Ola, Grab and Lyft, together with their vertical diversification such as Uber eats, although they are essentially mode-specific (though covering an increasingly expanding mix of intermediate modes, many of which are being defined for the first time, and encouraging shared rides in a more customer-friendly way than taxis have traditionally been able to do). Fundamentally, we increasingly see many variants on the conventional wisdom that are tantamount to delivery models that cannot operate as well under outdated regulations.

Smart Transition is the context in which we have to contemplate that anything goes, including MaaS, as long as it has a sensible customer and societal outcome, and one might hope an acceptance by government as the custodian of societal interests through a reformed governance (and funding) model (see Chapter 7). Although Uber was one of the first services to break the regulatory mould in many geographical jurisdictions, its likely long-term heritage might be the way in which some governments have recognised the need to allow any sensible reform in service delivery that benefits customers, to be supported by new regulations and legislation,[b] and this is precisely what MaaS is aspiring to do by providing a richer array of choices unconstrained by any rules about what modes are allowed. Governments are moving increasingly (in some countries at least) to a recognition that a customer focus is what service delivery is all about

---

a. Interestingly, New South Wales, Australia made a start with this is the 2014 Passenger transport Act where linking of specific vehicles to modes was removed.

b. To some extent we also saw this happen with the regulations to allow bus operators to register flexibly routed bus services in the UK in 2004.

('The customer comes first') and that modal protection should not be allowed unless there are serious threats to the integrity of the transport system. This last point is critical since a risk of degrading the transport network should be something unacceptable to government and society more generally.

At present there seems to be a sense that governments in many countries attach some amount of nirvana to MaaS; however we believe a realism that this is far from this belief is impending. Pangbourne et al. (2020) remind us of the challenges in transitioning to a possible MaaS future, which may have negative consequences on the broader goals of society, elicited through government. Drawing on transition theory in a setting of urban governance efficiency and equity, Pangborne et al. emphasise concerns surrounding rhetoric, specifically noting that:

1. Rhetoric conceptualisations are concrete enough to be applicable in the real context.
2. The rhetoric is critical of contemporary times and existing technological regime.
3. Rhetoric conceptualisations often provide very compelling arguments for social change.
4. The rhetoric underlines the technological impact that would render previous technological transitions almost irrelevant.

We need to highlight the real possibility that MaaS may be attractive for some but not all travel activities, being limited by its scalability, and one can imagine a situation where a number of car-based trips are outside of such a package, but that the package can appeal to a subset of travel currently undertaken. We call this *sub-MaaS* to modify the rhetoric that all trips can be integrated into a MaaS subscription plan (Tripi in Chapter 3 is an example of this approach). Even if it is often never explicit, it is very implicit in the propaganda. Crucially, we are interested in what this might mean for delivering on the broader goals of society as reflected typically in the goals and objectives underpinning strategic plans of governments, which includes new or revised regulations and contracts.

## 8.3 Moving beyond the interest of MaaS providers and users

> *...the sharing economy is being hyped up by those that stand to gain the most from it, that is, platform operators (Dredge and Gyimothy, 2015). The hyping takes the form of sponsored reports by consultants, lobbying of government by platform providers, website content and social media content*
>
> (Standing et al., 2019, p. 236)

MaaS has generated a significant amount of interest by the private sector, with interests as diverse as new start-up businesses that specialise in the development of digital apps through to organisations that see an opportunity to diversify their product offerings in a market where digital transformation is increasingly likely to increase the exposure of their core business activity.[c] Examples include insurance companies, ride sharing, sourcing and hailing car businesses (such as Uber, Ola, and Lyft), and private providers of public transport, where the latter is either under contract to government or operating in an economic deregulated market.

Although the market-led model has great appeal in supporting new commercial activity designed to not only offer improved services to the travelling public, its primary obligation is the commerciality of any new initiative. It is one thing to know what impact MaaS may have in a broader societal sense, it is another matter to determine the best way to secure a positive societal contribution, which is a key responsibility of government.

It has been suggested that MaaS has the potential to physically reshape the design of our cities and towns and improve the amenity for all users of streets and roads, particularly pedestrians. This includes changing parking, the form of our streets and how people interact with vehicles and the streetscape. If achievable, this will help shape amenity, liveability and social experiences, and support the development of smarter, more successful places in cities and regional areas (TfNSW, 2019). Much of this promotion (or aspiration) appears to be connected to autonomous vehicles (AVs) per se and not to MaaS, unless MaaS is able to be a conduit (supported by AVs) to reduced private car ownership that translates into reduced car kilometres. We discuss AVs later in more detail. A growing number of researchers believe, like Kent (2018) that people "… are generally not prepared to give up their private car and use shared car services."

Despite this scepticism, what is encouraging, as a very small start, is evidence in Australia for the growth in services that should become part of the multi-modal MaaS offering. New ridesharing services, such as Uber, Taxify, and Ola, are reshaping the market for point to point travel in NSW. The growing trend of carsharing and carpooling, driven by services such as GoGet, Car Next Door, Liftango, and SMove (whose cars are accessed via a public transport card such as Opal in Sydney), offer convenient choices for people who do not drive very often or do not own a car, for instance older people and young adults. GoGet—the pioneer of carsharing in Australia which operates on a "return to station" model, has, in 2018, over 100,000 members who have made over five million trips using its services. Car Next Door, which has over 90,000 members, estimates each carshare vehicle represents ten private cars that have been disposed of or avoided, resulting in a net reduction of nine vehicles on the road (Boyle and Associates, 2016). How much of this growth from existing and new markets will reduce public transport use and indeed have a positive benefit on the externality effects currently in place such as congestion is unknown.

c. But interestingly, interest has not translated into pilots or full scale roll out.

One big question is how scalable is this 'encouraging' evidence, since the numbers represent a miniscule amount of trip activity; however if it translates into a 5–10% reduction in car trip kilometres in major western cities, we might see significant reductions in traffic congestion, emissions and possibly gains in social exclusion. The matter of parking is also very ambiguous. While we might hope for a reduction in the demand for off street parking lots resulting in reduced capacity, there is likely to be an increase in the amount of curbside capacity used to pick up and drop off users of car based services, resulting in a transfer from off-street to on-street car activity. This has implications for the design of roads and curbside pavements and is of interest in a number of trial projects (e.g. Waverley Council in Sydney). However, these modal changes have not been within the MaaS setting but essentially PAYG, using uni-modal initiatives and it will be questioned as to whether the extension to a MaaS subscription model will add societal value over the evidence we already have under PAYG.

In contrast, some US based pundits, typified by research from Juniper Research (2018), suggest that MaaS has the potential to replace more than 2.3 billion urban private car journeys annually in the US by 2023. They suggest that while the theory behind MaaS' ability to reduce congestion is sound, implementing it in cities requires a high level of collaboration between governments, transport agencies, public and private sector transport companies and other parties. They predict that the growth of MaaS in the US will be slower than in countries with a stronger central government engagement because of the fragmentation of the state and federal system:

> *Stakeholder partnerships are fundamental to MaaS in order to develop a viable multi-modal system delivering significant cost- and time-savings to the user*
>
> (Juniper research analyst Nick Maynard)

However, we would argue that countries with stronger central governments typically have a more effective mainstream public transport system and hence may have greater resistance to a MaaS outcome that becomes overly car-based. There are as always, exceptions. A counterexample would be Switzerland, which has the weakest central government and strongest federalism and yet one of the best public transport systems. We suspect that moving out of private car ownership will be a gargantuan challenge, recognising under AVs that many people for many years will always wish to drive a private vehicle, or at least not share their AV with others, especially strangers.

McKinsey (2019) suggest an optimistic future featuring seamless mobility using technologies from smart traffic lights to autonomous vehicles (AVs) to preventive maintenance, to integrate all sorts of travel. An outcome would be fewer private cars, with people mixing and matching rail transit and low-cost, point-to-point travel in robo-taxis and autonomous shuttles. It means converting parking spaces into parks or gardens as well as widespread use of AVs, which is expected to result in many fewer traffic deaths. There are many points here of questionable merit.

If MaaS schemes become dominated by car based offers, like those cited above, what does it mean for conventional public transport, and government's response to a car dominated solution? Maybe in the future, the shared autonomous car in a safe platoon will act like public transport and so does it matter what the mode is? This, however, is likely to be less spatially efficient than purpose-built large vehicles and will possibly sabotage many of the intrinsic benefits (e.g. land use) of fixed route mass transit (see Chapter 2). This will be important to retain, especially if there is a growth in apartment blocks which do not have parking such as the Gothenberg example (see Chapter 7) for whom public transport options are important. The land use implications (in terms of density and where people will live and work) must be given closer scrutiny since the initial transition to sharing under MaaS without autonomous vehicles, and the subsequent roll out with a significant amount of autonomous vehicles, will change the location landscape, with even more diverse origin–destination patterns and potentially longer commutes expected. The peak car debate contributes to the decline in vehicles by the young segment. The one instrument that can protect a preferred land use and activity profile for our cities in particular is pricing and funding reform (especially to impact parking and congestion), and even competition for (in contrast to in) the market, which may be the greatest disruptive instrument available to government to achieve its desired objectives. This should be central to the new societal-responsible governance model underpinning MaaS and an opportunity not to be missed. We discuss this in more detail in a later section, especially in the context of sharing (in Chapter 2), where research suggests that the majority of consumers are much more interested in the financial rewards offered by a changed regime than any of the other arguments associated with good citizenry, carbon footprints and the other feel good attributes.

## 8.4 Some big questions currently without clear answers

There are some big questions which need some response, since they will dictate what might be the appeal to improving the performance of the transport network and delivering increasing societal value, in contrast to potential benefits to specific customers that translate negligibly to broader societal benefits.

1. What does a MaaS broker or aggregator bring? They can work with an integrated digital platform and have subscribers better informed as to the modal choices available on a PAYG basis (customers can be routed to the modal service provider platforms to book or do it through the brokers platform). Alternatively the broker can offer subscription packages which enable a one stop way of accessing the services defined by the chosen package including variations at an agreed price (including discounts, credits and debits across subscription periods). As credit cards become increasingly used in every modal transaction, it is likely that the credit card supplier (i.e. a bank) might become the clearing house (or defector broker or aggregator) with

the convenience of use across many geographical jurisdictions, locally and internationally, and no likely discounts.[d] What is missing (although this can change over time) is the information on travel options via a trip planning App and a range of financial and non-financial incentives tied to specific modal activity. But regardless of what model is adopted, how might we identify the likely benefits to the wider society? Will it lead to a switch away from or towards specific mode usage that impacts in a positive or negative on traffic flows (congestion), air pollution, health, and enhanced greenhouse gas emissions (the latter highly correlated with car fuel efficiency and kilometres driven), and levels of government subsidy? What will government have to do to support a societally desirable outcome?

2. Will commercially focussed service providers be interested in MaaS when subsidised public transport is at the core of MaaS and is indeed central to government policies? Without public transport, what are we actually getting? How might a car-based solution be appealing to government? It would have to demonstrate an ability to significantly reduce the use of private vehicles (even if ownership of private vehicles remains at least in the short to medium term) without adding congestion and negative environmental externalities (although electric vehicles will be a positive input, especially if we overlook the life cycle emissions associated with EVs and just focus on tailpipe). It might help over-crowded public transport? It is however encouraging that Uber announced the rolling out of their first-ever integration with public transport information at the end of August 2019.[e] In partnership with the Regional Transportation District (RTD),[f] Uber riders in Denver are able to plan their public transport journey with real-time information and end-to-end directions right in the Uber app. This is not, however, a MaaS integration through a broker, but a clever initiative by Uber to try and capture the

---

d. The more this is moved towards bank cards, the more disadvantaged are the people, typically lower paid, who do not have bank accounts.

e. Uber announced in August 2019 that when customers in Sydney enter their destination in the app, 'public transport' will come up as an option. "Nearby transport hubs, timetable and pricing information will be displayed on the screen of their smart phone, making them even more aware of alternative options to using a car," he said. "The journey is no longer about a single mode of transport, it's about a combination of modes to get to you your destination in the most convenient way." Arrival and departure times for trains, buses, ferries, and the metro will be shown on the app. It will also include directions for those commuters wishing to walk to and from public transport. It provides a lot of hope, and quite a bit of hype. There is no payment integration piece at all. All they are doing is integrating GTFS data into their app so you can see that there may be a public transport option available for the same or similar route to you. If you then want to take that option it's up to you to make your way there (via Uber or not if it's a distance) and then pay by your own means (Opal or Contactless). There is no deep linking or integration as such. You cannot plan multi-modal journeys such as an Uber to the train station and then train into town. It is just public transport information only for reference purpose. It is a step in the right direction, but at this stage it is just a small step. https://www.dailymail.co.uk/news/article-7296281/The-change-coming-Uber-Customers-able-pay-public-transport-rideshare-app.html?ito=rss-flipboard.

f. http://www.rtd-denver.com/.

first and last mile part of a conventional public transport journey. Will this result in reduced walking (hence health implications) and even the demise of local bus services which often serve rail hubs?

3. Can MaaS contribute to a progressive move towards a sharing culture that might lead to a reduction of car use (per person and per vehicle) and a consequent improvement in traffic congestion, or might it go the other way? All the while car based offerings are relatively inexpensive (If people forget about the fixed costs, the private car has low marginal costs compared to any other mode except bike), given the perception of costs that influence travel such as operating costs of cars, (noting that tolls cannot be avoided by switching to a shared vehicle provided through a business such as car next door, GoGet and Uber), the ability to secure enough shared travel away from the private car is questionable, although shedding the second car may have real prospects. The Zurich evidence below paints a gloomy picture.
4. However, if AVs are introduced into the MaaS mix, both bus and car, with eliminated driver costs, are we likely to see a significant reduction in the price of travel by shared cars as well as reduced public transport fares, or will the labour savings be transferred into high profits and reduced subsidies, maintaining the price of travel? This will have a profound impact on the modal mix and whether traffic flows will improve or deteriorate. A switch out of public transport to car based services may well increase car kilometres even if there is an increase in passenger occupancy. One hope on the horizon is that AVs should enable lower fares and charges simply because of the anticipated growing competition amongst current and new entrant car-based services. However, economies of scale in the provision of autonomous taxi operations might lead to a quick (international) consolidation of autonomous taxi operators and thus limit competition or even enable pricing much above marginal costs (Reck and Axhausen, 2019c). Further research in Switzerland (Bösch et al., 2018) suggests that there will be a change in the mix of costs, resulting in a much less advantageous cost profile for AVs and car based share mobility. The media-friendly grey technology literature tends to lack the focus on human mobility with a real risk that we design locations (cities, regions) for new kinds of car-based services rather than for people. Policy action is required now to avoid dysfunction as a new norm.
5. Under MaaS, when the broker or investor in a broker business is an incumbent operator, are they likely to be biased in favour of their own services? Jittrapirom et al. (2017) discuss this in relation to a (government) public transport authority taking the role of a broker. We recognise that such conflicts of interest could exist between private operators and therefore believe a government broker is a particularly challenging proposition since they might not only lack the incentive to innovate but also cause a potential conflict of interest, especially in cases where both public and private operators exist. Conflicts of interest may also exist between multiple private operators. Increasingly amongst Western economies, governments are removing

themselves from a service provision role (but still providing subsidy through a contract) but rather being involved at arm's length only (Wong and Hensher, 2018).

6. How might equity considerations be integrated into such privately structured and financed MaaS mobility services with a profit orientation, for example, special tariffs for children, retired persons and socially deprived peoples? Given a concern about a social safety net, what role might 'light touch' regulation play in the case of an economically deregulated scenario and for a government broker and the potential of regulatory oversight with government defining the market's terms of operations like environmental considerations (vehicle emissions) and subsidies (means-tested for social inclusion)? Singapore is a good example of light regulation as a way of seeing how well the market can deliver outcomes aligned with government plans.
7. Given all these (and other) uncertainties, it is clearly timely for government to be pro-active and set out some aspirations that define the landscape that they will create and support in a market for MaaS. However, they should not interfere directly unless there is evidence of pending outcomes that are not in the interest of increasing the overall benefits to society (or at best not leading to a worsening situation). We see government's role as the more traditional one of a regulator but one that does a better job by offering incentives, financial and non-financial, to market participants so as to deliver outcomes aligned with the societal goals.

## 8.5 MaaS and potential implications for levels of road congestion

How might the commentary above relate to the future of road congestion reduction, something that is claimed to be a major benefit of an era of intelligent mobility? This appears to be premised on one crucial consideration, the success in moving society to a regime of collaboration and connectivity, initially without autonomous vehicles, but subsequently with such vehicles. Collaboration is often associated with the sharing economy which can take at least two paths—shared and pooled (see Wong et al., 2020 and Chapter 2), or without others, for a particular 'point to point' or 'point via another point to point' trip. It is far from clear how much of the congestion challenge can be resolved through greater sharing of private cars (no matter whether they are autonomous or not), increasing occupancy, assuming a constant number of person trips. However, sharing of private cars could lead to increased trips overall through a higher number of trips per vehicle, and to greater congestion if the number of trips overall goes up.

The limited evidence on smart transition (predominantly associated with smart apps, opportunities to ride hail and dispose of a car), is simultaneously creating the promise of a system that can reduce demand (and hence congestion), but at the same time fulfilling previously unmet demand and creating new demand (e.g. Truong et al., 2017). Smart transition can, in principle, move society to a rentier model (Docherty et al., 2018) where the incentive for the mobility service provider is to generate as much mobility as possible (i.e. trips and kilometres) to maximise returns on capital (Karlsson et al., 2016). MaaS is a sub-player in the AV evolution, but clearly autonomous mobility will impact on the cost of transport and hence the MaaS subscription price if labour costs of taxi and bus drivers, for example, are eliminated; however Bösch et al. (2018) suggest that some costs will be saved but others will be introduced to shared asset providers, closing the gap for the full set of cost outlays (see below for details). We can expect capital costs will be higher initially and it remains an open question whether this will work out as an overall reduction.

What little evidence there is at present, based on simulated scenarios of futures, is informative, to some degree, but can it be relied on? We draw in part on the overview of this theme in Hensher (2017, 2018b). Studies of particular interest include one from the ITF/OECD, one from University of California Davis (Clewlow and Mishra, 2017), a recent one from Switzerland by Hörl et al. (2019) and a simulation undertaken by Hannon et al. of McKinsey (2019). The first two studies say nothing about the impact of autonomous cars or indeed any renewed future role of public transport and MaaS (except on demand buses)—they focus primarily on shared cars with a driver, the latter likely to be the basis of car travel for at least the next 20 years. If we can identify car ownership and use strategies that are effective, we may have the catalyst for a successful MaaS program.

The ITF/OECD (2017) modelled the impact of replacing all car and bus trips in a city with mobility provided through fleets of shared vehicles. They found that if all individually-owned private cars were removed from the city with shared vehicles only, there would be a significant drop in the number of vehicles required to service overall mobility demand, resulting also in greater equity of service across the city. However, the findings suggested an increase in car kilometres of 6.4% per day. When the assumption of perfect conditions breaks down, and 50% of private cars are assumed to remain, the system performance deteriorates with up to 90.9% more kilometres driven per day. This does not sound like a congestion buster? (Hensher, 2018a,b). This suggests more congestion, although the congestion levels may be more predictable (non-random) with improved reliability, and maybe a lower value of travel time savings and reliability willingness to pay. This study only forecasts a minor increase in travel times by having distributors and local streets absorb much of this increase—thereby ignoring the road hierarchy and bringing associated externalities.

The same study also investigated through simulation in Lisbon, Portugal scenarios where shared mobility is delivered by a shared taxi fleet of six-seat vehicles offering on-demand, door-to-door shared rides in conjunction with a fleet of eight-person and 16-person mini-buses (taxi-buses) that serve pop-up stops on demand and provide transfer-free rides. They tested scenarios where car owners could use their car for one, 2 or 3 days each working week, which corresponds to having 20%, 40%, and 60% of trips currently made by private car continuing to be made by that same mode.[g] The findings suggest that allowing for 60% of the private cars[h] brings almost no reduction in congestion, thus producing no support for a political argument in favour of introduction of shared mobility solutions. However, assuming that each private car is allowed 2 days per week of operation, this reduces vehicle kilometres at the peak hour by 13%, which is claimed to 'essentially makes congestion disappear'. The reduction of parking space needs is also visible (see Rantasila, 2015) and it is suggested that this would allow a benefit for pedestrians (and cyclists) in many parts of the city (assuming this space is not used for other endeavours).

Clewlow and Mishra (2017) presents findings from a travel and residential survey in seven major US cities (Boston, Chicago, Los Angeles, New York, San Francisco/Bay Area, Seattle, and Washington, DC), undertaken from 2014 to 2016, with a representative sample of urban and suburban populations. 4094 completed responses were collected, with 2217 from respondents residing in dense, urban neighbourhoods and 1877 from more suburban locations.[i] They show that directionally, based on mode substitution and ride-hailing frequency of use data, ride-hailing is likely to contribute to growth in vehicle miles travelled (VMT) in the major cities represented in this study.[j]

Of especial interest is the finding that ride-hailing users, on average, do not have noticeably fewer vehicles than their non-ride hailing counterparts, but have more vehicles than those who only use transit. While some amount of ride-hailing users reduce the miles that they personally drive, and 9% disposed of a vehicle, these miles return in the form of miles travelled in a ride-hailing vehicle. They found a strong correlation between increasing ride-hailing use and increasing rates of vehicle reduction. The reduction of vehicle ownership is primarily of value insomuch as it reduces total vehicle miles travelled (VMT), although the reduction in the number of vehicles in the system is encouraging.

---

g. A related issue and cautionary evidence is what happened when Athens allowed vehicles to be driven every other day (odd and even registration plates), albeit for pollution control. The outcome was an increase in the number of vehicles as households moved to buy more vehicles so they had a permitted vehicle for each day or they went for one of the exempted vehicles. It is not easy to stop people once they have a car, so reducing the number of vehicles overall has to be where we start.

h. The study found that if conventional cars were replaced with driverless cars that take either a single passenger at a time or several passengers together, as long as half of travel is still carried out by conventional cars, total vehicle miles travelled will increase from 30% to 90%, suggesting that even widespread sharing of driverless cars would mean greater congestion for a long time.

i. The authors correctly express concern about many other studies in the USA that have self-selection bias in that their samples are from locations where car ownership is typically much lower than normal, and the socio economic characteristics and density of the built environment are more supportive of not owning a car and using taxi-like services.

j. A recent US Department of Transport study of autonomous car sharing in Chicago predicted a 70% worsening of traffic congestion. 30% is the cited figure for San Francisco. Referenced in McCabe (2017) video talk.

What is currently unclear is the net vehicle miles travelled (VMT) adjustment due to the introduction of ride-hailing—has it gone up or down? And what are the likely longer-term impacts of these services, including the future of mainstream regular public transport, as ride-hailing companies operate a commercial model with a usage maximisation objective? Some ride sharing schemes are taxi replacement services which may involve additional vehicle kilometres in the pick up and drop off process and become substitutes to walking and public transport. Graehler et al. (2019) in a study of the main USA cities concluded that when Uber and Lyft enter a city, the app-based taxis decrease rail ridership by 1.29% per year and decrease bus ridership by 1.7%. The effect is cumulative with Uber and Lyft having reduced bus ridership in San Francisco a staggering 12.7% since they entered the market in 2010. Increased public transport service could counter the trend, but it would not be enough to make up for the decline. Graehler et al. (2019) estimated that San Francisco would have to increase bus service by 25% to offset the effects of Uber and Lyft in depressing ridership.

Furthermore, a recent Fehr and Peers (2019) study commissioned by Uber and Lyft estimates that additional miles driven while a driver waits for a ride request or is driving to pick up a passenger accounts for 40% of TNC vehicle miles in the Chicago metro region. This behaviour is particularly concerning, as it is adding to overall congestion while providing no tangible transportation value to residents. Between 2015 and 2018, the annual number of TNC trips in Chicago has grown 271%, and the TNP miles travelled with passengers have increased 344%. A 2018 Chicago Transit Authority (CTA) ridership survey revealed that TNCs are substituting for public transport, with overall losses between 2015 and 2018 of up to 8%. Of customers who use TNCs, 48% would have taken CTA if TNCs did not exist, and 31% said they take TNCs more since riding CTA less. Approximately 26 miles of road space is occupied in the downtown area by TNPs during a typical evening rush period (City of Chicago 2019). Every rider shifting from a bus or a train to a TNC service adds to congestion and mobile source emissions. The City of Chicago is undertaking in 2019–20 as congestion pricing study to try and tame congestion, which in large measure is growing under the influence of ridesharing and ridehailing.

There is nothing in this evidence to inform us about the role of autonomous vehicles and implications on MaaS. Whereas the studies reported above are related to driver based cars, a study by MacKenzie et al. (2016) estimates that autonomous cars can cut the cost of travel by as much as 80%, which in turn drives up kilometres travelled by 60%.[k] Clearly the price elasticity is at work and really does matter. MacKenzie suggests that "You are talking about a technology that promises to make travel safer, cheaper, and more convenient. And when you do that, you'd better expect people are going to do more of it."

Maciejewski and Bischoff (2018) investigate the influence of shared autonomous vehicle fleets replacing private cars by providing a taxi-like service but

k. To realise this savings, significant investment is required up front with a long term ROI model.

at a cost similar a private car being driven. MATSim, a multi-agent transport simulation platform for the city area of Berlin was used to investigate the levels of traffic congestion under scenarios that vary the replacement rate of private driver cars with shared autonomous cars under various assumptions of road capacity (vehicles per hour) increase. They use a congestion index defined as a delay ratio (the average travel delay (i.e. actual-free flow travel time)/average flow (uncongested) travel time) to assess the impact on traffic performance, and conclude that without any increase in road capacity level, the delay ratio will worsen (contributed to by empty vehicle trips and induced demand) and that after a 50% increase in capacity, we start to see a reduction of 0.5–2 absolute percentage points in the delay ratio depending on the replacement rate varying from 20% to 100%. The empty vehicle trips are being compensated for by improved road capacity due to efficient spacing of vehicles. Given a doubling of capacity, this range increases from 0.9 to 3.7, respectively, for 20%, 40%, 60%, 80%, and 100% replacement of the private driver cars. These simulated findings suggest is that the impact on congestion is dependent on whether shared autonomous cars can deliver greater road capacity as a consequence of a more efficient contribution to traffic flow, assisted in large part by reduced gaps between following vehicles and improved performance through intersections.

Bösch et al. (2018) and Hörl et al. (2019) undertook simulation work in Switzerland on the possible impact of autonomous mobility services, and provide evidence which questions the extent to which driverless cars and shared vehicles, even under MaaS, will indeed be financially appealing as well as reducing car kilometres. The Zurich study offers great insights which have a portability to many developed societies. The authors compared a base case (business as usual in terms of modal mix) with five scenarios for private car, private autonomous vehicle, autonomous taxi, and public transport. The scenarios are:

1. Base case, but with a 50% fare reduction for public transport
2. Adding AV taxis to the current mix
3. Adding AV taxis to the current mix but with a 50% price reduction for public transport
4. Adding private AV to the current mix
5. Adding private AV to the current mix but with a 50% price reduction for public transport

They initially calculated the expected cost per passenger kilometre (cost/pkm) for each mode under current occupancy and found that the passenger cost varies from 0.47CHF[1]/pkm for private car to 0.43CHF/pkm for shared private car, 0.43CHF/pkm for taxi and $0.25CHF/pkm for city bus. Approximately 0.17CHF/pkm (or 36.1%) of private car cost is a variable cost (mainly fuel); in contrast the other modes are all a price of service. Importantly, the switch from a private driver car to an autonomous car changes the mix of full costs/pkm with

1. On Franc is equivalent to 1 US dollar as at May 2019.

a higher incidence of depreciation (48% compared to 42%) but a reduction in fuel costs (down to 10% from 12%).

However, when we move to a non-owned shared mode such as the autonomous 'taxi', we see a massive reassignment of costs away from salaries (88%) to cleaning (29%), overhead and vehicle operation (20%), fuel (13%) and depreciation (18%). Maintenance and wear and tear also increases from a few percent points to over 11%. Although the cost/pkm will play an important role, and we do not expect large savings in moving from private car use to shared cars, when the number of vehicles on the road and the costs are accounted for, the authors find that switching to AVs will significantly increase vehicle kilometres travelled (VKT). They suggest a 50% increase, on average, of VKT, and nearly a 40% increase in number of vehicle trips. Even allowing for some errors in key assumptions, these findings are counter to what we hear in the popular press, in particular, on the benefits of AVs, linked to shared cars such as taxis, especially claims of reduced traffic congestion.

Hannon et al. (2019) modelled, in the USA, short (fewer than 2km), medium (2–10km), and long (more than ten kilometres) trips, differentiating between trips within the CBD and trips to and from the city and the suburbs. They also simulated the trade-offs that people make such as choosing between a more convenient but more expensive autonomous shuttle and a less convenient but lower priced bus, suggesting how these decisions could affect congestion in 2030. Their business as usual scenario, in the US context, paints a bleak picture—transport demand is likely to increase in line with population growth (about 15% by 2030), and greenhouse-gas (GHG) emissions could rise proportionally. City residents would travel in essentially the same ways as currently, and private cars would continue to account for up to 35% of passenger-kilometres. Average travel times are predicted to increase by 15% because capacity would be constrained. In the US, and we suspect elsewhere in western societies with car domination, without substantial change, this is the likely scenario: few cities, even the largest, have comprehensive plans that consider new and forthcoming technologies. An unconstrained autonomy scenario in which autonomous-driving technology advances (including shared AVs and rob-taxis), but regulators and governments do not keep up, suggests that such AVs become an attractive alternative to private-vehicle ownership, with the cost per mile of riding in a robo-taxi being about the same as the cost of owning a moderately priced private vehicle (see Zurich evidence which is similar), and that travellers could adopt them for individual or shared use for about 35% of their travel by 2030. They suggest that "the partial displacement of fixed-route buses by robo-taxis with flexible routing would increase the share of point-to-point trips, reducing waiting and walking times between transfers. If the robo-taxis were electric, GHG emissions would fall and air quality improve" (but the lifecycle emissions need recognition to account for the source of energy such as coal fired or green energy sources). Congestion, however, is predicted to not improve compared to the baseline, and it is expected to get worse. "The average time for a private car trip could increase as an increased convenience of robo-taxis draws more users onto the roads. Other travellers, anxious to avoid the crowded roads, could pack into trains. In all, we estimate that average travel times would be 15 percent higher compared with today's baseline scenario" (page 6).

Finally, a seamless mobility scenario is worth promoting, akin to the MaaS aspiration, would encourage the use of shared AVs through regulation and incentives, making it possible for residents to 'mix and match' rail transit and low-cost, point-to-point autonomous travel in robo-taxis, autonomous shuttles, and autonomous buses easily. The McKinsey analysis suggests that pooled AV shuttles could take 25% of the market (twice as much as in the unconstrained-autonomy scenario), and private cars and privately used robo-taxis could provide about 30% of passenger-kilometres in 2030, compared with 35% for private cars today. The difference includes intelligent traffic systems, advanced rail signalling, and connectivity-enabled predictive maintenance to boost network reliability and improving the performance of public transport in terms of availability, affordability, efficiency, convenience, and sustainability. They suggest that this could accommodate up to 30% more passenger-kilometres to 35% less per trip (affordability), increase the number of point-to-point trips by 50% (convenience), and, if AVs are electric, lower GHG emissions by up to 85% (sustainability).

Much of the simulated evidence is couched in terms of the introduction of autonomous vehicles and shared mobility (as if it will be easy to achieve). What does this all mean for MaaS? Using Zurich as an example, currently the variable costs of a private car trip in Zurich are 0.17CHF/pkm, and with typical occupancy of 1 or 2 person for most trips; this will always be considerably less expensive than the shared vehicle scenario. Given that the majority of motorists ignore the fixed cost when choosing to make a trip (focussing only on the marginal cost of the trip), it will be necessary to promote the full cost savings by relinquishing car ownership to make the shared car mode attractive in a MaaS package for individuals (or even households) who own one or more cars. Indeed the research by Ho et al. (2018, and Chapter 5) suggests that this segment of the population who use their own car extensively are unlikely to be interested in a MaaS bundled offering. Hence we have a significant challenge in establishing the appeal of MaaS (financially at least as well as convenience of specific modes) unless we can reduce private car ownership. MaaS may be best seen as a way of offering a plan for only a subset of travel activity, whereby the private car use is partially integrated into a shared vehicle offering while much of such travel (e.g. out of town and weekends) remains as is currently undertaken.

This hints at a possibility for many years to come that MaaS without any reform incentives to deal with use of the private car, will be no more than a niche product in terms of its impact of societal goals. There is no guarantee under any scenario that it will be scalable to become a mainstream mobility model. One reform that can help (in a very limited way initially) is road pricing reform built into the MaaS price as simply a component of such a price without any explicit reference to road pricing, which we would argue will become even more important if MaaS bundling is to be an attractive non-niche consideration. Such a pricing reform, for equity reasons, must be introduced throughout the road use environment and not simply 'hidden' within a MaaS package offer. This will remain a huge challenge for most governments who generally oppose road pricing reform (often without understanding the potential for buy in and votes from the population of voters—see Hensher and Mulley, 2014). We have shown in previous chapters some of the challenges in a fully specified MaaS subscription program with a mix of modes where some are currently subsidised and the likelihood that government may have to invest in some way in a successful MaaS product, which naturally risks a conflict of interest and a move to competition for the market in contrast to competition in the market. It is unlikely that government would be prepared to subsidise all entrants into the MaaS market, as affirmed by the Senior Minister of State in Singapore when he said at the Thredbo 16 conference (August 26, 2019) that government will continue to only subsidise the mainstream public transport input into a MaaS plan and has no intentions to support commercial car-based ride sharing participants in the MaaS mix.

As interest in shared mobility grows, facilitated in part by MaaS, with evidence thus far mainly focussing on switching between a privately owned car usage model to a car-based shared vehicle model, a broader question of interest becomes the mix of modes that will (might) be offered through the subscription plans that are starting to enter the market, or being actively considered, by mobility service providers (and how these ought to be allocated including the link with modal efficiency and land use—see Chapter 2). When autonomous vehicles are added into the mix in future years, and there is greater acceptance of sharing non-owned cars (in contrast to sharing existing public transport),[m] there are real prospects of significant changes in the performance of the transport network, especially roads.[n]

Pangbourne et al. (2020) make a very important point. MaaS rhetoric promises unfettered freedom and instantaneous mobility to individuals within the context of a finite transport network. MaaS Global advertises its application as 'mobility on a whim', promoting directly this idea of individual unfettered freedom. However, this promise of freedom is on a collision trajectory with a challenge of simultaneous demand for travel in a transport network with a finite capacity, in which the main transport policy objectives are to reduce congestion (and the impacts that has on emissions, journey times and urban quality of life) and to reduce greenhouse gas emissions and air pollution. By modelling MaaS packages on those used in telecoms, the impression is given that any desired

m. This also implies a greater level of personal intimacy—how acceptable this is has yet to be adequately tested.

n. All this depends on the pricing model. One of the serious impediments to sharing is the way in which the private car is a low marginal cost mode, especially in comparison to shared cars, public transport etc. MaaS relies on people being prepared to understand the full costs of car ownership.

trip can have a door-to-door solution supplied on demand. "Here, a fundamental error is made, as the transport network has a finite capacity, and thus everyone cannot travel at once" (c.f. Pangbourne et al., 2018). The commercial imperative of the car-based suppliers under MaaS and indeed even as a stand-alone PAYG provider, creates challenges for government in how it might contain growth that is profit-centred and has no respect for the creation of negative externalities. A serious review of the regulatory setting is in order, earlier than later, to anticipate some of these downside societal impacts, which are likely to be more about AVs than MaaS.

## 8.6 MaaS and the future of conventional public transport

The question remains—how much of the kilometres travelled on the roads by shared vehicles will be car based and result in significant reductions in conventional public transport use (Hensher, 2017)? Will this also make traffic congestion worse, even if more predictable, but in a safer mobility environment, or not? Maybe the advent of the small bus will become nothing more than a higher vehicle occupancy shared car, which may be a good thing and it is almost inevitable that it will become the bus mode under a demand-responsive system[o]?

There is limited evidence that public transport use is being reduced by the business models of ride-hailing brokers like Uber or Lyft that make impulsive door-to-door service exceptionally convenient (Clewlow and Mishra, 2017). Having shared vehicles available through MaaS could magnify this effect, leaving high-capacity, fixed route modes in the cold. This would make the widespread adoption of shared self-driving vehicles much easier. The spatial land use effects of this technological development are also in need of thorough investigation to ensure that further sprawl does not result. Alternatively, this could spawn a new generation of attractive first and last mile solutions (1LM) which sees traditional public transport operators moving in to, or at least arranging, 1LM provision?

As the multi-modal brokerage model is typically promoted as based on incorporating car-based solutions that provide more options for non-car owners, such as car-share or taxi, the obvious convenience of these for door-to-door service will undoubtedly impact on the use of traditional public transport,

o. An important question is to what extent conventional fixed route timetabled bus services will be replaced by demand responsive bus services (DRTs), and importantly what this will mean for future large bus needs and contracting models. DRTs can be built into existing contracts (as variations) under tendered or negotiated contracts; however the author argues that DRTs should be part of an economically deregulated market, at least initially, as a way of encouraging competition. If as might be expected in some jurisdictions, the DRT appeal is in replacing regular public transport (RPT) services with DRTs because of the thinness of the market, then a natural monopoly setting may evolve which suggests that a single operator makes sense. But this does not have to be the incumbent RPT provider, especially where the buses are small and not available under a shared cost model with the incumbent RPT services.

particularly fixed-route scheduled buses, yet public transport is the backbone of MaaS [despite for example the Finnish approach (see Chapter 3) failing to engage public transport operators adequately]. Whereas the public transport system is required to serve all of society, the mobility companies are private as is their rich accumulation of data about ridership take up and pricing response, with shared mobility often seen as blurring the line between public and private transport. This raises the inevitable question of the role of subsidy (in general or for special groups on equity grounds), and how this can be handled within a full economically deregulated shared mobility setting[p]? One doubts that governments will want to offer such a subsidy across the board, although it is noteworthy than many if not most have been doing this for many years with regular public transport services; however the difference is that they either own such services through a public monopoly model or support public transport services through an contract regime which is either negotiated or tendered, with a recognition of a spatial natural monopoly setting. This does not mean that all service providers may enter and receive a subsidy entitlement, which will lead to chaos in forward budgeting of governments (and predictable court action when governments fall short in subsidy funding given their budget commitment). A possible way forward is presented in Section 8.10.

MaaS (Australia),[q] amongst others however, argues that without public transport at the centre of MaaS complemented with on-demand transport covering the first and last mile, as stated above, it will not succeed in delivering mobility solutions that are more than simply commercial propositions designed to make money for car-based services, and will not deliver on the goals and expectations of government and society more broadly. There is no reference however to the type of public transport and whether we are moving to a low capacity flexible small bus scenario that has the potential to detract from the high capacity needs of large cities. It is a balancing act—optimising the supply and demand chains of the transport services without compromising the intended goals and objectives. This will require all transport providers and MaaS operators to collaborate transparently (the commercial model yet to be contested/trialled). This creates a real challenge for a number of the players in this space who have a vehement interest in a car-based solution, but who are reticent about joining forces in a subscription plan with conventional public transport modes, which they believe will be loss making. This raises important questions about

p. In some countries (e.g. the UK), there seems to be a distinction whereby concessions such as older people fares are paid back to the operators in full (after a deduction for taking account of cheaper fares leading to extra journeys) which are perhaps the equity grounds type of 'subsidy', and the more general subsidy because Revenues are less than Costs. There are also 'commercial' type fares where discounted fares are offered such as to the unemployed and students on the basis that they will make more journeys as a result.

q. We thank Hany Eldaly [Managing Director and Co-founder of MaaS (Australia)] for discussions on this theme and the commitment that MaaS (Australia) has to ensuring public transport is in the mix (MaaS Australia).

how the packages can be designed to allow for internal cross subsidy[r] and still deliver an acceptable return on investment, while at the same time not requiring government subsidy, and hence allowing the MaaS model to be delivered under a truly free market setting.[s] MaaS (Australia) envisions that mobility ecosystem benefits will be realised by establishing a trusted partnership between the public and private sector and unlocking the access to data.

The 'limited' evidence as presented above suggests that if the cost of mobility drops under a CCS model (after accounting for removing ownership and hence costs, and eventually the widespread presence of autonomous cars), then we should expect more road based travel (i.e. increased passenger kilometres), but what is unclear is whether the move to sharing will reduce vehicle kilometres—it may be fewer vehicles doing more kilometres since they will be on the road for many more hours (being more temporally efficient) than the privately owned vehicle. If you believe some pundits, this is the model that will evolve as the business model of the growing number of competing ride sharing and ride sourcing services, forcing prices down[t] and increasing the hours that any one car has to be on the road to recover the commercial objective (aligned with arguments given by Hollands, 2015). Conventional public transport needs to heed this warning, as does government, given an obligation to reduce traffic congestion and emissions.

Part of the solution in protecting the future of public transport may rest with future government funding models, especially if the current provider side subsidy regime for public transport is replaced with a user-side controlled scheme[u] that gives users control on where subsidy is allocated given what public transport trips they choose. This will also engender a competitive process as mobility providers compete to attract customers, and hence is expected to result in a much more efficient level of subsidy provision and hopefully modal mix of offers. There is a proviso, however that package providers do not move in to 'help' clients spend their money and of course taking a sizeable cut themselves.

If it results in reduced demand for public transport services and increased demand for shared car services, government will have to decide how much of conventional public transport should continue to be provided, both in the MaaS package and separate from such packages. It is likely that conventional rail

r. This is the basis of an ITLS study on community transport in NSW (Mulley et al., 2019).

s. There is a lot of value add from the data collected by apps; hence if this has real value in a MaaS context, then this value can be used to deflate the MaaS package price. In the UK, although less in Australia, for example, there is a lot of advertising around leasing of cars (for individuals, not necessarily firms). These are all inclusive lease prices (car, repairs, maintenance, and in some cases road tax). The more this becomes the way in which people buy their cars, the more the MaaS package will look less expensive as the marginal cost of the car use will be including all the costs rather than just fuel.

t. Including low labour costs for drivers, which is a criticism of many Uber services; and with driverless cars in the future these costs will be even lower (possibly halved), making car based travel very popular at the risk of a future role for public transport.

u. As is potentially going to happen for with the community transport sector in New South Wales.

(and bus rapid transit) will remain as the backbone of the transport network (even if scaled back where services are no longer justified), but the rest of the public transport system (essentially bus based and increasingly demand responsive) might be folded into the new mobility model. With autonomous buses, we might also expect a reduction in the cost of travel unless the gains are taken up by government in reducing subsidy while maintaining fares.

A recent example of such a bus is 'Auto Pilot', a self-driving bus project spearheaded by operator Nobina, launched on 24 January 2018 a first of its kind in Scandinavia (see http://www.truckandbus.net.au/swede-self-drive-mini-busses-hit-roads-stockholm/, Accessed 12 September 2019). The minibuses each carry 11 passengers (six seated and no steering wheel) use LiDAR technology ('Light Detection and Ranging'), an array of sensors that enable self-driving vehicles to 'see' what is around them so they can safely navigate roads. At present, in the one kilometre trial the bus is staffed with a 'host', who keeps watch over the vehicle and closes the door once all passengers have boarded.

In summary, will MaaS schemes be dominated by car based offers? What does it mean for conventional public transport, and government's response to a car dominated solution? Does it matter what modes are in the mix? Maybe in the future the autonomous car in a safe platoon will act like public transport and so does it not matter what the mode is? Issues of public acceptability will be important here and the type of journey lengths envisaged. This, however, is likely to be less spatially efficient than purpose-built large vehicles (and higher cost autonomous or not, being unable to reap economies of scale from shared components-engines, etc.) and possibly sabotage many of the intrinsic benefits (e.g. land use) of fixed route mass transit. The land use implications (in terms of density and where people will live and work) must be given closer scrutiny since the initial transition to sharing under MaaS without autonomous vehicles, and the subsequent roll out with a significant amount of autonomous vehicles, will change the location landscape, with even more diverse origin–destination patterns and longer commutes expected. The one instrument that can protect a preferred land use and activity profile for our cities in particular is pricing and funding reform, which may be the greatest disruptive instrument available to government to achieve its desired objectives. This should be central to the new governance model and an opportunity not to be missed.

## 8.7 The multimodal conundrum for MaaS

MaaS is promoted as a multimodal single platform integration. While attractive in principle, it is far from clear what the implications of this might mean for performance of the transport network. We can draw on the theoretical literature on first best pricing in economics to highlight some of the potential downside (and upside) consequences of MaaS.

Beginning with Tabuchi (1993), he considers the properties of the bimodal equilibrium between private and public transport under different pricing regimes. Instead of assuming static congestion for the car, Tabuchi assumes a dynamic bottleneck that arises when the flow of cars exceeds the capacity of the road (Vickrey, 1969). With a highly stylised model that ignores travel time as a cost for bus [assumed to have its own dedicated corridor as in Bus Rapid Transit (BRT)] and rail users and capacity constraints, Tabuchi shows for rail public transport only that as demand grows it is more attractive to have a rail based alternative competing with cars, due to economies of scale in the former and congestion externality in the latter mode. Subsequently, Danielis and Marcucci (2002) extended Tabuchi's two-mode approach to include budget constraints on rail operations, and Huang (2002) introduced a stochastic (logit) modal choice model. The contrary argument is that if a shared mobility solution evolves for all modes (notably car-based), then we might anticipate an improvement in road congestion (a relaxation of the capacity constraint, at least initially) in mixed traffic lanes and hence public transport becomes less attractive.

A different approach was presented by Kraus and Yoshida (2002) who adopted the highway bottleneck model of Vickrey (1969) for the modelling of rail commuting, assuming that users arrive at stations at the same time as trains do. They show that the average users cost increases with demand, i.e. the opposite result to the decreasing average users cost of all of the Mohring's type of models, a result explained in part because the length of the peak period is not fixed, such that as demand grows, the peak period enlarges (i.e. some passengers take earlier trains), which increases the schedule delay cost at the destination, given that the desired arrival time is fixed. Kraus and Yoshida (2002) provide an important insight into how the scheduling considerations of users affect average costs of travelling; however their approach is less appropriate for modelling high frequency services, in which it has been empirically observed that passengers arrive at stations or bus stops randomly at a more or less constant rate. Therefore the waiting time at stops exists even if the capacity constraint is not binding, and consequently, the economies of scale induced by increasing frequency should be accounted for. A switch under MaaS to car-based offerings can take pressure off a crowded (i.e. congested) public transport network, and as long as we can obtain reduced car use through sharing, there are likely to be positive societal and user benefits.

Not only are additional benefits for users associated with a more frequent public transport service, costs could also be incurred if providing extra bus kilometres has a negative effect on speeds for both buses and cars. In this case, an increase in frequency can augment total average cost, and Mohring's (1972) scale economies argument for bus subsidies could no longer apply, as shown in Mohring (1983). Nonetheless, there are a number of strategies that can be used to make bus transport more efficient, in order to minimise or avoid the congestion related to high bus frequency. An example is the provision of faster fare collection systems at bus stops, as analysed by Tirachini and Hensher (2011) who, using an optimisation model for congested bus corridors, show that increasing total costs are observed for high demand services if passengers are allowed to pay fares on-board buses, and frequency is over 120 veh/h, but decreasing total costs are still obtained even for higher frequencies when the fare payment is performed off-board buses. With electronic cashless ticketing and tap on and off (now enhanced by the ability to use bank cards) this concern will diminish. All in all, MaaS may impact on public transport through reduced use (switching to multiple occupancy or sharing car-based offers) but may also benefit public transport where it is at carrying capacity as appears to be a common phenomenon in many large cities where crowding on public transport is a bad as congestion on the roads. The net cffect of subsidy is unclear other than the fare box contribution will most likely decrease. Mohring's economies of scale argument under shared multimodal mobility may be on shaky ground, even though we believe that mainstream public transport is highly likely to continue to operate within MaaS and/or outside of MaaS.

## 8.8 Health

The current approach of packaging by the month (as with mobile phone contracts) with the only alternative being PAYG (which typically have higher unit costs), is poorly designed to support the established knowledge that individuals should undertake a minimum level of physical activity each day or across the week to maintain their physical and mental well-being. Healthier options, such as walking or cycling, are not prominent in MaaS products which are predicated on monetisable modes, and which also obscure the unit costs of public transport, although the arrival of bike sharing schemes offers possibilities to remedy this. For many people, the efficient way to achieve minimum recommended levels of physical activity might be to switch some shorter journeys to active travel (walking or cycling), or alight from the bus one stop earlier! Having a MaaS package might result in a neglect of these minimum amounts of active travel through its door-to-door promise. The research by Mulley and Ho (2017), however, suggests this is not the best way—the better advice is to walk to more destinations.

Health benefits can occur at a number of levels in terms of potential reduction in walking as people switch to first and last mile motorised modes. If we can reduce private car ownership then we might see a sharing of cars to reduce emissions, which has a positive impact on air quality (hence interaction between emissions and health). However it is unclear how much of that travel replaces public transport use, which is a negative outcome in terms of emissions unless the future car-based offerings are driven by green energy, even allowing for the fact that buses are slowing moving to electrification.

An interesting potentially positive unintended consequence of MaaS when there is a switch away from large buses in busy metropolitan areas is a reduction in crowding or an avoidance of it when sharing a car (where a seat must be guaranteed) or a small bus where standing may not be permitted. This could mean more vehicle kilometres in the road environment but an avoidance of discomfort associated with crowding. This has potential health benefits when the spread of colds and flu is allowed for in crowded buses and trains and close proximity to other passengers which has a higher likelihood of spreading with a greater volume of people in a vehicle.

The impacts of the crowding phenomenon on passengers' health and well-being is extremely complex to analyse. Attached to the discomfort of sharing a limited space with several people are multiple physical and psychological factors that intervene in the perception of crowding and its effects. Amongst the reasons for the aversion of public transport users to waiting and travelling in crowded conditions, we can name increased anxiety (Cheng, 2010), stress and feeling of exhaustion (Lundberg, 1976; Mohd Mahudin et al., 2011), perceptions of risk to personal safety and security (Cox et al., 2006; Katz and Rahman, 2010),[v] feelings of invasion of privacy (Wardman and Whelan, 2011), propensity to arrive late at work (Mohd Mahudin et al., 2011), and the difficulty of using buses and trains with increased physical frailty (Xenia and Tyler, 2018).

Besides anxiety and stress, other symptoms have also been found to be related to high levels of crowding. Using data from Kuala Lumpur, Mohd Mahudin et al. (2011) found that commuters with greater levels of stress and exhaustion attributed to crowding, reported more somatic symptoms like headaches, tension, stiff muscles and sleeplessness. The propensity to be late at work is found to be a spillover effect of rail crowding, in cases in which passengers have to let an overcrowded train pass (or decide to do so in hope that the next train will be less crowded, sometimes unsure of the exact time the next train will arrive).

## 8.9 Greater government influence in MaaS provision

An important issue is the extent to which we can rely on the market to deliver desirable societal outcomes and hence a recognition that the public sector may have to increase its direct involvement and possibly enlarge the scope of public transport authorities (Smith et al., 2018a), something which we commonly observe in a number of European countries, although not all (for example in the UK they have given up on public transport authorities) and something that many pundits remain unconvinced about such centralised control. This might entail the public sector adopting the MaaS integrator and MaaS operator roles in addition to its regulatory and planning roles, driving MaaS developments by orchestrating and funding development, implementation and operation. Importantly this does not strictly mean that public transport authorities internally adopt the new roles, they could direct or control MaaS developments by procuring development and operation of MaaS integrator and MaaS operator services from private actors (i.e. according to the current division of roles as purchaser and

v. Cox et al. (2006) suggest that the relationship between crowding and personal security may be contingent upon crime type, as a crowded environment may discourage muggings, but at the same time make easier pick pocketing and verbal and physical abuse.

service providers). The rationale for such engagement of the public sector can be aligned with at least three objectives. The first objective is to contribute to societal good through facilitating a modal shift from private cars to 'servitised' modes (e.g. Sochor et al., 2016, 2018; Sochor and Sarasini, 2017). The second objective is a recognition that public transport is the backbone of MaaS as it is "the only superior alternative to individual private car use able to fulfil the lion's share of trips" (UITP, 2016b, p. 3 and 2016a). Thirdly, public and private actors might have conflicting goals, notably a private MaaS operator objective to maximise revenue by promoting as many and as expensive trips as possible. The public sector however would tend to strive towards reducing the amount of travel, given accessibility needs, and increasing the modal share of PT, which is an product less expensive modal option compared to, for example car sharing modes. Thus public control is arguably desired to steer the development towards societal good. Moreover, some contend that the business opportunity in adopting the new roles in the MaaS ecosystem are limited or non-existent, due to small margins within the sector, large administration costs, and a lack of proof of the end-users' willingness to pay (Smith et al., 2017). As discussed in the next section, public funding might be needed to catalyse the development and diffusion of MaaS, but only if there is a demonstrable public benefit. There could instead be a non-transport cross-subsidy strategy which is often used in many expensive transport settings, the best example being high speed rail in Japan here hotel and retail investments cross-subsidise the rail system. We might anticipate this happening over time with MaaS as it matures with discounts at retail outlets and points to spend on sustainable activities.

A growing concern is the current structure of the mobility ecosystem. A Siemens in Germany concluded that, even though many efforts have been made to integrate and digitalize existing transportation services, the reality is, "...we still have hundreds of digital '*Mobility island systems*' and in some cases many analog problems were just translated to digital ones" (Guilarte, 2019). As more service providers enter the market, the risk of a growing lack of integration with unified user accounts increases. Governments in particular are anticipated to be concerned and not supportive of this development since it will haemorrhage the opportunity to developing a system wide network of opportunities that can be moulded more effectively into the fabric of a sustainable and socially acceptable mobility environment. We see a crucial role for the public sector (primarily through its regulatory role) to ensure that all participants in the mobility supply chain can take advantage, without limits of the diversified portfolio of opportunities, to execute their mobility preferences. In some countries, government has taken the lead in developing the open data agenda, e.g. data.gov.uk.

A long-term benefit might include a mobility data hub that could help leverage future public policies like tax incentives (e.g. when passengers use more environmentally friendly transport modes), linking kilometres travelled by a transport mode factor—if we take rail as a baseline, it pollutes 5–10× less than a bus, 10–20× less than plane and 50–100× than a car, ignoring the full life cycle emissions which are complicated by the source of energy generated. Such an approach should include an inter-operable point-based system that rewards users by usage, mode of transport, emissions, delays and data sharing. Access to such incentives would only be possible by having a MaaS supplier agreeing to make their platform translational with a government mandated standard, and we anticipate that this should be enough to both be attractive to potential subscribers and potential aggregators.

## 8.10 Government's role in pricing and subsidy

Without exception, all modes associated with MaaS will use infrastructure that is provided by the public sector (and hence the tax payer), be it roads or rail tracks. To date, much of transport provision is subject to pricing controls set by governments, although there are a growing number of mobility providers whose pricing models are subject only to market forces, such as car based services and active modes such as e bikes. One of the most challenging features of a MaaS subscription model is the mixing of commercial and non-commercial services, where the latter typically are public transport modes that receive substantial subsidy (fare box revenue being inadequate to even recover variable costs in some places[w]). Such low fares have evolved over many years, in part associated with the argument of competitive neutrality with the car rather than some fine-tuned justification on equity (or income distribution) grounds.

If MaaS is to succeed in integrating all modes into a single subscription offer, then it has to come to grips with the concern that some parties have about participating under a pricing model that is unlikely to be subsidised and yet which contains modes that have previously been subsidised and which potential subscribers will require if they are to switch from a PAYG model to a MaaS multi-modal bundle. If MaaS ends up being simply a single integrated app to access all modes on a PAYG basis, then Maas might miss out on delivering the significant benefits to the transport system, even if the app has inbuilt planning and information providing capability. The only way that subsidised and non-subsidised services might co-exist in a single MaaS offering is through demonstrating that it will grow the market for non-subsidised services and/or if there is a rewards/loyalty program that supports lower priced packages that are less expensive than purchases of each service separately. We doubt that the convenience of a one-stop shop will be enough by itself to sway customers without some financial appeal, despite some commentators suggesting that there is a willingness to pay for an integrated all embracing card even if there is no discount as found when Edwards and Mulley (2004) looked at the soft benefits of a university smart card with the potential to add on other services such as gym membership and parking.

w. It is an interesting observation that in Hong Kong where there is no subsidy needed, there is no talk of MaaS!

So what does this mean for government? If there is a belief in a MaaS model delivering improved customer service and possibly other advantages that improve the performance of the transport network (especially if sharing becomes more acceptable through a subscription plan which is far from clear), then government may wish to further subsidise the MaaS plan as a way of supporting lower priced PT. This has a number of interesting implications—will commercially focussed operators be interested in participating since they may be controlled through the package by government regulations, and will there be a limit imposed on the number of service providers (through competitive tendering) to ensure that the services subsidised by government will attract enough patronage? This may well be the Achilles heel of the future of MaaS, resulting in an outcome that is very similar to what we currently see evolving as stand-alone competing modes supported by competitive digital platforms. In the Australian context, Queensland is going the other way and having a SEQ app, at least at the start, rather than the plethora as seen in NSW. We now discuss the idea of extended optional subsidies in more detail.

Given the commentary above, a theme that is emerging as we investigate the role that MaaS might play in the future is the role that the public sector will have in the delivery to market of MaaS products. There are a growing number of views, ranging from the public sector remaining as the arms-length regulator who has no active engagement in participation of delivering a specific MaaS product and, in addition to its involvement in public transport operations (actively or through subsidy provision), having an active role in the delivery of a MaaS product through its investment in a business (equity) and/or managing a MaaS offering.

Separately, and adding a complication, is the generally accepted position that public transport must be central to the provision of a MaaS offering otherwise it will be nothing more than an extension of existing stand-alone car-based mobility services (with the exception of bicycles) such as Uber, GoGet, and Car next door. If conventional public transport is to be in the mix of MaaS services, this inevitably means that subsidised public transport will have to join with commercially-focussed private sector mobility services to define a MaaS bundle, offered through a subscription plan as high level MaaS (see Chapter 1) or as PAYG, under an integrated multimodal App for information, booking and payment which we call low level MaaS.

With public subsidy (to conventional public transport and community transport) in the mix, we have a challenge as to how MaaS might be delivered into the market by suppliers who have a contract with a broker (or aggregator) to deliver service to customers through a subscription plan that will need to be financially more appealing than PAYG. However, even if public transport is subsidised in MaaS, and as long as the subsidy is not more than what public transport is subsidised outside of a MaaS plan, there should in principle, at least, be no issue with *existing levels* of subsidised public transport being offered as part of the bundle in as many MaaS businesses as are interested in entering the market.[x] But as set out below, there might be real opportunities for government to use the MaaS setting to achieve a number of societal objectives through further subsidy incentives.[y]

The providers of public transport who fund the services (as distinct from those organisations who operate them—typically contracted under a gross cost contract), would not (or should not) have any issues under such a plan, and do not need to be a broker, but simply be treated like any supplier of mobility services into a MaaS offering. It is possible that the presence of subsidised public transport (at the same level as all existing public transport) might appeal to other modal suppliers who participate, since it exposes them to potentially new market opportunities of customers used to choosing public transport,[z] who now can be better informed about the role of other mobility options that may suit in a small or large way over time. But it could go another way—namely commercial suppliers may be nervous about participating if public transport becomes the dominant mode of choice in the mix. This topic has been discussed in more detail in Chapter 6.

Alternatively, the public sector may wish to be an active participant in the brokerage role, which under an economic deregulated MaaS model would inevitably cause many problems of conflicts of interest let alone the risk of stretching their resources as the number of MaaS brokers grow (although the issue is controversial—MaaS may simply be no more than a niche offering). Being the regulator and provider in a selective number of MaaS offerings (but not all such offerings in the same market) is almost certainly a case of unfair competition and regulatory conflict. However, in time the market may evolve into one of a very few players (not necessarily a natural monopoly—possibly an oligopoly), and government may see, through MaaS, a mechanism to reduce private car use through promoting the sharing appeal of MaaS, and hence wish to have some control over the evolution of MaaS.

One possible way to do this is to use competitive tendering (or franchising) that has attached to it a value for money proposition designed to offer financial incentives, much like optimal subsidy, to achieve broad social welfare and

x. A necessary condition is that all MaaS plans have the same level of subsidy for public transport—this could be less or indeed more (if you want to nudge behaviour) than the subsidy outside a MaaS bundle. If we take this to the next stage, a competitive market could mean that MaaS operators get different levels of subsidy—why not? The challenge is affordability to government.

y. Where government subsidises all public transport tickets (as in Sweden and Australia) or it subsidises certain peoples' use of public transport (as in Finland), this makes it more or less straight forward to include public transport in privately managed MaaS bundles. One would need more info about the users in the latter case. In Sweden, there is no discussion on whether or not MaaS providers should be able to resell subsidised public transport tickets (we discuss if they should get commissions on top of that), but MaaS Global can only resell single public transport tickets to the unsubsidised price.

z. For commercial unsubsidised services in an economic deregulated market, operators may choose who to give a subsidy to and thus influence the market by cartel behaviour? Fair trading behaviour is only legislated between operators.

efficiency objectives. In promoting tendering, we are mindful of the financial burden (including implementation costs) from the public purse of subsidising too many MaaS offerings. Specifically, government may offer an attractive subsidy (that is better than current subsidy levels for public transport) for MaaS bundles (and not just the already subsidised (outside of MaaS) public transport component) designed to encourage subscription *as long as subscribers, for example, agree to reduce car use by an agreed amount*, as captured through GPS technology built into cars.[aa] This very specific societal objective, often promoted by strategic plans of governments, forces the subscriber (be it an individual, a group such as a household) to think about behaviour change issues at sign-up. While the aggregator would manage an appropriate bundle price, government has an opportunity to use MaaS to support some societal objectives through essentially paying the broker to fund the bundle price through the subscriber and subsidy contributions. If potential practical and ethical problems are mitigated, this seems a potentially attractive way to meet an objective of reduced car use; but unlike road pricing reform, attacking it from an angle that might be politically more palatable. If a subscriber does not own or use a car, then other incentives might be considered that are also aligned with societal objectives.

Through benchmarking and monitoring, the full agreed financial gain to travellers, through the app being used by subscribers, can only be obtained where the agreed level of *private car use reduction* is achieved and verified (e.g. via an on-board unit) (with some possible partial reduction permissible in the initial period(s) with a lesser subsidy support as appropriate until the achievable realistic levels of reduced car use are identified). This can be 'gamified', i.e. competition for subsidies and levels of car reduction. The level may vary according to whether the private car is electric or not. Otherwise the MaaS plan (under the same broker) reverts to a less attractive bundle price that might still be better than purchasing a mobility service from each provider separately (under PAYG[ab]), although there is a challenge here as to how price discounts and/or non-financial rewards might be funded. The subsidy offered would clearly have to support all mobility services within the bundled MaaS offering, although it can be designed in such a way that some modes which are deemed more environmentally friendly (reducing emissions and congestion) or health benefit inducing (cleaner air and more active travel) or improving transport accessibility, it might attract a greater level of optimal subsidy.

This idea should have great appeal to all stakeholders and might be the only basis within which the public sector becomes active and ensures no conflict of

---

aa. In general, travel behaviour change should follow sufficient incentives; however it is appealing to identify some very specific incentives that government is willing to support financially as part of their mandate. An important consideration is to properly segment the market and appeal appropriately to the relevant segments, with subsidy divided up differently in line with societal benefits.

ab. People may just opt for PAYG in the first place because they feel it is simpler and more familiar. Hence, marketing the concept of MaaS and its benefits becomes very important and there must be a role for government in this.

interest between its role as a regulator and its role in securing specific global goals and objectives which it has a mandate to deliver on. It does not have to be, and we would suggest should not be, the active broker. Government hence can remain a regulator, and fulfil a role as a champion for MaaS, supporting and enabling its development through policy guidance and legislation, with its operating arm charged with providing public transport as a supplier only, with broker entry into a subsidised MaaS offering only permissible through a competitive tendered contracting model. This contract will have conditions that have to be met in terms of specific levels of subsidy being allowed when the broader societal objectives, which are likely to differ across geographical jurisdictions (e.g. Sweden versus Finland—see Chapters 3 and 7), are met.[ac] Under this model, government will be best suited as a monitoring agency (even if they outsource this task to a benchmarking specialist to achieve independent objective outcomes), with data required to be supplied to the monitoring agency in order to pay the subsidy. Where the broker fails to deliver on the KPIs, the subsidy is not paid and hence a shortfall must be funded by the broker. This provides a mechanism to ensure that the designed subscription bundles are geared to attracting customers from those that align with the agreed (and quantified to minimise ambiguity) societal obligations. Government can reserve the right to cancel the contract and retender (provided this is clearly articulated in the terms of the contract that is subsidy linked).

Importantly, the tendering process can allow for more than one successful bidder,[ad] unlike conventional public transport contracts where competition for the market (in contrast to competition in the market) results in only one successful bidder (presumed to be the most efficient operator under natural monopoly) and is commonly limited to a much smaller geographical jurisdiction than is required to deliver a very locationally flexible MaaS product, operational nationwide. A MaaS offering may still be offered under free market entry, but one wonders whether it would survive financially; one suspects this is unlikely. While there is a potential problem with tendering, compared to open APIs, in that the government has to specify what it wants, which might limit the action space for external MaaS providers, this may be necessary if public subsidy levels beyond the current standard public transport subsidy to all public transport becomes an instrument to grow MaaS participation aligned to achieving a broad base of societal objectives.

We acknowledge however that there will be challenges in implementing such a plan. These will include the need to (i) agree on what the societal goals are, (ii) develop short-term and long-term KPIs for these goals, and (iii) analyse whether or not the services are delivering on the KPIs. For instance, if the main

ac. Simply put, compliance with a societal objective such as a specific reduction in car use must be satisfied. The subsidised price cannot be guaranteed to be a sufficient incentive to shift behaviour and thus meet the social objectives? It is easy to capture relevant data from Apps, and in the case of car use it will require data on prior car use to establish a level of reduction.

ad. West Sweden is currently trying to initiate an open/ongoing tender for mobility providers.

goals are to reduce car usage and exclusion from the transport system, we need good data on how the users of the services travelled prior to adopting the service. This has remained a problem when developing the contractual framework for mobility partners in West Sweden.

In summary, we believe that apart from the regulatory role of government (administered through a public sector agency), there is a very appealing separate role for government in supporting an optimally subsidised MaaS program under very specific conditions for subscription plans that can deliver on the societal goals and objectives that provide the basis for justifying optimal subsidies. This subsidy logic is no different to what is currently the situation with stand-alone contracts for modal services. Alternatively, MaaS products with a discount model funded from any source can deliver simile outcomes to customers but not necessarily linked to societal objectives; hence the approach being suggested has very general appeal as a way of offering a financial incentive as a mechanism to ensure that a MaaS bundle is preferred to a PAYGO model. Without this we speculate that the MaaS idea will have very limited customer support and will at best be a niche offering with no prospects of scalability.

## 8.11 Conclusions

Whenever we attend a conference on future mobility and autonomous cars, we are told by experts in the technology space, especially those from telecommunications businesses, that congestion will be a thing of the past and all our roads will perform at totally safe free flow levels with optimised spacing between vehicles, as well as intersection and lane merging controls to ensure free flow performance at all locations along a road.[ae] Vehicle-to-infrastructure communication will make the city function like a giant computer, with a central operating system that everything flows into. As appealing as this prediction is, one wonders how much faith can be placed on this speculation. What is likely to occur, however, is that the information obtained, after being compiled and analysed by a central platform, will help maintain the traffic flow and direct traffic intelligently, but impact on levels of congestion in a directionally unclear manner, and adapt the infrastructure to meet acute requirements. These assertions appear to fail to recognise the implications of evolving car-based business models focussed on profits. There is a hint here about the possible role of government and whether user or provider side subsidy may be required (maybe less than currently outlaid on conventional public transport) if it ensures a business model that respects the needs of the city over the needs of the commercial operator. All of this can occur without, as well as with, MaaS.

ae. At a recent conference we heard from the Chief Scientist of Telstra (Australia) who claimed that we will soon have 5G communications controlling autonomous vehicles that will be the basis of operating our road network with all communication built into the vehicles (no modification required to roads), resulting in the complete elimination of traffic congestion.

With a fixed amount of road network capacity, if the popularity of the collaborative and connected economy actually takes hold, with or without vehicles being autonomous (and regardless of the fuel source, although this may impact favourably on the cost of car usage if electricity and hence attract even more ridership), we might expect congestion to continue to exist, albeit as more predictable (i.e. less due to random circumstances; lower uncertain travel time variability), and hence the case for efficient road user charging that accommodates congestion impacts will remain real. This will also be required as a mechanism to pay for the roads (as increased support for hypothecation mounts).

It is almost impossible to think of an argument that would result in fewer car kilometres on the roads under even a shared mobility model (which has the greatest prospects), especially if the claim is to also satisfy pent up latent mobility demand and round the clock commercial imperatives. What might be expected is that intelligent mobility opportunities will buy a number of years of growth in automobility in such a way that it will take pressure off the need to invest in currently planned future road investment (which will be a good thing), but will require imposing meaningful road user charges. Encouragingly, such reformed road user charges will no longer be imposed on individuals (where the real sensitivity exists), but on mobility brokers who deliver the shared mobility services. Breaking the nexus between ownership and mobility should also break the resistance to supporting road pricing reform at the individual traveller and voter level.

In the debate on traffic congestion, we need to stop looking just at cars. What if there was a smart infrastructure that connected road, rail, and other modes of transportation in such a way that all of them worked together to serve the mobility needs of the modern urban population? It is in this context that the congestion debate should be positioned. As McCabe (2017) suggests, MaaS may well be a fraud if it is car centric, and that if all of the arguments associated with car sharing are currently designed to get more people using cars without protecting the future of public transport, we are likely to see congestion getting worse, not better (after allowing for positive initiatives such as automated roads and reduced vehicle size in platoon settings).

What may well be the saviour is ensuring that a public transport contribution to the mix is preserved as a basis of moving large numbers of travellers who prefer it or find it a necessary option to a car-based offer, and we have efficient road user charging and reformed public funding. If, as is suggested, car use will drop in price as we move to a sharing non ownership society with autonomous electric vehicles, the market will deliver higher levels of demand for such services (exactly what the technology and app developers are hoping for), and thus simple economics without efficient road user charging is likely to deliver congestion growth. So will we end back at a position where the savings associated with selling a car and moving to a non-ownership model with relatively low costs of usage actually discourage travel by a car mode? The central theme of this chapter is that even with significant sharing of vehicles that are not privately owned, we are unlikely ever to fully tame congestion through the smart technology initiative (Cars are still cars-geometrically unchanged by technology). Road pricing must come to the rescue as well as a new public transport funding model by government designed to switch control of subsidy to users and away from providers as a way of creating a competitive market for mobility contracts that support public transport. The greatest disruption may, in time, be created by pricing and funding reform. There are many implied recommendations in this book, but the highlights should focus on ways to ensure that deregulated mobility contracts, if this is the way they will be delivered to the market, serve the relevant geographical jurisdiction in line with societal objectives. Also we would support a position that mobility contract providers contribute financially through a road user charge associated with the services that use government provides assets (hiding this charge in the subscription price); and that public transport remains part of the future mix of multimodal service provision (even where there is a closer definition of a car and a small bus as distinguished in a sharing model by only the carrying capacity).

Future MaaS planning and implementation needs to keep the following points front of mind:

- It must be multi-modal and door to door to recognise the diversity of community needs and delivery capability.
- It needs to be mindful of societal goals and possible opportunities to incentivise MaaS with optional subsidies that are linked to outcomes aligned with broader government objectives.
- It needs to offer an integrated pricing scheme across all (or many) modes, ideally with a one stop payment.
- It must match the needs of actual and potential users through flexible packaging and pricing.
- It must deliver greater choice than exists currently, with easy entry and participation.
- It must open up the possibility of a shift to the sharing economy, where asset ownership, such as car ownership, is increasingly not necessary, provided it guarantees access to preferred modes of transport when required.

By itself, MaaS is not a panacea for modern problems of traffic congestion and emissions. It needs to address all of the pain points in transport, connecting with such solutions as road pricing reform and incentives to reduce private car ownership (or at least use of such vehicles).

Chapter 9

# Future challenges

**Chapter outline**



## 9.1 Introduction

This chapter draws together the overall conclusions arising from the investigation of 'MaaS, Past, Present, and Future'. An early starting point, and recurring theme, was discussion of "what is MaaS?" Chapter 3 presented the various definitions put forward in the literature for MaaS. Whilst this book has not developed its own definition, it recognises the definition of MaaS must have some essential components. These essential components identify MaaS as a type of service that creates/improves alignments between different transportation services within a sector/domain/ecosystem using a digital channel (or App) to offer unified information, booking opportunities and a unified payment system (e.g. a multimodal travel planner that allows booking along with a mobility wallet), as well as possibly bundles and incentives etc. (i.e. a more advanced MaaS product such as UbiGo or Whim).

The examination of the different aspects of MaaS in this book leads us to the conclusion that MaaS is *not* a paradigm change in mobility management. It is nevertheless an appealing concept which, if implemented in the way that has inspired researchers and the market to date, could make a step change in the way transport services are delivered in our cities (and maybe also in our more rural and regional areas), and contribute to sustainability objectives and wider imperatives such as climate change.

This concluding chapter recaps the contribution of this book by revisiting the questions of the global debate identified in Chapter 3 to examine how many of these questions now have answers, informed by the other chapters in the book, to identify those areas where there are 'still more questions than answers', and to compile a list of unanswered questions which need to be the preoccupation of future researchers.

Understanding Mobility as a Service (MaaS). https://doi.org/10.1016/B978-0-12-820044-5.00009-9
© 2020 Elsevier Inc. All rights reserved.

## 9.2 Revisiting the questions of the global debate

This section revisits, in turn, each of the 10 questions of global debate, of Chapter 3, relating to the development of Mobility as a Service (MaaS) over the last 5 years. The aim is to confirm the insights derived from each of the chapters in this book and to identify further questions raised.

*Question 1: Who is MaaS most attractive to?*

In Chapter 3 this was identified as a basic question. Yet there is still no conclusive answer, given that most trials have been of limited duration and often poorly documented.

Chapter 5 however offers some answers in terms of the market demand for various MaaS products if this question is interpreted as whether customers are willing to pay for different aspects of the service. In Section 9.1 above, one of the essential components of MaaS is identified as improving alignment between transportation services using digital channels. Chapter 5 considers the willingness of travellers to pay for the app (representing a single, customer-facing digital channel) and found that whilst a smart app is valued, both in Sydney, Australia, and Tyneside, UK, the respondents to the survey were unwilling to pay for it. However, this can be contrasted with a similar question posed to respondents in Zurich, Switzerland, where the willingness to pay for a smart app that integrated all journeys into a journey planner and provided a uniform payment system was in excess of USD $100 per month (Guidon et al., 2020).

MaaS development is still at an early stage and so identifying the segment of the population for whom MaaS might be attractive can also be considered by looking to what we already know about potential early adopters. Chapter 4 in looking at the pilots and trials discusses this and identifies potential early adopters as already being comfortable with multi-modal travel, concerned about the environment and more infrequent users of a car. Curiosity and inertia appear to play important roles in the early adopters or others interest in MaaS.

In terms of modes, the research evidence points to some modes within a MaaS scheme as being more important to potential users than others. Public transport and car sharing appear to be preferred modes with point to point modes such as taxis and Uber considered as less essential. Other modes such as car-rental and bike-share are (still) more debatable as being important modes of a MaaS scheme. Users of the preferred modes are more likely to find MaaS attractive, which corresponds with earlier findings on habitual travel behaviour (Gärling and Axhausen, 2003).

In terms of vertical equity, if MaaS is to be inclusive and to provide for all walks of life, it is critical that a credit card or debit card is not the only means by which payment can be made. In many developing countries, there is much more of a cash economy with many of the poorer members of society having no formal bank accounts: to make MaaS attractive to this segment of the population, the ability to have a pre-charged smart card, or similar, for payment is essential.

In summary, the various strands of literature are beginning to provide answers, but they are not yet so numerous so as to understand if context is the all important feature, or whether there are commonalities which can be used as building bricks to identify who MaaS might appeal to. The findings from pilots and ongoing schemes can provide some more information and these are considered in the next question.

*Question 2: How can more pilots be encouraged for learning?*

Chapter 4 rather turns this question around from how to encourage more pilots to how more can be learnt from pilots more generally.

Chapter 4 gave three key messages to pilots to provide better learning for MaaS implementation. First, there needs to be better evaluation of existing pilots or trials and pilots and trials of the future. There are only a handful of detailed evaluations of which UbiGo is a good example. There are signs that some current pilots will be better evaluated (EC2B, Gothenburg, Tripi, Sydney and Mobil-Flat, Augsburg, Germany) but these will not necessarily be evaluated in a comparable way to ensure that transferability and generalisability of the results will ensue. It would be admirable if the Swedish roadmap for MaaS could be more universally adopted whereby this roadmap requires the development of an open MaaS database and the evaluation of trials or pilots in a standardised way to benefit from Swedish Innovation Agency funding.

The evidence from Chapter 4 suggests that it is not necessarily *more* trials that we need but that we need more transparent reporting of longer trials or pilots, and trials or pilots which involve larger sample sizes of users. These are essential to understand and witness the implications of potential long-term effects and whether or not MaaS is scalable. Whim in Helsinki is the only long-term and large-scale implementation of MaaS and its evaluation is compromised by commercial sensitivity. Chapter 4 recommends that governments should take a lead in this and, in the UK, it seems this is being put forward by the House of Commons Transport Committee (2018) with their enquiry into MaaS with a call for pilot studies to be funded and the Scottish Government establishing a MaaS Investment fund.

Pilots or trials to date have looked at the characteristics and socio demographics of users. But Chapter 4 argues that this needs to be done in a more systematic way to identify which market segments react to which incentives and products so that more targeted MaaS solutions can be made. This is not just a market imperative but an imperative for greater take up which in turn has a better chance of meeting societal aims and objectives too. Slow take up may indeed suggest that MaaS is, at best, a niche product or one that in general is unlikely to deliver outcomes that attract users (and investors in a business model). This may also in part be due to the early offerings of MaaS which if not popular will set back promoting and justifying its positive features. Findings from Whim in Helsinki indicates its take up is dominated by millennials with lower expectations of car ownership. Moreover, the trials or pilots to date have been largely urban in nature, although this is more discussed under the next question.

*Question 3: Will MaaS be too expensive to deliver beyond high density areas?*
Chapter 3, Table 3.2 shows the clear majority of MaaS schemes around the world—whether in pilot, trial or operational format—are based in urban areas. MyCicero in Italy is a notable scheme for also applying outside the urban area but nevertheless has an overarching urban focus. Apart from this, Table 3.2 shows that other MaaS schemes applying to rural areas are quite “Low MaaS” and are little more than journey planners.

However, beyond the urban focus, scholars as well as practitioners have lately started investigating rural applications of MaaS, but so far as we are aware, only in the Nordic countries (e.g. Berg et al., 2019; Eckhardt et al., 2018). One interesting example of a national level initiative is the Finnish Rural MaaS communication project (referred to in Chapter 3). Finland is also home to the world’s first Rural MaaS project: the Ministry of Agriculture and Forestry-led project aimed at creating a national vision for MaaS in rural and sparsely populated areas.

It is a question for further research as to whether MaaS will be viable only in situations similar to the high density European cities. Or, taking another approach, research should consider what adaptations or changes might be needed for MaaS to work in lower densities. Rural and regional areas may provide a setting to offer something that is less ambitious in terms of the MaaS ecosystem, perhaps with a specific focus on tourism.

Playing devil’s advocate, if more sustainable travel and the reduction of congestion is its primary objective of MaaS, does it matter if MaaS does not happen in rural areas since the objective primarily relates to urban conditions?

*Question 4: Who are the key stakeholders in the MaaS ecosystem?*
In terms of the key stakeholders, Chapter 6 identifies three stakeholder roles important for delivering MaaS (note that a single entity can fulfil all of these roles as in the case of Augsburg, Germany): the broker/aggregator as an integrator, mode-specific operators and non-mobility operators. However, there are a number of different contenders, particularly for the broker/aggregator role. Should it be government when government also has a role in regulating the market? This issue, as discussed in Chapter 6, is a continuing point of debate. So far, there appears to be a varied approach to whether government takes the broker/aggregator role or not and, as Chapter 6 indicates, in the end it is likely to be spatially contextual. There is already a difference between, for example,

the Finnish approach where government is enabling MaaS to develop through the requirement to allow third party sale of single tickets and in NSW, Australia, where government appears to be keen to encourage start-ups and existing businesses to take the role of broker in a test of a potential MaaS delivery model. It is not yet clear which approach might provide the more successful outcome, although it will be important to be watchful of potential anti-competitive behaviour between the different modes making up the MaaS modal mix.

Additionally, and following work undertaken by the UK's Transport Systems Catapult (Transport Systems Catapult, 2016), it is clear that the data provider—who acts as a data broker to service the data and information sharing requirements of the transport operators and broker—is another key stakeholder in the MaaS ecosystem. The customer, too, who consumes the MaaS offer should not be forgotten as an important stakeholder. A further stakeholder could be added in the form of the MaaS Champion who can provide strong leadership (a role taken, for example, by the Finnish Government). The candidates for these roles and the extent and nature of engagement have not yet been well defined although there are a number of candidates (Government, local authority, private sector, or transport operator). This is an area for further research.

*Question 5: What are the critical factors affecting the delivery of MaaS?*

The technical requirements for MaaS such as the requirement for interoperability between ecosystems; digital connectivity; data and API sharing (MaaS Scotland, 2018) are well established. Much less is known in terms of user (i.e. consumer) requirements or indeed what the business community is prepared to supply.

On the demand side, a key finding from Chapter 5 is that the travelling public do not want only to have a subscription or bundle of mobility, they want to have a choice of payment method. Incentives and discounts built into subscriptions appeal to some customers whereas others want a pay per ride (or PAYG). Customers appear to be heterogeneous in all the settings examined, in both Chapters 3 and 4, with no pattern of payment method being preferred in a particular spatial context or particular jurisdiction. Interestingly, Whim as a MaaS provider is offering different payment options in different markets. For example, in the Helsinki market, Whim offers both PAYG and monthly subsription models but in other markets such as West Midlands, the UK Whim only offers a PAYG option (with an earlier failed attempt at introducing a subscription plan). There is also no real agreement yet as to which payment option is preferred and in Australia, PAYG has been found to be more attractive by one research team (Vij et al., 2018) but in our own research, we found subscription models were much preferred. The evidence in both studies is drawn from stated preference surveys and not market trials.

The supply side issues are considered under *Question 9.*

*Question 6: What are the potential problem areas for MaaS?*

This is a crucial question in terms of the forward trajectory of MaaS. The history of "failed" schemes captured by Table 3.2 would suggest that there are problems to be overcome. Chapter 4, in examining what we have 'learnt' from MaaS trials contributes a number of problems to be overcome (see *Question 2* above). Other bodies, such as the UK Parliament Transport Select Committee (2018) have raised a number of transport related issues that could become problematic such as an increase in the use of taxis and private hire vehicles (PHVs) at the expense of other modes may contribute to worsening traffic congestion; MaaS may also contribute to worsening digital and social exclusion. It is also possible that MaaS, instead of building public transport mode share may abstract from it, leaving public transport less well patronaged and potentially requiring greater subsidy.

Chapter 7 describes a number of governance issues which are problematic for the development and diffusion of MaaS including the way in which the private car enjoys many benefits, including tax benefits in many jurisdictions, the difficulty of providing regulatory support for MaaS because of the speed at which change is occurring, the absence of tools and processes for harnessing public and private collaboration and the mismatch between trialled MaaS offerings and perceived mobility need. The Chapter proposes five strands of strategy to overcome these institutional barriers but acknowledges that these are unproven and require further research.

*Question 7: Is there too much hype? Is MaaS capable of making it to mainstream?*

The key message of Chapter 2 is that MaaS is predicated on providing a unique opportunity to improve the efficiency of our transport networks and the sustainability of our cities by reducing car ownership and car dependence. However, MaaS, by integrating modes to provide a more efficient trip, aided by digital technologies and bundled subscription products, promises an outlook yet to be realised. So 'Hype' or the 'MaaS bubble' will remain terms being applied to discussions of MaaS until empirical research can clarify the impact of MaaS on travel behaviour.

It is clear that the coming of age in the digital world is advanced as motivating the MaaS premise and that new applications continue to enter the market place. As an example, a new digital payments platform was launched in Sydney, Australia, by the State government in 2019. Opal Connect is designed to provide an integrated and convenient ticketing system in a single digital account, connected to a credit or debit card. The Opal Connect account can be used to sign in to different transport operator's apps to book and pay for their travel with the potential in the future to support a bundled transport subscription service. The pace of change in this domain is fast with the Opal Connect development and delivery being just one example of significant development that has taken place over the few months of writing this book. Conversely, as described in Chapter 4, Stadtwerke Augsburg “jump-started” to offering subscription bundles (level three in Sochor et al., 2018) before offering a fully integrated mobility app. This allowed them to focus on the critical bundle design aspect of MaaS and not be hampered by technology related barriers (at least initially).

However, as Chapter 5 identifies ‘MaaS is more than an App’ and to make it to mainstream there are a number of obstacles to overcome, as detailed in the responses to the questions above. Chapter 3 also posed a number of issues under this question that remain unanswered although critical for underpinning a mainstream MaaS. These were: How will the attitudes towards sharing and the move away from asset owning be accomplished? Will this begin with the younger generation and grow as this generation ages and is replaced by the next younger generation? Is a true multi-modal MaaS likely to appeal most in geographical jurisdictions where travellers are already using a mix of available modes? How will this impact on land use and the eventual shape of our cities—will they become more compact or will MaaS, in making mobility easier, lead to greater sprawl? These have been added to the unanswered questions below.

*Question 8: What does success look like for MaaS?*

When looking at criteria for success, it is important to recognise that by itself, MaaS cannot be expected to be the panacea for the modern problems of traffic congestion and emissions. It is also the case that this question must recognise MaaS development is still in its infancy. One of the limiting factors when commenting on what success may look like is the paucity of detailed evaluation studies of MaaS trials. The need to achieve critical mass for MaaS schemes is one obvious measure of success. More widely in society there are changing attitudes towards sharing and this provides an opportunity for more sustainable transport solutions.

Throughout this book there are issues which have been identified as success elements. Chapter 8, in particular, provides some clear pointers for future MaaS planning and implementation. First, MaaS must be more than an app, it must provide information and an opportunity to make door to door travel using multi-modal options available through an integrated payment facility. Second, MaaS must be alert to societal goals and government could be willing to incentivise MaaS with optional subsidies to achieve broader government objectives. For example, a MaaS scheme that provides incentives and rewards for greater public transport use could be subsidised by a government wanting to reduce private car use. MaaS will also be regarded as having success when it has made inroads to changing travel behaviour to be more part of a sharing economy, where asset ownership, such as private car ownership, is increasingly not necessary. However, successful MaaS by itself may not be enough to achieve societal goals as, even with significant sharing of vehicles that are not privately owned, congestion is unlikely to be 'cured'. Road pricing, together with a new public transport funding model by government, designed to switch control of subsidy to users and away from providers, is needed to reinforce the opportunities MaaS presents and as a way of creating a competitive market for mobility contracts that support public transport.

This question can also be answered in part by reference to the 'Five tests for 'Good MaaS'' offered by Linton and Bray (2019) which echo the discussion above. The questions are: Does it incentivise public transport use? Does it help reduce congestion and pollution? Is it socially inclusive (is it affordable; accessible in a non-digital way; providing good geographical coverage; providing information and options for those with additional mobility needs)? Is there a culture of openness and data sharing? and Does it encourage active lifestyles? Indeed, these questions hint at the possibility that without any reform incentives to deal with use of the private car, MaaS cannot be anything more than a niche product in terms of its impact on societal goals or scalable to a mainstream mobility model.

*Question 9: Are the business models still too much in their infancy?*

*Question 5* considered the demand side issues critical to the delivery of MaaS. On the supply side, Chapter 6 provides quantitative and empirical evidence on business preferences as informed by a stated choice study undertaken with the business community, including mode-specific and non-mobility stakeholders. Interestingly, in the context of *Question 3* above, the business community showed a preference for stable but arm's length government involvement with the opportunity to compete and without undue requirements for financial support. The chapter identifies possible contracts in terms of their modal mixes, equity stake and potential value proposition of the business (amongst other contract attributes). We are still at the very beginning of the journey and the small size of trials is evidence of evolving business models where stakeholders are still finding their roles.

*Question 10: Opportunity or threat from autonomous vehicles?*

As noted in Chapter 3, the implications of AVs for the development and sustainability of MaaS has received less attention in the debate. It is widely expected that AVs will have the potential for greater door to door solutions which is something that can also be expected of MaaS. AVs also have the capability to reduce the costs of transport. The impact of AVs is discussed in Chapter 8.

However, with a fixed amount of road network capacity, the emergence of a collaborative and connected economy is unlikely to remove congestion—with or without vehicles being autonomous (and regardless of the fuel source). Congestion might be more predictable but, as discussed in *Question 8*, there will still be a need for efficient road user charging to both attend to congestion and as a mechanism to pay for roads. So, within a MaaS context, AVs can only help by providing opportunity for more *interlinked* travel options but from a policy point of view, AVs should not be thought of as a panacea for urban congestion.

## 9.3 Unanswered and unasked questions: Framing the future research directions

This book highlights that a MaaS future embraces a very appealing mobility strategy. However, with MaaS still being in its infancy, many questions remain unanswered and, as a result of the writing of this book, unasked. This section draws together these issues and questions as a way of posing some future research imperatives.

There are inevitably many more questions than answers in knowing how intelligent mobility will change the way people live, work and travel, and its values in relation to sustainability objectives. The evidence so far in this book suggests that MaaS may not be a game changer. Chapter 3 shows few ongoing MaaS schemes which are highly integrated. Chapter 5 suggests that customers may not be willing to pay a lot for MaaS services. Chapter 7 identifies critical governance issues and Chapter 8 discusses many issues relating to broader transport and societal goals. To achieve the vision that MaaS proposes, something more is needed than a smart phone app—innovations to improve sustainability (alternative fuels) and politically (addressing congestion through better pricing than can be provided by fuel excise) and social and cultural attitudinal changes to engender greater positive attitudes towards sharing.

How future technology innovation in other fields will impact on transport is an unasked question. One example is blockchain, a Distributed Ledger Technology (DLT) which is expected to have application to MaaS. With DLT, each member in a network stores an identical ledger or database which takes the form of a chronological chain of unique groups of information called "blocks" (Transport Systems Catapult, 2018). Blockchain can be used to facilitate sharing of trusted information across a network of stakeholders. In the case of MaaS, "blockchain represents an opportunity to mitigate against centralised platform issues [i.e., a tendency towards monopoly power] with open, transparent, decentralised principles" (Transport Systems Catapult, 2018).

Turning now to future research, the global debate is still continuing on these questions and more research is needed.

*Question 3: Will MaaS be too expensive to deliver beyond high density areas?*

We need more information here as to the role of population density in the delivery of MaaS. If public transport is the core of urban MaaS, it may well be that changes to the MaaS ecosystem are required to make MaaS a reality in lower density areas. Promoting on-demand bus services as MaaS is highly misleading.

*Question 4: Who are the key stakeholders in the MaaS ecosystem?*

More work needs to be done on identifying the roles and potential candidates for the data provider and the MaaS Champion. The need for a data provider is unequivocal, but little attention has been paid to who this should be and what 'rules' should be implemented to ensure privacy and indeed sharing of information. In many spheres of transport policy, a Champion has been instrumental in moving forward the debate to the point of implementation: Enrique Peñalosa and the implementation of the BRT in Bogotá, Ken Livingstone and the congestion charging in London are notable examples.

A question is prompted by the trials in Augsburg and Whim in Birmingham. Augsburg has a centralised stakeholder relationship with Stadtwerke Augsburg, as a municipal utilities company, at the centre of the MaaS trial able to co-ordinate internally and 'sign up' mobility providers. This contrasts with Whim in the West Midlands in the UK, operating as a MaaS scheme but without the centralised 'benefits' of Stadtwerke Augsburg. Whim has not achieved a good selection of modal options for its MaaS scheme through only signing up a small subset of the mobility offerings available in Birmingham. The research question is 'what are the governance arrangements necessary to ensure a full set of mobility options are included in the MaaS scheme'?

*Question 5: What are the critical factors affecting the delivery of MaaS?*

How MaaS is financed and what sort of incentives need to be offered to both customers and suppliers are areas where more research information would be helpful.

Research that explores the current behaviour of travellers and the characteristics of early adopters would be helpful to place MaaS in the suite of transport options available to future travel markets. In terms of governance, governments need to be trained to look for consistency in service delivery, and for stakeholder groups to get the relevant skills so as to deliver MaaS.

The technical issues are not fully resolved in the sense of how many and which users have the equipment to actually use a MaaS app? What happens, for example, to people who do not have a smart phone or do not have a debit/credit card for payment? What other access strategies might be considered? Further research is needed on different segments of the population rather than being dependent on the results of trials and the socio-demographics of trial participants.

The digital divide is also relevant. Whim is predicated on internet access and/or having the appropriate digital infrastructure. It is perhaps not surprising that MaaS started in Finland where wifi access is good. How important is pervasive internet connection to MaaS take up?

*Question 6: What are the potential problem areas for MaaS?*

The governance strategies outlined in Chapter 7 do not have empirical underpinning and require research to identify if they would indeed be helpful in reducing institutional barriers.

*Question 7: Is there too much hype? Is MaaS capable of making it to mainstream?*

Some longer-term questions were raised under this question above and require further research and/or inclusion in the evaluation of MaaS trials. These include: How will the attitudes towards sharing and the move away from asset owning be accomplished? Will this begin with the younger generation and grow as this generation ages and is replaced by the next younger generation? Is a true multi-modal MaaS likely to appeal most in geographical jurisdictions where travellers are already using a mix of available modes? How will this impact on land use and the eventual shape of our cities—will they become more compact or will MaaS, in making mobility easier, lead to greater sprawl?

## 9.4 Final words

One aim of this book is to take stock of where we are at present and what are some of the big challenges in the future if MaaS is to become an appealing reality. Needing more research is an inevitable conclusion—providing an evidence base for unanswered and unasked questions is a research imperative. However, whilst some of the research questions above may be investigated in isolation from a working MaaS ecosystem, there will be never be a substitute to the overarching conclusion of Chapter 4—we need bigger and better trials, and trials which are properly evaluated.

# References


Aapaoja, A., Eckhardt, J., Nykänen, L., Sochor, J., 2017. MaaS service combinations for different geographical areas. In: Paper Presented at the 24th World Congress on Intelligent Transportation Systems, Montreal.

Alemi, F., Circella, G., Handy, S., Mokhtarian, P., 2018. What influences travelers to use Uber? Exploring the factors affecting the adoption of on-demand ride services in California. Travel Behav. Soc. 13, 88–104.

Alexander, L.P., González, M.C., 2015. Assessing the impact of real-time ridesharing on urban traffic using mobile phone data. In: Paper Presented at the 4th International Workshop on Urban Computing (UrbComp), Sydney, Australia.

Ambrosino, G., Nelson, J.D., Romanazzo, M. (Eds.), 2004. Demand Responsive Transport Services: Towards the Flexible Mobility Agency. ENEA, Rome.

Ambrosino, G., Nelson, J., Boero, M., 2016. Enabling intermodal urban transport through complementary services: from Flexible Mobility Services to the Shared Use Mobility Agency. Res. Transp. Econ. 59, 179–184.

Amey, A., Attanucci, J., Mishalani, R., 2011. Real-time ridesharing: opportunities and challenges in using mobile phone technology to improve rideshare services. Transp. Res. Rec. 2217, 103–110. https://doi.org/10.3141/2217-13.

Antons, D., Piller, F.T., 2015. Opening the black box of "not invented here": attitudes, decision biases, and behavioral consequences. Acad. Manag. Perspect. 29 (2), 193–217.

Arthur D. Little, 2018. The Future of Mobility 3.0—Reinventing Mobility in the Era of Disruption and Creativity. Retrieved from: http://www.adlittle.com/futuremobilitylab/assets/file/ADL_UITP_Future%20of%20Mobility3.0-min.pdf.

Arup, 2019. The Future of Mobility and MaaS Governance and Orchestration. Retrieved from: https://www.arup.com/perspectives/publications/promotional-materials/section/the-future-of-mobility-and-maas.

Atkins, 2015. Journeys of the Future—Introducing Mobility as a Service. Retrieved from: https://www.atkinsglobal.com/~/media/Files/A/Atkins-Corporate/uk-and-europe/uk-thought-leadership/reports/Journeys%20of%20the%20future_300315.pdf.

Audouin, M., Finger, M., 2018. The development of Mobility-as-a-Service in the Helsinki metropolitan area: a multi-level governance analysis. Res. Transp. Bus. Manag. 27, 24–35. https://doi.org/10.1016/j.rtbm.2018.09.001.

Bakker, E., Walker, H., Harland, C., 2006. Organizing for collaborative procurement: an initial conceptual framework. In: Advancing Public Procurement: Practices, Innovation and Knowledge-Sharing, pp. 14–44.

Bardhi, F., Eckhardt, G.M., 2012. Access-based consumption: the case of car sharing. J. Consum. Res. 39 (4), 881–898.

Becker, H., Becker, F., Abe, R., Abou-Zeid, M., Becker, T., Bekhor, S., et al., 2020. Impact of vehicle automation and electric propulsion on production costs for mobility services worldwide. In: Paper Presented at the 99th Transportation Research Board (TRB) Annual Meeting, Washington, DC.

Beirão, G., Sarsfield Cabral, J.A., 2007. Understanding attitudes towards public transport and private car: a qualitative study. Transp. Policy 14 (6), 478–489. https://doi.org/10.1016/j.tranpol.2007.04.009.

Berg, J., Arby, H., Fredricson, M., Holmberg, P.-E., Darijan, Å.H., Persson, J.S., Tufvesson, E., 2019. Kombinerade mobilitetstjänster på landsbygd och i mindre tätorter—resultat från förstudien KomILand (VTI rapport 986). Retrieved from: http://vti.diva-portal.org/smash/get/diva2:1252359/FULLTEXT01.pdf.

Bly, P.H., Webster, F.V., Pounds, S., 1980. Effects of subsidies on urban public transport. Transportation 9 (4), 311–331.

Boethius, O., Arby, H., 2011. Den flexible trafikanten—En affärsmodell för en samlad mobilitetstjänst. (Gothenburg).

Boone, S., Steinberger, S., Wafa, Z., 2018. Mobility as a service: examining transit agency–ride-hailing partnerships. In: Paper Presented at the 97th Transportation Research Board (TRB) Annual Meeting, Washington, DC.

Bösch, P.M., Becker, F., Becker, H., Axhausen, K.W., 2018. Cost-based analysis of autonomous mobility services. Transp. Policy 64, 76–91. https://doi.org/10.1016/j.tranpol.2017.09.005.

Boyle, P., Associates, 2016. The Impact of Car Share Services in Australia. International Car Sharing Association. 13 October 2016. Retrieved from http://phillipboyle.com.au/wp-content/uploads/2016/10/Carsharing-Association-FINAL-Report-4.0.pdf.

Bozeman, B., Kingsley, G., 1998. Risk culture in public and private organizations. Public Adm. Rev. 58 (2), 109–118. https://doi.org/10.2307/976358.

Brendel, A.B., Mandrella, M., 2016. Information systems in the context of sustainable mobility services: a literature review and directions for future research. In: Paper Presented at 22nd Americas Conference on Information Systems, San Diego, CA.

Caiati, V., Rasouli, S., Timmermans, H., 2020. Bundling, pricing schemes and extra features preferences for mobility as a service: sequential portfolio choice experiment. Transp. Res. A Policy Pract. 131, 123–148.

CB Insights, 2016. Big auto's scramble for auto tech partnerships, investments, and M&A [Online]. New York, United States. Available at https://www.cbinsights.com/blog/auto-corporates-investment-ma-timeline. (Accessed February 12, 2017).

Chalmers, 2013. Framtidens resetjänst för storstadshushåll—UbiGo. Retrieved from: https://www.chalmers.se/en/areas-of-advance/Transport/news/Pages/Framtidens-resetj%C3%A4nst-f%C3%B6r-storstadshush%C3%A5ll-%E2%80%93-UbiGo-.aspx.

Cheng, Y.H., 2010. Exploring passenger anxiety associated with train travel. Transportation 37 (6), 875–896.

Chowdhury, S., Ceder, A., 2016. Users' willingness to ride an integrated public-transport service: a literature review. Transp. Policy 48, 183–195. https://doi.org/10.1016/j.tranpol.2016.03.007.

City of Chicago, 2019. Transportation Network Providers and Congestion in the City of Chicago. City of Chicago.

Clewlow, R.R., Mishra, G.S., 2017. Disruptive transportation: the adoption, utilization, and impacts of ride-hailing in the United States. Research Report – UCD-ITS-RR-17-07, October, Institute of Transportation Studies, University of California, Davis.

Cohen, B., 2018. Mobility as a Service (MaaS) and Mobility on Demand (MOD) via Blockchain. Retrieved from: https://medium.com/iomob/mobility-as-a-service-maas-and-mobility-on-demand-mod-via-blockchain-64e36a2f6676.

Competition act, Pub. L. No. 2008:579., 2008. (2008-06-18).

Cottrill, C., 2020. MaaS surveillance: privacy considerations in mobility as a service. In: Hensher, D.A., Mulley, C. (Eds.), Transportation Research Part A: Policy and Practice. Special Issue on Developments in Mobility as a Service (MaaS) and Intelligent Mobility.

Cox, T., Houdmont, J., Griffiths, A., 2006. Rail passenger crowding, stress, health and safety in Britain. Transp. Res. A Policy Pract. 40 (3), 244–258.

Cramer, J., Krueger, A.B., 2016. Disruptive change in the taxi business: the case of Uber. Am. Econ. Rev. 106 (5), 177–182. https://doi.org/10.1257/aer.p20161002.

Currie, G., Fournier, N., 2019. Why most DRT/Micro-Transits fail—What the survivors tell us about progress. In: Paper Presented at the 16th International Conference on Competition and Ownership in Land Passenger Transport (Thredbo 16), Singapore.

Danielis, R., Marcucci, E., 2002. Bottleneck road congestion pricing with a competing railroad service. Transp. Res. E 38 (5), 379–388.

Datson, J., 2016. Mobility as a Service—Exploring the Opportunity for Mobility as a Service in the UK. Retrieved from: https://ts.catapult.org.uk/intelligent-mobility/im-resources/maasreport/.

Daziano, R.A., Sarrias, M., Leard, B., 2017. Are consumers willing to pay to let cars drive for them? Analyzing response to autonomous vehicles. Transp. Res. Part C Emerg. Technol. 78, 150–164. https://doi.org/10.1016/j.trc.2017.03.003.

De Borger, B., Kerstens, K., 2007. The performance of bus-transit operators. In: Hensher, D.A., Button, K.J. (Eds.), Handbook of Transport Modelling, second ed. Handbooks in Transport, vol. 1. Elsevier, Oxford, pp. 693–714.

De Reuver, M., Bouwman, H., Haaker, T., 2013. Business model road mapping: a practical approach to come from an existing to a desired business model. Int. J. Innov. Manag. 17, 1340006.

Delbosc, A., Currie, G., 2013. Causes of youth licensing decline: a synthesis of evidence. Transp. Rev. 33 (3), 271–290.

Delbosc, A., Mokhtarian, P., 2018. Face to Facebook: the relationship between social media and social travel. Transp. Policy 68, 20–27. https://doi.org/10.1016/j.tranpol.2018.04.005.

Delbosc, A., Nakanishi, H., 2017. A life course perspective on the travel of Australian millennials. Transp. Res. A Policy Pract. 104, 319–336.

Delbosc, A., McDonald, N., Stokes, G., Lucas, K., Circella, G., Lee, Y., 2019. Millennials in cities: comparing travel behaviour trends across six case study regions. Cities 90, 1–14. https://doi.org/10.1016/j.cities.2019.01.023.

Deloitte, 2019. New Zealand Transport Agency—Review of Connected Journeys Solutions. Retrieved from: https://nzta.govt.nz/assets/About-us/docs/deloitte-review-of-cjs-may-2019.pdf.

Department of the Environment, Transport and the Regions, 1998. A New Deal for Transport: Better for Everyone. The Stationery Office London.

Docherty, I., Marsden, G., Anable, J., 2018. The governance of smart mobility. Transp. Res. A Policy Pract. 115, 114–125. https://doi.org/10.1016/j.tra.2017.09.012.

Dodgson, J., Preston, J., 1991. The issues. In: Competition Ownership of Bus and Coach Services. Transportation Planning and Technology, vol. 15, pp. 135–143.

Dredge, D., Gyimothy, S., 2015. The collaborative economy and tourism: critical perspectives, questionable claims and silenced voices. Tour. Recreat. Res. 40 (3), 286–302.

Eckhardt, J., Nykänen, L., Aapaoja, A., Niemi, P., 2018. MaaS in rural areas—case Finland. Res. Transp. Bus. Manag. 27, 75–83. https://doi.org/10.1016/j.rtbm.2018.09.005.

Edler, J., Georghiou, L., 2007. Public procurement and innovation—resurrecting the demand side. Res. Policy 36 (7), 949–963.

Edwards, S., Mulley, C., 2004. How can soft benefits increase the viability of multi-application smart card schemes? In: Paper Presented at 11th World Congress on Intelligent Transport Systems (ITS), Nagoya, Japan.

Enoch, M.P., 2015. How a rapid modal convergence into a universal automated taxi service could be the future for local passenger transport. Tech. Anal. Strat. Manag. 27 (8), 910–924.

ESP Group, 2019. NaviGoGo: Scotland's First MaaS Pilot. Retrieved from: https://static1.squarespace.com/static/5cee5bd0687a1500015b5a9f/t/5d5c0a6c3e4b3a0001242602/1566313071168/NaviGoGo-Pilot-report.pdf.

Fagnant, D.J., Kockelman, K.M., Bansal, P., 2015. Operations of a shared autonomous vehicle fleet for the Austin, Texas market. Transp. Res. Board 2563 (1), 98–106.

Falconer, R., Zhou, T., Felder, M., 2018. Mobility-as-a-Service—The Value Proposition for the Public and Our Urban Systems. Retrieved from: https://www.arup.com/publications/research/section/maas-the-value-proposition.

Fehr and Peers, 2019. What Are TNCs' Share of VMT? Retrieved from: https://www.fehrandpeers.com/what-are-tncs-share-of-vmt/.

Finger, M., 2015. Mobility-as-a-Services: From the Helsinki Experience to a European Model? European Transport Regulation Observer. https://doi.org/10.2870/07981.

Fioreze, T., de Gruijter, M., Geurs, K., 2019. On the likelihood of using mobility-as-a-service: a case study on innovative mobility services among residents in the Netherlands. Case Stud. Transp. Policy. 7, 790–801.

Foster, C., Golay, J., 1986. Some curious old practices and their relevance to equilibrium in bus competition. J. Transp. Econ. Policy 20 (2), 191–216.

Gardner, B., Abraham, C., 2007. What drives car use? A grounded theory analysis of commuters' reasons for driving. Transport. Res. F: Traffic Psychol. Behav. 10 (3), 187–200.

Gärling, T., Axhausen, K.W., 2003. Introduction: habitual travel choice. Transportation 30 (1), 1–11. https://doi.org/10.1023/a:1021230223001.

Geels, F.W., Schot, J., 2007. Typology of sociotechnical transition pathways. Res. Policy 36 (3), 399–417.

Ghanbari, A., Álvarez San-Jaime, O., Casey, T., Markendahl, J., 2015. Repositioning in value chain for smart city ecosystems: a viable strategy for historical telecom actors. In: Paper Presented at 2015 Regional Conference of the International Telecommunications Society (ITS), Los Angeles, USA.

Goh, P.S., Swee, A., 2017. Singapore's experience with transition to bus contracting model. In: Paper Presented at 15th International Conference on Competition and Ownership in Land Passenger Transport (Thredbo 15), Stockholm, Sweden.

Goodin, R.E., March, J.G., Olsen, J.P., 2013. The Logic of Appropriateness. Oxford University Press.

Goodwin, P., Van Dender, K., 2013. 'Peak car'—themes and issues. Transp. Rev. 33 (3), 243–254.

Graehler, M., Mucci, R., Erhardt, G., 2019. Understanding the recent transit ridership decline in major US cities: service cuts or 1 emerging modes? In: Paper Presented at the 98th Annual Meeting of the Transportation Research Board, Washington, DC.

Grotenhuis, J.-W., Wiegmans, B.W., Rietveld, P., 2007. The desired quality of integrated multimodal travel information in public transport: customer needs for time and effort savings. Transp. Policy 14 (1), 27–38. https://doi.org/10.1016/j.tranpol.2006.07.001.

Guidon, S., Wicki, M., Bernauer, T., Axhausen, K., 2020. Transportation service bundling—for whose benefit? Consumer valuation of pure bundling in the passenger transportation market. In: Hensher, D.A., Mulley, C. (Eds.), Transportation Research Part A: Policy and Practice. Special Issue on Developments in Mobility as a Service (MaaS) and Intelligent Mobility. https://doi.org/10.1016/j.tra.2019.09.023.

Guilarte, A.G., 2019. Blockchain Based Open Mobility Marketplace. LinkedIn. 3 May 2019. Retrieved from: https://www.linkedin.com/pulse/blockchain-based-open-mobility-marketplace-andres-g-guilarte/.

Gwilliam, K., 2008. Bus transport: is there a regulatory cycle? In: Hensher, D.A. (Ed.), Transportation Research Part A: Policy and Practice. Institutional Reform in Land Passenger Transport, vol. 42, pp. 1183–1194.

Hannon, E., Knupfer, S., Stern, S., Nijssen, J.T., 2019. The Road to Seamless Urban Mobility. McKinsey & Company. Retrieved from: https://www.mckinsey.com/business-functions/sustainability/our-insights/the-road-to-seamless-urban-mobility.

Harb, M., Xiao, Y., Circella, G., Mokhtarian, P.L., Walker, J.L., 2018. Projecting travelers into a world of self-driving vehicles: estimating travel behavior implications via a naturalistic experiment. Transportation 45 (6), 1671–1685.

Harper, C.D., Hendrickson, C.T., Mangones, S., Samaras, C., 2016. Estimating potential increases in travel with autonomous vehicles for the non-driving, elderly and people with travel-restrictive medical conditions. Transp. Res. Part C Emerg. Technol. 72, 1–9. https://doi.org/10.1016/j.trc.2016.09.003.

Hartikainen, A., Pitkänen, J.-P., Riihelä, A., Räsänen, J., Sacs, I., Sirkiä, A., Uteng, A., 2019. Whimpact: Insights From the World's First MOBILITY-as-a-Service (MaaS) System. Retrieved from: https://ramboll.com/whimpact.

Heikkilä, S., 2014. Mobility as a Service—A Proposal for Action for the Public Administration, Case Helsinki. (Master of Science in Technology). Aalto University, Helsinki. Retrieved from: https://aaltodoc.aalto.fi/handle/123456789/13133.

Hensher, D.A., 2010. Hypothetical bias, choice experiments and willingness to pay. Transp. Res. B 44, 735–752.

Hensher, D.A., 2017. Future bus transport contracts under a mobility as a service (MaaS) regime in the digital age: are they likely to change? Transp. Res. A Policy Pract. 98, 86–96. https://doi.org/10.1016/j.tra.2017.02.006.

Hensher, D.A., 2018a. Public service contracts: the economics of reform with special reference to the bus sector. In: COWIE, J., ISON, S. (Eds.), The Routledge Handbook of Transport Economics. Routledge, London.

Hensher, D.A., 2018b. Tackling road congestion—what might it look like in the future under a collaborative and connected mobility model? Transp. Policy 66, A1–A8. https://doi.org/10.1016/j.tranpol.2018.02.007.

Hensher, D.A., Mulley, C., 2014. Complementing distance based charges with discounted registration fees in the reform of road user charges: the impact for motorists and government revenue. Transportation 41 (4), 697–715.

Hensher, D.A., Rose, J.M., Greene, W.H., 2015. Applied Choice Analysis, second ed. Cambridge University Press, Cambridge.

Hensher, D.A., Ho, C., Mulley, C., 2016. Disruption costs in bus contract transitions. In: Muñoz, J.C., Hensher, D.A., Steel, R. (Eds.), Research in Transportation Economics. Competition and Ownership in Land Passenger Transport (Selected Papers From the Thredbo 14 conference), vol. 59, pp. 75–85.

Hesselgren, M., Sjöman, M., Pernestål, A., 2019. Understanding user practices in mobility service systems: results from studying large scale corporate MaaS in practice. Travel Behav. Soc. https://doi.org/10.1016/j.tbs.2018.12.005.

Hietanen, S., 2014. 'Mobility as a Service'—the new transport model? ITS & Transport Management Supplement. Eur. Secur. 12 (2), 2–4. Retrieved from: http://www.itsineurope.com/its10/media/press_clippings/ITS%20Supp_et214.pdf.

Ho, C.Q., Hensher, D.A., Mulley, C., Wong, Y.Z., 2018. Potential uptake and willingness-to-pay for mobility as a service (MaaS): a stated choice study. Transp. Res. A Policy Pract. 117, 302–318. https://doi.org/10.1016/j.tra.2018.08.025.

Ho, C.Q., Mulley, C., Hensher, D.A., 2020. Public preferences for mobility as a service: insights from stated preference surveys. Transp. Res. A Policy Pract. 131, 70–90.

Hollands, R., 2015. Critical interventions into the corporate smart city. Camb. J. Reg. Econ. Soc. 8 (1), 61–77. Retrieved from: http://refhub.elsevier.com/S0965-8564(16)31102-8/h0105.

Holmberg, P.-E., Collado, M., Sarasini, S., Williander, M., 2016. Mobility as a Service (MaaS): Describing the Framework. Retrieved from: https://www.viktoria.se/publications/mobility-as-a-service-maas-describing-the-framework.

Hörl, S., Becker, F., Dubernet, T., Axhausen, K.W., 2019. Induzierter Verkehr durch autonome Fahrzeuge: Eine Abschätzung. final report SVI 2016/001, Schriftenreihe, 1650, UVEK, Bern.

House of Commons Transport Committee, 2018. Mobility as a Service: Eighth Report of Session 2017–19. Retrieved from: https://publications.parliament.uk/pa/cm201719/cmselect/cmtrans/590/590.pdf.

Huang, H.-J., 2002. Pricing and logit-based mode choice models of a transit and highway system with elastic demand. Eur. J. Oper. Res. 140 (3), 562–570.

Huhtala-Jenks, K., 2019. MaaS of the Month: Whim—Insights From the World's First Mobility as a Service (MaaS) Operator. Retrieved from: https://maas-alliance.eu/wp-content/uploads/sites/7/2019/06/MaaS-of-the-Month-Whim-Final.pdf.

Huhtala-Jenks, K., Forsblom, M., 2015. Mobility as a Service—The New Transport Paradigm, 12–14. Retrieved from: http://asp.vejtid.dk/Artikler/2015/08/8173.pdf.

International Transport Forum, 2017. Shared Mobility—Innovation for Liveable Cities. ITF and OECD, Paris.

Isaksson, K., Oldbury, K., Hedegaard Sørensen, C., Paulsson, A., Smith, G., Rignell, M., 2019. Problembilder som formar framtidens mobilitet—exemplet "mobilitet som tjänst" i kollektivtrafikplanering. In: Syssner, J. (Ed.), Ett nytt kontrakt för samhällsbyggande.

ITS Australia, 2018. Mobility as a Service in Australia: Customer Insights and Opportunities.

ITS World Congress 2017, 2017. ITS World Congress 2017 Awards. Retrieved from: http://itsworldcongress2017.org/awards/.

Jittrapirom, P., Caiati, V., Feneri, A.-M., Ebrahimigharehbaghi, S., Alonso-González, M.J., Narayan, J., 2017. Mobility as a Service: a critical review of definitions, assessments of schemes, and key challenges. Urban Plan. 2, 13–25. https://doi.org/10.17645/up.v2i2.931.

Jittrapirom, P., Marchau, V., van der Heijden, R., Meurs, H., 2018a. Dynamic adaptive policymaking for implementing Mobility-as-a-Service (MaaS). Res. Transp. Bus. Manag. 27, 46–55. https://doi.org/10.1016/j.rtbm.2018.07.001.

Jittrapirom, P., Marchau, V., van der Heijden, R., Meurs, H., 2018b. Future implementation of mobility as a service (MaaS): results of an international Delphi study. Travel Behav. Soc. https://doi.org/10.1016/j.tbs.2018.12.004.

Juniper Research, 2018. Helsinki Leads in Mobility-as-a-Service. SmartCitiesWorld. 5 September 2018. Retrieved from: https://www.smartcitiesworld.net/news/news/helsinki-leads-in-mobility-as-a-service-3308.

K2 Swedish Knowledge Centre for Public Transport, 2017. Strategic Case: Mobility-as-a-Service (MaaS). Retrieved from: http://www.k2centrum.se/fou-omr%C3%A5den/integrerade-mobilitetstj%C3%A4nster.

Kamargianni, M., Matyas, M., 2017. The business ecosystem of mobility-as-a-service. In: Paper Presented at the 96th Transportation Research Board (TRB) Annual Meeting, Washington, DC. Retrieved from: http://discovery.ucl.ac.uk/10037890/.

Kamargianni, M., Li, W., Matyas, M., 2016a. A Comprehensive Review of "Mobility as a Service" Systems, Washington, DC.
Kamargianni, M., Li, W., Matyas, M., Schäfer, A., 2016b. A critical review of new mobility services for urban transport. Transp. Res. Procedia 14, 3294–3303. https://doi.org/10.1016/j.trpro.2016.05.277.
Kamargianni, M., Matyas, M., Li, W., Muscat, J., 2018a. Londoners' Attitudes Towards Car-Ownership and Mobility-as-a-Service: Impact Assessment and Opportunities That Lie Ahead. Retrieved from: https://www.ucl.ac.uk/consultants/images/casestudies/maas.
Kamargianni, M., Matyas, M., Li, W., Muscat, J., Yfantis, L., 2018b. The MaaS Dictionary. Retrieved from: https://docs.wixstatic.com/ugd/a2135d_d6ffa2fee2834782b4ec9a75c1957f55.pdf.
Karlsson, I.C.M., Sochor, J., Strömberg, H., 2016. Developing the 'service' in mobility as a service: experiences from a field trial of an innovative travel brokerage. Transp. Res. Procedia 14, 3265–3273. Retrieved from: http://www.sciencedirect.com/science/article/pii/S2352146516302794.
Karlsson, I.C.M., Mukhtar-Landgren, D., Lund, E., Sarasini, S., Smith, G., Sochor, J., Wendle, B., 2017a. Mobility-as-a-Service: a tentative framework for analysing institutional conditions. In: Paper Presented at the 45th European Transport Conference, Barcelona.
Karlsson, I.C.M., Sochor, J., Aapaoja, A., Eckhardt, J., König, D., 2017b. Deliverable Nr 4—Impact Assessment. Retrieved from: https://research.chalmers.se/publication/248829.
Karlsson, I.C.M., Mukhtar-Landgren, D., Smith, G., Koglin, T., Kronsell, A., Lund, E., et al., 2020. Development and implementation of mobility-as-service—a qualitative study of barriers and enabling factors. In: Hensher, D.A., Mulley, C. (Eds.), Transportation Research Part A: Policy and Practice. Special Issue on Developments in Mobility as a Service (MaaS) and Intelligent Mobility. https://doi.org/10.1016/j.tra.2019.09.028.
Katz, D., Rahman, M.M., 2010. Levels of overcrowding in bus system of Dhaka, Bangladesh. Transp. Res. Rec. 2143 (1), 85–91.
Kent, J., 2018. Will Autonomous Cars Lead to Less Car Ownership? Retrieved from: https://sydney.edu.au/news-opinion/news/2018/12/11/will-autonomous-cars-lead-to-less-car-ownership-.html.
Kesteloot, R., 2019. MaaS in Flanders: creating value through cooperation/competition. In: Paper Presented at the UITP Global Public Transport Summit, Stockholm.
König, D., Eckhardt, J., Aapaoja, A., Sochor, J., Karlsson, I.C.M., 2016. Deliverable Nr 3—Business and Operator Models for MaaS. Retrieved from: https://research.chalmers.se/publication/239795.
KPMG, 2017. Reimagine Places: Mobility as a Service. Retrieved from: http://kpmg.com/uk/reimagine-maas.
Kraus, M., Yoshida, Y., 2002. The commuter's time-of-use decision and optimal pricing and service in urban mass transit. J. Urban Econ. 51 (1), 170–195.
Kronsell, A., Mukhtar-Landgren, D., 2018. Experimental governance: the role of municipalities in urban living labs. Eur. Plan. Stud. 26, 988–1007.
Kuhn, T.S., 1962. The Structure of Scientific Revolutions, first ed. University of Chicago press.
Kuhnimhof, T., Zumkeller, D., Chlond, B., 2013. Who made peak car, and how? A breakdown of trends over four decades in four countries. Transp. Rev. 33 (3), 325–342.
Kyriakidis, M., Happee, R., de Winter, J.C., 2015. Public opinion on automated driving: results of an international questionnaire among 5000 respondents. Transport. Res. F: Traffic Psychol. Behav. 32, 127–140. https://doi.org/10.1016/j.trf.2015.04.014.
Law on public transport, Pub. L. No. 2010:1065., 2010. (2010/07/14).
Law on the application of eu state aid rules, Pub. L. No. 2013:388., 2013. (2013-05-30).

Li, Y., Voege, T., 2017. Mobility as a Service (MaaS): challenges of implementation and policy required. J. Transp. Technol. 7 (2), 95–106. https://doi.org/10.4236/jtts.2017.72007.

Linton, C., Bray, J., 2019. MaaS Movement? Urban Transport Group. Retrieved from: http://www.urbantransportgroup.org/system/files/general-docs/Urban%20Transport%20Group%20%E2%80%93%20Maas%20movement%20report_AW.pdf.

Local goverment act, Pub. L. No. 2017:725., 2017. (2017-06-22).

Loorbach, D., 2007. Transition Management: New Mode of Governance for Sustainable Development. International Books, Utrecht.

Lundberg, U., 1976. Urban commuting: crowdedness and catecholamine excretion. J. Hum. Stress. 2 (3), 26–36.

Lyons, G., 2016. Getting smart about urban mobility—aligning the paradigms of smart and sustainable. Transp. Res. A Policy Pract. 115, 4–14. https://doi.org/10.1016/j.tra.2016.12.001.

Lyons, G., Hammond, P., Mackay, K., 2019. The importance of user perspective in the evolution of MaaS. In: Hensher, D.A., Mulley, C. (Eds.), Transportation Research Part A: Policy and Practice. Special Issue on Developments in Mobility as a Service (MaaS) and Intelligent Mobility, vol. 121, pp. 22–36. https://doi.org/10.1016/j.tra.2018.12.010.

MaaS Alliance, 2017. White Paper: Guidelines & Recommendations to Create the Foundations for a Thriving MaaS Ecosystem. Retrieved from: https://maas-alliance.eu/wp-content/uploads/sites/7/2017/09/MaaS-WhitePaper_final_040917-2.pdf.

MaaS Alliance, 2018a. What is MaaS? Retrieved from: http://maas-alliance.eu/homepage/what-is-maas/.

MaaS Alliance, 2018b. The European Mobility as a Service Alliance. Retrieved from: https://maas-alliance.eu/european-mobility-service-alliance/.

MaaS Global, 2016. What is Mobility as a Service (MaaS)? Retrieved from: https://maas.global/what-is-mobility-as-a-service-maas/.

MaaS Global, 2018. MaaS as a Concept. Retrieved from: https://maas.global/maas-as-a-concept/.

MaaS Global, 2019a. A Brief History of MaaS Global, the Company Behind the Whim app. Retrieved from: https://whimapp.com/history-of-maas-global/.

MaaS Global, 2019b. MaaS Global Completes €29.5M Funding Round. [Press release]. Retrieved from: https://whimapp.com/maas-global-completes-e29-5m-funding-round/.

MaaS Global, 2019c. Sampo's Blog: Why Freedom of Mobility is at the Center of Dealing With the Climate Crisis. Retrieved from: https://whimapp.com/why-freedom-of-mobility-is-at-the-center-of-dealing-with-climate-crisis/.

MaaS Scotland, 2018. Mobility as a Service: Positioning Scotland for an Emerging Global Market. MaaS Scotland White Paper, January. Retrieved from: https://maas-alliance.eu/wp-content/uploads/sites/7/2018/02/MaaS-Positioning-Scotland-for-an-Emerging-Global-Market_PUBLIC.pdf.

Maciejewski, M., Bischoff, J., 2016. Congestion effects of autonomous taxi fleets. Transport.

Maciejewski, M., Bischoff, J., 2018. Congestion effects on autonomous taxi fleets. Transport 33 (4), 971–980. https://doi.org/10.3846/16484142.2017.1347827.

MacKenzie, et al., 2016. In: Lowy, J. (Ed.), Will Robot Cars Drive Traffic Congestion off a Cliff? Associated Press. Retrieved from: https://www.pbs.org/newshour/nation/will-robot-cars-drive-traffic-congestion-off-a-cliff.

March, J.G., Olsen, J.P., 1989. Rediscovering Institutions: The Organizational Basis of Politics. Free Press.

Marchetti, C., 1994. Anthropological invariants in travel behavior. Technol. Forecast. Soc. Chang. 47 (1), 75–88.

Martin, E., Shaheen, S., 2011. The impact of carsharing on public transit and non-motorized travel: an exploration of North American carsharing survey data. Energies 4 (11), 2094–2114.

Martinez, L., Crist, P., 2015. Urban Mobility System Upgrade: How Shared Self-Driving Cars Could Change City Traffic. International Transport Forum, Paris.

Matyas, M., Kamargianni, M., 2018. The potential of mobility as a service bundles as a mobility management tool. Transportation, 1–18. https://doi.org/10.1007/s11116-018-9913-4.

Mayas, M., Kamargianni, M., 2017. Stated preference design for exploring demand for "mobility as a service" plans. In: Paper Presented at the International Choice Modelling Conference, Cape Town, South Africa.

Mazzucato, M., 2015. The Entrepreneurial State: Debunking Public vs. Private Sector Myths. vol. 1. Anthem Press.

McCabe, G., 2017. Is mobility as a service a fraud? In: Presentation at the 2017 Bus Industry Confederation (BIC) National Conference, Hobart, November 2017.

McCarthy, L., Delbosc, A., Currie, G., Molloy, A., 2019. 'Transit Faithfuls' or 'Transit Leavers'? Understanding mobility trajectories of new parents. Transp. Policy 78, 105–112. https://doi.org/10.1016/j.tranpol.2019.04.007.

McDonald, N.C., 2015. Are millennials really the "go-nowhere" generation? J. Am. Plan. Assoc. 81 (2), 90–103. https://doi.org/10.1080/01944363.2015.1057196.

McKinsey, 2019. The Road to Seamless Urban Mobility. Retrieved from: https://www.mckinsey.com/business-functions/sustainability-and-resource-productivity/our-insights/the-road-to-seamless-urban-mobility.

McKinsey, & Bloomberg, 2016. An Integrated Perspective on the Future of Mobility. McKinsey & Company/Bloomberg New Energy Finance, New York, NY/London.

Merkert, R., Wong, Y.Z., 2020. Workshop 3: emerging business models and implications for the transport ecosystem. In: Leong, W., Wong, Y.D., Hensher, D.A., Steel, R. (Eds.), Research in Transportation Economics. Competition and Ownership in Land Passenger Transport (Selected Papers From the Thredbo 16 Conference), (Forthcoming).

Merkert, R., Bushell, J., Beck, M., 2020. Collaboration as a service (CaaS) to fully integrate public transportation—lessons from long distance travel to reimagine Mobility as a Service. In: Hensher, D.A., Mulley, C. (Eds.), Transportation Research Part A: Policy and Practice. Special Issue on Developments in Mobility as a Service (MaaS) and Intelligent Mobility.

Metz, D., 2013. Peak car and beyond: the fourth era of travel. Transp. Rev. 33 (3), 255–270.

Meurs, H., Sharmeen, F., Marchau, V., van der Heijden, R., 2020. Organizing integrated services in mobility-as-a-service systems: principles of alliance formation applied to a MaaS-pilot in The Netherlands. Transp. Res. A (Special Issue on developments in Mobility as a Service (MaaS) and intelligent mobility). https://doi.org/10.1016/j.tra.2019.09.036.

Meyer, J.W., 1994. Rationalized environments. In: Scott, W.R., Meyer (Eds.), Institutional Environments and Organizations. SAGE Publications, Newbury Park, pp. 28–54.

Mohd Mahudin, N.D., Cox, T., Griffiths, A., 2011. Modelling the spillover effects of rail passenger crowding on individual well being and organisational behaviour. In: Pratelli, A., Brebbia, C.A. (Eds.), Urban Transport XVII, Urban Transport and the Environment in the 21st Century. WIT Transactions on the Built Environment, WIT Press, pp. 227–238.

Mohring, H., 1972. Optimization and scale economies in urban bus transportation. Am. Econ. Rev. 62 (4), 591–604.

Mohring, H., 1983. Minibuses in urban transportation. J. Urban Econ. 14 (3), 293–317.

MuConsult, 2017. Mobility as a Service. Bouwstenen voor keuzen I&M. Retrieved from: https://dutchmobilityinnovations.com/fileattachment?file=ppBLeK%2BP7fmK2X67eeSZhQ%3D%3D&v=1.

Mukhtar-Landgren, D., Smith, G., 2019. Perceived action spaces for public actors in the development of Mobility as a Service. Eur. Transp. Res. Rev. 11 (1), 32. https://doi.org/10.1186/s12544-019-0363-7.

Mukhtar-Landgren, D., Karlsson, I.C.M., Koglin, T., Kronsell, A., Lund, E., Sarasini, S., et al., 2016. Institutional conditions for integrated mobility services (IMS): Towards a framework for analysis (Working Paper No. 2016:16). Retrieved from: http://www.k2centrum.se/sites/default/files/institutional_conditions_for_integrated_mobility_services_ims_wp_2016-16_1.pdf.

Mulley, C., 2017. Mobility as a services (MaaS)—does it have critical mass? Transp. Rev. 37 (3), 247–251. https://doi.org/10.1080/01441647.2017.1280932.

Mulley, C., Daniels, R., 2012. Quantifying the role of a flexible transport service in reducing the accessibility gap in low density areas: a case-study in north-West Sydney. Res. Transp. Bus. Manag. 3, 12–23.

Mulley, C., Ho, C., 2017. Understanding the determinants of walking as the basis for social marketing public health messaging. In: Mulley, C., Gebel, K., Ding, D. (Eds.), Walking: Connecting Sustainable Transport with Health. Emerald Group Publishing Limited, Bingley, pp. 41–59.

Mulley, C., Kronsell, A., 2018. Workshop 7 report—The 'uberisation' of public transport and mobility as a service (MaaS): implications for future mainstream public transport. In: Alexandersson, G., Hensher, D.A., Steel, R. (Eds.), Research in Transportation Economics. Competition and Ownership in Land Passenger Transport (Selected Papers From the Thredbo 15 Conference), vol. 69, pp. 568–572.

Mulley, C., Moutou, C.J., 2015. Not too late to learn from the Sydney Olympics experience: opportunities offered by multimodality in current transport policy. Cities 45, 117–122. https://doi.org/10.1016/j.cities.2014.10.004.

Mulley, C., Nelson, J.D., 2009. Flexible transport services: a new market opportunity for public transport. Res. Transp. Econ. 25 (1), 39–45. https://doi.org/10.1016/j.retrec.2009.08.008.

Mulley, C., Nelson, J.D., Wright, S., 2018. Community transport meets mobility as a service: on the road to a new a flexible future. Res. Transp. Econ, 1–9. https://doi.org/10.1016/j.retrec.2018.02.004. (in press).

Mulley, C., Nelson, J.D., Hensher, D.A., 2019. Intelligent mobility and mobility as a service. In: Stanley, J., Hensher, D.A. (Eds.), A Research Agenda for Transport Policy. Edward Elgar Publishing, Cheltenham.

Mulley, C., Ho, C., Balbontin, C., Hensher, D.A., Stevens, L., Nelson, J., Wright, S., 2020. Mobility as a Service in Community Transport in Australia: can it provide a sustainable future? In: Transportation Research Part A: Policy and Practice. Special Issue on Developments in Mobility as a Service (Maas) and Intelligent Mobility.

Musk, E., 2016. Master Plan, Part Deux. Tesla Motors. Retrieved from: https://www.tesla.com/blog/master-plan-part-deux.

National Academy of Sciences, 2019. Partnerships Between Transit Agencies and Transportation Network Companies. The National Academies Press, Washington, DC.

Nelson, J.D., Wright, S., Masson, B., Ambrosino, G., Naniopoulos, A., 2010. Recent developments in flexible transport services. Res. Transp. Econ. 29, 243–248.

Nielsen, G., Nelson, J., Mulley, C., Tegner, G., Lind, G., Lange, T., 2005. Public Transport—Planning the Networks. Best Practice Guide, vol. 2. HiTrans, Stavanger, Norway.

Noland, R.B., 2019. Trip patterns and revenue of shared e-scooters in Louisville, Kentucky. Transp. Find. https://doi.org/10.32866/7747.

Nordin, F., 2011. The risks of providing services. J. Serv. Manag. 22 (3), 390–408. https://doi.org/10.1108/09564231111136881.

Pangbourne, K., Stead, D., Mladenović, M., Milakis, D., 2018. The case of Mobility as a Service: a critical reflection on challenges for urban transport and mobility governance. In: Marsden, G., Reardon, L. (Eds.), Governance of the Smart Mobility Transition. Emerald Publishing Limited, Bingley, pp. 33–48.

Pangbourne, K., Stead, D., Mladenović, M., Milakis, D., 2020. Questioning Mobility as a Service: unanticipated societal and governance implications. In: Hensher, D.A., Mulley, C. (Eds.), Transportation Research Part A: Policy and Practice. Special Issue on Developments in Mobility as a Service (MaaS) and Intelligent Mobility.

Payre, W., Cestac, J., Delhomme, P., 2014. Intention to use a fully automated car: attitudes and a priori acceptability. Transport. Res. F: Traffic Psychol. Behav. 27 (Part B), 252–263. https://doi.org/10.1016/j.trf.2014.04.009.

Perera, S., Ho, C., Hensher, D.A., 2019. Resurgence of demand responsive transit services—insights from BRIDJ trials in Inner West of Sydney. In: Paper Presented at the Thredbo 16 International Conference Series on Competition and Ownership in Land Passenger Transport, Singapore.

Pernestål Brenden, A., Holmberg, P.-E., Smith, G., Laurell, A., Kramers, A., 2017. Roadmap for Combined Mobility as a Service in Sweden. Retrieved from: https://kompis.me/wp-content/uploads/2018/01/roadmapp_eng_10jan_2018-1.pdf.

Polis Seminar, 2018. CIVITAS Webinar: Can Mobility as a Service Contribute to Sustainable Mobility and How to Establish It Successfully? Retrieved from: https://www.polisnetwork.eu/publicnews/1713/48/CIVITAS-Webinar-Can-Mobility-as-a-Service-contribute-to-sustainable-mobility-and-how-to-establish-it-successfully.

Polydoropoulou, A., Pagoni, I., Tsirimpa, A., Roumboutsos, A., Kamargianni, M., Tsouros, I., 2020. Prototype business models for Mobility-as-a-Service. In: Hensher, D.A., Mulley, C. (Eds.), Transportation Research Part A: Policy and Practice, Special Issue on Developments in Mobility as a Service (MaaS) and Intelligent Mobility. https://doi.org/10.1016/j.tra.2019.09.035.

Preston, J., 1992a. Competition policy and the British bus industry: the case of mergers. In: Talvitie, A., Hensher, D.A., Beesley, M.E. (Eds.), Privatization and Deregulation in Passenger Transportation: Selected Proceedings of the 2nd International Conference, Tampere, Finland, pp. 99–115.

Preston, J., 1992b. Report for workshop 2: understanding competition and anti-trust behaviour. In: Talvitie, A., Hensher, D.A., Beesley, M.E. (Eds.), Privatization and Deregulation in Passenger Transportation: Selected Proceedings of the 2nd International Conference, Tampere, Finland, pp. 133–140.

Preston, J., 2010. What's so funny about peace, love and transport integration? Res. Transp. Econ. 29 (1), 329–338. https://doi.org/10.1016/j.retrec.2010.07.042.

Pucher, J., Markstedt, A., Hirschman, I., 1983. Impacts of subsidies on the costs of urban public transport. J. Transp. Econ. Policy 17 (2), 155–176.

Ramboll, 2019. Whimpact: Insights From the World's First Mobility-as-a-Service (maas) System.

Rantasila, K., 2015. The impact of Mobility as a Service concept to land use in Finnish context. In: Paper Presented at the 2015 Sustainable International Conference on Sustainable Mobility Applications, Renewables and Technology (SMART), Kuwait. Retrieved from: http://ieeexplore.ieee.org/abstract/document/7399229/.

Ratilainen, H., 2017. Mobility-as-a-Service: Exploring Consumer Preferences for MaaS Subscription Packages Using a Stated Choice Experiment.

Rayle, L., Dai, D., Chan, N., Cervero, R., Shaheen, S., 2016. Just a better taxi? A survey-based comparison of taxis, transit, and ridesourcing services in San Francisco. Transp. Policy 45, 168–178.

Reck, D.J., Axhausen, K.W., 2019a. Learning From the MaaS Experience in Augsburg, Germany. Arbeitsberichte Verkehrs- und Raumplanung, 1469, IVT, ETH Zürich, Zürich.

Reck, D.J., Axhausen, K.W., 2019b. Subsidized Ridesourcing for the First/Last Mile: How Valuable for Whom? Working Paper, Arbeitsberichte Verkehrs- und Raumplanung, 1441, IVT, ETH Zürich, Zürich.

Reck, D.J., Axhausen, K.W., 2019c. Autonomous taxi operations: market structure, competitive dynamics and regulatory implications. In: Paper Presented at the 98th Annual Meeting of the Transportation Research Board, Washington, DC.

Reck, D.J., Axhausen, K.W., 2020. How much of which mode? Using revealed preference data to design MaaS plans. In: Paper Presented at the 99th Annual Meeting of the Transportation Research Board, Washington, DC.

Regulation (2007) no 1370/2007, EUR-lex, 1370/2007 Stat. (EUR-lex 2007 2017-10-23).

Riksbyggen, 2016. Länge Leve BRF Viva. Retrieved from: https://www.riksbyggen.se/globalassets/1-riksbyggen/2-bostad/1-bostadsratter/vastra-gotaland/brf-viva/bofakta_brf_viva_web.pdf.

Rogers, E.M., 1995. Diffusion of Innovations. Simon and Schuster, New York.

Romanyuk, J., 2018. Mobility as a Service—Hype or the Future of Transportation? (Master of Science in Economics and Business Administration) Aalto University.

Rural-MaaS, 2017. Rural-MaaS project. Retrieved from: http://www.vtt.fi/sites/maaseutumaas/. (in Finnish only).

SAE International, 2018. Taxonomy and definitions for terms related to shared mobility and enabling technologies. In: Surface Transportation Recommended Practice. Retrieved from: https://www.sae.org/standards/content/j3163_201809/.

Samtrafiken, 2017. Förarbete—Swedish Mobility Program (SMP). Retrieved from: https://samtrafiken.se/wp-content/uploads/2017/02/F%C3%B6rarbete-Swedish-Mobility-Program.pdf.

Sarasini, S., Sochor, J., Arby, H., 2017. What characterises a sustainable MaaS business model? In: Paper Presented at the 1st International Conference on Mobility as a Service (ICOMaaS), Tampere, Finland.

Schaller, B., 2017. Empty Seats, Full Streets: Fixing Manhattan's Traffic Problem. Schaller Consulting. December, 1(3).

Schoeman, I., Schoeman, C., 2017. Alignment of spatial, transportation and environmental planning: practices underpinning strategic approaches in developing countries. In: Schoeman, I. (Ed.), Transportation, Land Use and Integration: Applications in Developing Countries. WIT Press, Southampton, pp. 119–151.

Scott, W.R., 2014. Institutions and Organizations: Ideas, Interests and Identities, fourth ed. SAGE Publications, Thousand Oaks.

Shaheen, S.A., Chan, N., 2016. Mobility and the sharing economy: potential to facilitate the first- and last-mile public transit connections. Built Environ. 42 (4), 573–588. https://doi.org/10.2148/benv.42.4.573.

Shaheen, S., Cohen, A., Yelchuru, B., Sarkhili, S., 2017. Mobility on Demand Operational Concept Report. Produced for US Department of Transportation. Retrieved from: http://innovativemobility.org/wp-content/uploads/Mobility-on-Demand-Operational-Concept-Report-2017.pdf.

Shaheen, S.A., Cohen, A.P., Jaffee, M., 2018. Innovative Mobility: Carsharing Outlook—Carsharing Market Overview, Analysis, and Trends, Spring 2018. Transportation Sustainability Research Center—University Of California, Berkeley.

Shergold, I., Lyons, G., Hubers, C., 2015. Future mobility in an ageing society—where are we heading? J. Transp. Health 2 (1), 86–94. https://doi.org/10.1016/j.jth.2014.10.005.

Sigala, M., 2019. The 'Sharing Economy' Simply Dresses Up Our Consumerist Tendencies in a More Palatable Ideology. Retrieved from: http://theconversation.com/the-sharing-economy-simply-dresses-up-our-consumerist-tendencies-in-a-more-palatable-ideology-99090.

Sipe, N., Pojani, D., 2018. For Mobility as a Service (MaaS) to solve our transport woes, some things need to change. The Conversation. November 19, 2018. Retrieved from: https://theconversation.com/for-mobility-as-a-service-maas-to-solve-our-transport-woes-some-things-need-to-change-105119.

Smith, G., Akram, A., 2017. Outbound open innovation in the public sector: the roles of intermediaries. In: Paper Presented at the 4th World Open Innovation Conference (WOIC), San Fransicso.
Smith, G., Hensher, D.A., 2019. Towards a framework for Mobility-as-a-Service policies. In: Paper Presented at the Thredbo 16—The International Conference Series on Competition and Ownership in Land Passenger Transport, Singapore.
Smith, G., Sochor, J., Karlsson, I.C.M., 2017. Procuring Mobility as a Service: exploring dialogues with potential bidders in West Sweden. In: Paper Presented at the 24th World Congress on Intelligent Transportation Systems, Montreal.
Smith, G., Sochor, J., Karlsson, I.C.M., 2018a. Mobility as a service: development scenarios and implications for public transport. Res. Transp. Econ. 69, 592–599. https://doi.org/10.1016/j.retrec.2018.04.001.
Smith, G., Sochor, J., Sarasini, S., 2018b. Mobility as a service: comparing developments in Sweden and Finland. Res. Transp. Bus. Manag. 27, 36–45. https://doi.org/10.1016/j.rtbm.2018.09.004.
Smith, G., Sarasini, S., Karlsson, I.C.M., Mukhtar-Landgren, D., Sochor, J., 2019a. Governing mobility as a service: insights from sweden and finland. In: Finger, M., Audouin, M. (Eds.), The Governance of Smart Transportation Systems: Towards New Organizational Structures for the Development of Integrated, Electric, Automated and Shared Mobility. Springer International Publishing, https://doi.org/10.1007/978-3-319-96526-0_9.
Smith, G., Sochor, J., Karlsson, I.C.M., 2019b. Public–private innovation: barriers in the case of mobility as a service in West Sweden. Public Manag. Rev. 21 (1), 116–137. https://doi.org/10.1080/14719037.2018.1462399.
Smith, G., Sochor, J., Karlsson, I.C.M., 2019c. Adopting Mobility-as-a-Service: an empirical analysis of end-users' experiences. In: ICoMaaS 2019 Proceedings Tampere, Finland, pp. 85–97.
Smith, G., Sochor, J., Karlsson, I.C.M., 2020. Intermediary MaaS Integrators: a Case Study on Hopes and Fears. In: Hensher, D.A., Mulley, C. (Eds.), Transportation Research Part A: Policy and Practice. Special Issue on Developments in Mobility as a Service (MaaS) and Intelligent Mobility. https://doi.org/10.1016/j.tra.2019.09.024.
Sochor, J., Sarasini, S., 2017. More than the sum of its parts? The Finnish public's perspectives on Mobility-as-a-Service and ITS. In: Paper Presented at the 12th European Congress on Intelligent Transportation Systems, Strasbourg.
Sochor, J., Strömberg, H., Karlsson, M., 2014. Travelers' motives for adopting a new, innovative travel service: insights from the ubigo field operational test in gothenburg, Sweden. In: Paper Presented at the 21st World Congress on Intelligent Transport Systems, Detroit.
Sochor, J., Strömberg, H., Karlsson, I.C.M., 2015a. The Added Value of a New, Innovative Travel Service: Insights From the UbiGo Field Operational Test in Gothenburg, Sweden. Springer International Publishing, Cham.
Sochor, J., Strömberg, H., Karlsson, I.C.M., 2015b. Implementing mobility as a service: challenges in integrating user, commercial, and societal perspectives. Transp. Res. Rec, 1–9. https://doi.org/10.3141/2536-01.
Sochor, J., Karlsson, I.C.M., Strömberg, H., 2016. Trying out Mobility as a Service: experiences from a field trial and implications for understanding demand. Transp. Res. Rec. 2542 (1), 57–64. https://doi.org/10.3141/2542-07.
Sochor, J., Arby, H., Karlsson, I.C.M., Sarasini, S., 2018. A topological approach to mobility as a service: a proposed tool for understanding requirements and effects, and for aiding the integration of societal goals. Res. Transp. Bus. Manag. 27, 3–14. https://doi.org/10.1016/j.rtbm.2018.12.003.
Standing, C., Standing, S., Biermann, S., 2019. The implications of the sharing economy for transport. Transp. Rev. 39 (2), 226–242.
Stanley, J., Hensher, D.A., Wong, Y.Z., 2019. Disruptive Technology and Moving People in Our Cities and Regions. Bus Industry Confederation, Canberra, ACT.

Storme, T., De Vos, J., De Paepe, L., Witlox, F., 2020. Limitations to the car-substitution effect of MaaS. Findings from a Belgian pilot study. In: De Vos, J., De Paepe, L., Hensher, D.A., Mulley, C. (Eds.), Transportation Research Part A: Policy and Practice. Special Issue on Developments in Mobility as a Service (MaaS) and Intelligent Mobility, vol. 131, pp. 196–205.

Stremersch, S., Tellis, G.J., 2002. Strategic bundling of products and prices: a new synthesis for marketing. J. Mark. 66 (1), 55–72. https://doi.org/10.1509/jmkg.66.1.55.18455.

Strömberg, H., Rexfelt, O., Karlsson, I.C.M., Sochor, J., 2016. Trying on change—trialability as a change moderator for sustainable travel behaviour. Travel Behav. Soc. 4, 60–68. https://doi.org/10.1016/j.tbs.2016.01.002.

Strömberg, H., Karlsson, I.C.M., Sochor, J., 2018. Inviting travelers to the smorgasbord of sustainable urban transport: evidence from a maas field trial. Transportation 45 (6), 1655–1670. https://doi.org/10.1007/s11116-018-9946-8.

Strömdahl, A., Arby, H., Kuschel, M., Karlsson, I.C.M., Billger, M., Holmberg, P.-E., 2014. Samverkansprojekt: Go:Smart. Retrieved from: http://mistratest.ita.chalmers.se/sites/default/files/samverkansprojekt_gosmart_udi_slutrapport_bfas_gosmart_final_jg.pdf.

Swedish Agency for Public Management, 2014. Nya myndigheter på transportområdet: Fördjupningsfrågor för uppföljning av trafikverket och transportstyrelsen (2014:33). Retrieved from: http://www.statskontoret.se/globalassets/publikationer/2014/201433.pdf.

Swedish Transport Agency, 2019. Kollektivtrafik. Retrieved from: https://www.transportstyrelsen.se/sv/vagtrafik/Yrkestrafik/Kollektivtrafik/.

Tabuchi, T., 1993. Bottleneck congestion and modal split. J. Urban Econ. 34 (3), 414–431.

Teece, D.J., 2010. Business models, business strategy and innovation. Long Range Plan. 43 (2–3), 172–194.

Teubner, T., Flath, C.M., 2015. The economics of multi-hop ride sharing. Bus. Inf. Syst. Eng. 57 (5), 311–324.

TfNSW, 2018. Tech Companies Chosen to Develop Mobility Solutions. Retrieved from: https://www.transport.nsw.gov.au/news-and-events/media-releases/tech-companies-chosen-to-develop-mobility-solutions.

TfNSW, 2019. Connected and automated vehicles plan. In: Future Transport, 2056. TfNSW, Sydney.

Tirachini, A., Hensher, D.A., 2011. Bus congestion, optimal infrastructure investment and the choice of a fare collection system in dedicated bus corridors. Transp. Res. B 45 (5), 828–844.

Torfing, J., 2016. Collaborative Innovation in the Public Sector. Georgetown University Press.

Transport Analysis, 2016. Nya tjänster för rapport delad mobilitet. Retrieved from: https://www.trafa.se/globalassets/rapporter/2016/rapport-2016_15-nya-tjanster-for-delad-mobilitet.pdf.

Transport Systems Catapult, 2016. Mobility as a Service: Exploring the Opportunity for Mobility as a Service in the UK. TSC. Retrieved from: https://ts.catapult.org.uk/wp-content/uploads/2016/08/Mobility-as-a-Service_Exploring-the-Opportunity-for-MaaS-in-the-UK-Download.pdf.

Transport Systems Catapult, 2018. Blockchain disruption in transport. In: Are You Decentralised Yet? Transport Systems Catapult Concept Paper, July 2018. Retrieved from: https://s3-eu-west-1.amazonaws.com/media.ts.catapult/wp-content/uploads/2018/06/06105742/Blockchain-Disruption-in-Transport-Concept-Paper.pdf.

Truong, L.T., De Gruyter, C., Currie, G., Delbosc, A., 2017. Estimating the trip generation impacts of autonomous vehicles in car travel in Victoria, Australia. Transportation 44 (6), 1279–1292.

UITP, 2011. Becoming a Real Mobility Provider—Combined Mobility: Public Transport in Synergy With Other Modes Like Car-Sharing, Taxi and Cycling (Position Paper). UITP, Brussels.

UITP, 2016a. World's First Example of Mobility as a Service Now Live in Hannover. Retrieved from: https://www.uitp.org/news/maas-hannover.

UITP, 2016b. Mobility as a Service: An Alternative to Owning a Car. Retrieved from: https://www.uitp.org/news/maas-finland.

UITP Policy Brief, 2019. Ready for MaaS? Easier Mobility for Citizens and Better Data for Cities. Retrieved from: https://www.uitp.org/sites/default/files/cck-focus-papers-files/Policy%20Brief_MaaS_V3_final_web_0.pdf.

UK Parliament Transport Select Committee, 2018. Mobility as a Service. Eighth Report of Session 2017-19. Published 19.12.18. Retrieved from: https://publications.parliament.uk/pa/cm201719/cmselect/cmtrans/590/full-report.html.

Urry, J., 2004. The 'system' of automobility. Theory Cult. Soc. 21 (4–5), 25–39. https://doi.org/10.1177/0263276404046059.

Utriainen, R., Pöllänen, M., 2018. Review on mobility as a service in scientific publications. Res. Transp. Bus. Manag. 27, 15–23.

van Welie, M.J., Cherunya, P.C., Truffer, B., Murphy, J.T., 2018. Analysing transition pathways in developing cities: the case of Nairobi's splintered sanitation regime. Technol. Forecast. Soc. Chang. 137, 259–271. https://doi.org/10.1016/j.techfore.2018.07.059.

Veeneman, W., 2019. Public transport in a sharing environment. In: Advances in Transport Policy and Planning. The Sharing Economy and the Relevance for Transport, vol. 4, pp. 39–57.

Veeneman, W., Smith, A., 2016. Workshop 2 report: effective institutional design, regulatory frameworks and contract strategies. In: Muñoz, J.C., Hensher, D.A., Steel, R. (Eds.), Research in Transportation Economics. Competition and Ownership in Land Passenger Transport (Selected Papers From the Thredbo 14 Conference), vol. 59, pp. 60–64.

Vickrey, W.S., 1969. Congestion theory and transport investment. Am. Econ. Rev. 59 (2), 251–260.

Vij, A., Ryan, S., Sampson, S., Harris, S., 2018. Consumer preferences for mobility-as-a-service (MaaS) in Australia. In: Paper Presented at the 40th Australasian Transport Research Forum (ATRF), Darwin, Australia.

Vuchic, V.R., 2005. Urban Transit: Operations, Planning and Economics. John Wiley & Sons, Hoboken, NJ.

Walker, J., 2008. Purpose-driven public transport: creating a clear conversation about public transport goals. J. Transp. Geogr. 16 (6), 436–442.

Walker, J., 2012. Human Transit: How Clearer Thinking About Public Transit Can Enrich Our Communities and Our Lives. Island Press, Washington, DC.

Wardman, M., Whelan, G.A., 2011. Twenty years of rail crowding valuation studies: evidence and lessons from British experience. Transp. Rev. 31 (3), 379–398.

Weckström, C., Ullah, W., Mladenović, M.N., Nelson, J.D., Givoni, M., Bussman, S., 2018. User perspectives on emerging mobility services: ex post analysis of Kutsuplus pilot. Res. Transp. Bus. Manag. 27, 84–97.

Williamson, O.E., 2010. Transaction cost economics: the natural progression. Am. Econ. Rev. 100 (3), 673–690. https://doi.org/10.1257/aer.100.3.673.

Woldeamanuel, M., Nguyen, D., 2018. Perceived benefits and concerns of autonomous vehicles: an exploratory study of millennials' sentiments of an emerging market. Res. Transp. Econ. 71, 44–53.

Wong, Y.Z., 2015. Distance Decay and Commuting Peaks: Evidence From Mining Transit Smartcard Data in Canberra, Australia. (Bachelor of Philosophy (Honours) in Science). Australian National University, Canberra, ACT.

Wong, Y.Z., 2018. Mobility as a service (MaaS): what does it mean for the NSW bus & coach industry? Bulletin, June 2018, pp. 11–17.

Wong, Y.Z., 2019a. Clarify contractual framework for data sharing in public transport to unlock sustainable multi-stakeholder mobility systems. Sharing of Data in Public Transport: Governance and Sustainability. Retrieved from: https://asiapacific.uitp.org/clarify-contractual-framework-data-sharing-public-transport-unlock-sustainable-multi-stakeholder.

Wong, Y.Z., 2019b. The future of data sharing contractual setting in the context of mobility as a service. Sharing of Data in Public Transport: Governance and Sustainability. Retrieved from: https://asiapacific.uitp.org/future-data-sharing-contractual-setting-context-mobility-service.

Wong, Y.Z., 2019c. Whimpact: more questions than answers. In: Thinking Outside the Box. Retrieved from: https://sydney.edu.au/business/news-and-events/news/2019/04/30/whimpact--more-questions-than-answers.html.

Wong, Y.Z., Hensher, D.A., 2018. The Thredbo story: a journey of competition and ownership in land passenger transport. In: Alexandersson, G., Hensher, D.A., Steel, R. (Eds.), Research in Transportation Economics. Competition and Ownership in Land Passenger Transport (Selected Papers From the Thredbo 15 Conference), 69, pp. 9–22. https://doi.org/10.1016/j.retrec.2018.04.003.

Wong, Y.Z., Hensher, D.A., Mulley, C., 2018. Stated preference design for mobility as a service (MaaS) broker/aggregator contracts. In: Paper Presented at the 40th Australasian Transport Research Forum (ATRF), Darwin, Australia.

Wong, Y.Z., Hensher, D.A., Mulley, C., 2019. Delivering mobility as a service (MaaS) through a broker/aggregator business model. In: Paper Presented at the 16th International Conference on Competition and Ownership in Land Passenger Transport (Thredbo 16), Singapore.

Wong, Y.Z., Hensher, D.A., Mulley, C., 2020. Mobility as a service (MaaS): charting a future context. In: Hensher, D.A., Mulley, C. (Eds.), Transportation Research Part A: Policy and Practice. Special Issue on Developments in Mobility as a Service (MaaS) and Intelligent Mobility, vol. 131, pp. 5–19. https://doi.org/10.1016/j.tra.2019.09.030.

Xenia, K., Tyler, N., 2018. Maintaining balance on a moving bus: the importance of three-peak steps whilst walking on the lower-deck. Transp. Res. A Policy Pract. 116, 484–496.

Zachariah, J., Gao, J., Kornhauser, A., Mufti, T., 2014. Uncongested mobility for all: a proposal for an area wide autonomous taxi system in New Jersey. In: Paper Presented at the Transportation Research Board 93rd Annual Meeting, Washington, DC.

# Index

Note: Page numbers followed by *f* indicate figures and *t* indicate tables.

## I



## L



## M